Narratives on Becoming

Identity and Lifelong Learning

A Volume in
I Am What I Become: Constructing Identities as Lifelong Learners

Series Editors

Jo Ann Gammel, Sue L. Motulsky, and Amy Rutstein-Riley
Lesley University

I Am What I Become:
Constructing Identities as Lifelong Learners

Jo Ann Gammel, Sue Motulsky, and Amy Rutstein-Riley, Editors

Narratives on Becoming: Identity and Lifelong Learning (2021)
edited by Emilie Clucas Leaderman, Jennifer S. Jefferson,
Jo Ann Gammel, Sue L. Motulsky, and Amy Rutstein-Riley

Identity and Lifelong Learning: Becoming Through Lived Experience (2021)
edited by Sue Motulsky, Jo Ann Gammel, and Amy Rutstein-Riley

Identity and Lifelong Learning in Higher Education (2020)
edited by Jo Ann Gammel, Sue Motulsky, and Amy Rutstein-Riley

Narratives on Becoming

Identity and Lifelong Learning

Editors

Emilie Clucas Leaderman
Boston College

Jennifer S. Jefferson
Endicott College

Jo Ann Gammel
Lesley University

Sue L. Motulsky
Lesley University

Amy Rutstein-Riley
Lesley University

INFORMATION AGE PUBLISHING, INC.
Charlotte, NC • www.infoagepub.com

Library of Congress Cataloging-in-Publication Data

CIP record for this book is available from the Library of Congress
http://www.loc.gov

ISBNs: 978-1-64802-480-1 (Paperback)

  978-1-64802-481-8 (Hardcover)

  978-1-64802-482-5 (ebook)

CONTENTS

PREFACE

**Jo Ann Gammel, Sue L. Motulsky, Amy Rutstein-Riley,
Emilie Clucas Leaderman, and Jennifer S. Jefferson**

There was a time, not that long ago, when adulthood marked the end of learning and the beginning of work and family, and retirement marked the beginning of decline. Identity was stable and often dictated by work, race, gender, and class. That time is no longer.

Today human growth and development does not peak at age 40 and decline after age 65. Emerging adulthood theory, with its new developmental stage following adolescence, suggests that adulthood does not even truly begin until the late 20s and growth continues into old age until death. Learning is ongoing throughout the lifespan and occurs in a variety of formal and informal settings. Adult learning is no longer unidirectional from teacher to student, limited to brick-and-mortar settings or structured education programs, nor is it age restricted. Along with the evolution of views on human development and learning comes a social constructivist perspective on identity. No longer is identity singular and fixed, but rather, identity is composed of multiple, intersecting layers that are dynamic and fluid. Identities are constructed and re-constructed through life experiences, in interaction with cultural and relational contexts. To quote

Narratives on Becoming: Identity and Lifelong Learning, pp. vii–xiii
Copyright © 2021 by Information Age Publishing
All rights of reproduction in any form reserved.

Ruthellen Josselson (1996), "Identity is what we make of ourselves within a society that is making something of us" (p. 28).

Learning and identity development are lifetime processes of becoming. To discuss the construction, revision and often transformation of identity in the context of learning, we chose the term "becoming." We believe that "the process-oriented term becoming, rather than achieving, is preferred to describe this unfolding, as it embodies flexible, dynamic, and open-ended ... explorations rather than close-ended or static end points" (Athan, 2020, p. 448). The construction of self, of interest to scholars and practitioners in adult development, adult learning, and psychology is an ongoing process, with the self both forming and being formed by lived experience in privileged and oppressive contexts. Intersecting identities and the power dynamics within them shape how learners define themselves and others and how they make meaning of their experiences in the world. Understanding the importance of identity in learning is "critical to advancing our understanding of the learning process and our creation of effective, inclusive educational environments" (Zaytoun, 2005, p. 8).

INTRODUCTION TO THE SERIES

I Am What I Become: Constructing Identities as Lifelong Learners is an insightful and diverse collection of empirical research and narrative essays in identity development, adult development, and adult learning. The purpose of this series is to publish contributions that highlight the intimate and intricate connections between learning and identity. Our aim is to promote reflection and research at the intersection of identity and adult learning at any point across the adult lifespan and in any space where learning occurs: in school, at work, or in the community.

Many of the contributions in this series examine identity and learning within marginalized and understudied groups. People from marginalized populations, whether based on gender, race, ethnicity, social class, sexual minority, disability status, or another identity, learn to perform their identities differently in diverse settings. Insights about how identity is constructed within diverse adult learning contexts can assist researchers and practitioners in understanding the sociocultural factors that inform adult development, education, and learning. Many of these works discuss how gender, race, class, ethnicity, sexual orientation, ability, religion, nationality, language, and the complex mix of these identities play a significant role in how learners define themselves and others and how their meaning-making shapes their experience in the world. In addition to chapters that span diverse identities, cultural contexts, and international settings, contributions also focus on identity development and adult learning at all points across adulthood, from emerging adults to the elderly.

The series aims to assist our readers in understanding and nurturing adults who are always in the process of becoming. We invite readers who are adult educators, adult development scholars, counselors, psychologists, social workers, and sociologists, along with education and training professionals in formal and informal learning settings, to revel in the rich array of qualitative research designs, methods, and findings, as well as the autobiographic and narrative essays that transform and expand our understanding of the lived experience of people both like us and unlike us, from the United States and beyond.

OUR STORIES

As university educators, the three series editors share interests within identity, adult development, and adult learning, although we have our own professional identities and particular scholarly interests. Jo Ann is an adult educator interested in mentoring adult doctoral students; Sue is a developmental and vocational psychologist interested in career transition, gender, cultural and relational identity, and sexual minority career development; and Amy is a sociologist focused on the well-being of adolescent and young adult girls. We proposed a volume on identity and lifelong learning that would highlight the many ways adults construct and change their identities as they encounter new contexts and new challenges. We envisioned chapters that would locate adult identity development and revision through formal or informal learning in professional, educational, or community settings. These settings include higher education, adult or community education, professional development, or informal learning through transitions, cultural exploration, or life experiences.

Our call for proposals resulted in 150 responses, much more than the two dozen or so that we expected. We were astonished. We seemed to have struck a chord. With such a rich mix of stories to tell, we opted to create a series. To achieve our aim of publishing multiple volumes, we invited two colleagues to serve as editors for the third volume. Emilie Clucas Leaderman is an educator and higher education consultant committed to facilitating equitable learning environments and centering learner experiences in institutional decisions. Jennifer S. Jefferson is a community college administrator dedicated to social justice; she brings significant experience teaching writers and supporting adult learners. As higher education practitioners, we approached the chapters in Volume 3 with the goal of elevating author voices so that readers could encounter collective facets of learning and identity.

The contributors are mostly, although not exclusively, higher education faculty members, administrators, and students interested in adult learning and development. The stories in this series are often deeply personal. Some are self-portraits exploring issues of transition, intersecting identities, and oppression. Others are qualitative research studies exploring identity development in context or teaching and learning experiences in specific cultural and international populations across the adult lifespan. Each chapter is a story of learners (who may be the authors themselves or their participants) and each reflects on identity as it is considered and reconsidered in a particular learning environment.

OVERVIEW OF THE THREE VOLUMES OF THE SERIES

Volume 1, *Identity and Lifelong Learning in Higher Education* (2020), contains chapters by and about postsecondary educators and students. Chapters selected for this volume include stories of traditional-age students in bachelor's degree programs, adult learners in community college and 4-year degree programs, graduate or doctoral students, and senior scholars reflecting on a lifetime of learning and becoming. Authors examine multiple and intersecting identities using a variety of methods including autoethnography, phenomenology, and narrative research. Many employ a critical lens such as feminism, critical race theory, or critical pedagogy to examine issues of power in formal learning settings. Practitioners offer unique pedagogical strategies based on new ideas that come from reflection and rigorous research. Together these chapters enhance our understanding of the inextricable link between learning and identity.

Chapters in Volume 2, *Identity and Lifelong Learning: Becoming through Lived Experience* (2020), focus on identity and learning within informal settings and life experiences rather than formal educational environments. The contributions showcase the many ways that identity development and learning occur within cultural domains, through developmental and identity challenges or transitions in career or role, and in a variety of spaces from assisted living facilities to makerspaces. These chapters highlight identity and learning across the adult lifespan from millennials and emerging adults to midlife and older adults. The studies take place in South Africa, Singapore, and South Korea as well as in both rural and urban settings in the United States. The authors examine cultural, relational, and social identity exploration and learning through experiences of immigrant women, domestic workers in two international contexts, hearing children of deaf parents, African American and Latinx career and family legacies, women becoming mothers, artist identity formation, and women in career transition. Included in this volume are phenomenological and ethnographic qualitative studies, autoethnographies, case studies, and narratives that engage the reader about the myriad ways that adult development, learning, and identity connect and influence each other.

Volume 3, *Narratives on Becoming: Identity and Lifelong Learning*, contains extraordinary essays that share a personal narrative lens or autobiographical/ethnographic methodology. Authors are from Canada, China, Dominican Republic, Germany, Malaysia, Mexico, New Zealand, South Korea, and the United States, and include community workers, doctoral students, and educators. Nearly half of the chapters are coauthored, collaborative stories. These chapters provide insights into the intersectional identities and learning of writers. These authors present powerful stories that identify the ways relationships, environments, culture, travel, and values shape their identities, use literacy, teaching, and learning as vehicles for experimenting with new identities, negotiate multiple identities, contexts, and transitions involved in becoming, and construct meaning from the multiple paths that comprise the journey of lifelong learning

Stories are powerful learning tools. Editing the chapters in this series has contributed to enlarging our own understanding of identity and lifelong learning and we hope it will do the same for our readers. Reading the contributions, we received has made us reflect more deeply on our own identities and ways of learning. As qualitative researchers, we are used to attending to the voices of others and reflecting on our own positionality. Yet we were not prepared for the rich diversity of studies and narratives from authors who were hungry for the opportunity to tell their stories or those of others. We were often deeply moved by the power of these chapters and their ability to bring to light the voices of so many people in multiple cultural and educational contexts. We are honored to bring these voices to a larger audience through this series. "We need to tune in to the stories of change we hear all around us, the stories each of us tells ourselves about who we were, who we are now, and who we may be in the future" (McAdams et al., 2001, p. xx).

OVERVIEW OF VOLUME 3

Narratives on Becoming: Identity and Lifelong Learning, Volume 3 in the series, *I Am What I Become: Constructing Identities as Lifelong Learners*, explores a myriad of ways that authors' personal and professional growth has influenced identity development. These reflections and insights reveal that intersectionality influences individual meaning-making processes, demonstrating how various trajectories, settings, cultures, and personal connections impact the process of becoming. This volume reminds us that lifelong learning takes multiple shapes and happens everywhere. Through their narrative essays and ethnographic/autobiographical accounts, these authors illuminate the power of transformational learning during life-changing events and transitions, including teaching abroad, becoming a parent, living with illness, learning as a doctoral student, educating for social justice, serving as a school leader, being a university professor at an HBCU, and living as an outsider. These chapters use both collaborative and individual voices, adding to the rich tapestry of adult learning.

Volume 3 chapters reveal some shared experiences in the process of becoming. These themes, such as learning from failure, reconstruction of self, transformation through multicultural experiences, reciprocal learning as a teacher/mentor/educator, female support for multi-generational families of women, pursuit as a reader/writer, and class mobility and the path to academic identity, contribute to understanding how individuals view themselves and their world. In editing authors' first-hand accounts, we posed questions to prompt inner dialogue and critical reflection about their lived experiences. Our goal was not to interrogate where they were in their learning, but rather to encourage sharing their journeys and the factors that shaped them. We view writer insights as crucial in understanding the nuances involved in intersectionality and lifelong learning. As one author articulated,

> These are the stories that need telling, not the tales of the bumpy road en route to a better life, but the stories of transgressing, transforming, and integrating ... stories of the personal work required to reject duality; stories in which we recognize how education provides the language we need to conceptualize and talk about transformation; and stories in which we come to understand our agency in negotiating our own identities. (Eamer, 2021, Chapter 5, *Confessions of a Transplanted Mind: 'Second Street' Stories of Transgressing, Transforming, and Integrating*)

Eamer noted that, in defining their identities, individuals engage in diligent inquiry and reflection, which allow them to recognize the power that lies within their personal transformation.

As we write this preface, we are in the midst of the 2020 COVID-19 pandemic. George Floyd was recently killed, and the Black Lives Matter movement has experienced a resurgence. These current events shaped the questions we asked ourselves about the significance of this volume. In working to address problems that persist in higher education, such as systemic racism and disparities in educational access and quality, we viewed it as essential to prioritize understanding the diversity, identity, and intersectionality that comprise adult learner populations.

In her discussion of creating engaged learning environments, bell hooks (1994) wrote, "our capacity to generate excitement is deeply affected by our interest in one another, in hearing one another's voices, in recognizing one another's presence" (p. 8). By critically listening to personal narratives and asking clarifying questions, we can start to uncover our own biases and misinformation that often maintain the status quo. As two White women working in higher education administrative and consulting roles in the United States, we were deeply conscious of how the stories of our authors resonated with us through our own specific cultural and identity lenses, and that these lenses reflect a relatively narrow worldview. As such, after many conversations about how to group the chapters and in what order to present them, we decided on alphabetizing by author. While this is nevertheless still a choice and the format of the book still linear, we encourage you to read these chapters in whatever order they speak to you. We hope that as you read, you will notice your own assumptions, reactions, and surprises; perhaps you will reflect on your positionality and choose to share this experience with colleagues.

We are grateful to the authors for their contributions to this third volume on *Narratives on Becoming: Identity and Lifelong Learning*. We anticipate that these stories will promote further dialogue and research, and that they will influence pedagogy and practice in adult development, education, identity development, counseling, and psychology. Most of all, we hope that by reading these narratives, you come to see the world through different lenses. We hope that this reading deepens your own process of becoming.

REFERENCES

Athan, A. M. (2020). Reproductive identity: An emerging concept. *American Psychologist, 75*(4), 445–456. http://dx.doi.org/10.1037/amp0000623

Eamer, A. (2021). Confessions of a Transplanted Mind: 'Second Street' Stories of Transgressing, Transforming, and Integrating. In E. Clucas Leaderman, J. S. Jefferson, J. Gammel, S. L. Motulsky, & A. Rutstein-Riley (Eds.), *Narratives on becoming: Identity and lifelong learning* (Vol. 3). Information Age Publishing.

hooks, b. (1994). *Teaching to transgress: Education as the practice of freedom*. Routledge.

Josselson, R. (1996). *Revising herself: Women's identity from college to midlife*. Oxford University Press.

McAdams, D., Josselson, R., & Lieblich, A. (Eds.). (2001). *Turns in the road: Narrative studies of lives in transition*. American Psychological Association.

Zaytoun, K. D. (2005). Identity and learning: The inextricable link. *About Campus, 9*(6), 8–15. https://doi.org/10.1002/abc.112

CHAPTER 1

I AM THE WARRIOR I AM BECOMING THROUGH *CURRERE* AND TRANSFORMATIVE ADULT LEARNING

Susan R. Adams
Butler University

INTRODUCTION

In 2002, after having done everything I could to prevent it, my life fell apart. My husband moved out just a few days shy of our 16th wedding anniversary. Our three middle school-aged children were devastated. Our friends and family were shocked. My worst fears came to life and for the first few months, this new reality consumed every waking hour.

I am a talker, an oral processor, a person who is quick to speak in a group and who is always willing to say what is on my mind. To everyone's surprise, my own included, I got very quiet in the weeks that followed our separation. My goal each day that summer was to simply function as best I could in front of my kids and to provide as much normalcy for them as possible.

Narratives on Becoming: Identity and Lifelong Learning, pp. 1–13

But any time I was alone, I turned off every device and most of the lights and sank into my thinking spot on the couch where I silently labored to reimagine my future.

This was hard, exhausting work, work I desperately wished to avoid. I felt my perceived failure wash over me in endless waves of humiliation. The deep pain of rejection and loss only relented during sleep, but like some sort of ghoul, this pain grimly waited for me to form my first conscious thought each morning when it resumed its silent torture of my heart and mind.

For many people, divorce provides release from an untenable situation, but for me, the end of my marriage signaled the death of my dreams for my family and for the future I believed I would share with my husband. My new status as a single person triggered an identity crisis. Who was I supposed to be now? And how could I navigate this upheaval that touched every aspect of my life and my identity? What new life was possible? As I often do when my life takes a turn, I headed to the library and read everything I could by women who had risen above life's challenges. As Buddhist teacher Pema Chödrön (2016) observed,

> When things are shaky and nothing is working, we might realize that we are on the verge of something. We might realize that this is a very vulnerable and tender place, and that tenderness can go either way. We can shut down and feel resentful or we can touch in on that throbbing quality. (p. 9)

I decided to lean into the discomfort and see what new learning might come from it. Gradually I realized I had a choice: I could resign myself to bitterness, disappointment, and defeat, or I could learn *about* what I perceived to be my failure and learn *from* my failure.

The failure of my marriage had profound professional and economic implications. To survive financially, I scrambled quickly and took a high school English as Second Language (ESL) position. As a secondary Spanish teacher, I naively assumed I was equipped to take on the challenge of teaching English to high school immigrant students and accepted the position with the promise I would complete the licensure requirements through university coursework within the year. I was initially overwhelmed by how much there was to learn about teaching ESL, but I soon found that focusing on this new challenge energized me and the graduate studies provided immense relief from the pain in my personal life.

Going back to graduate school at night with three middle school kids was no easy feat. Heading to the local university for 3-hour evening classes 2 or 4 nights per week for a year meant that too often the kids were home alone; sometimes one unlucky child waited slumped on a bench in the hall for me to finish class. But despite these challenges, the unexpected joy of thinking, discussing, and considering new perspectives was addictive. I quickly finished the licensure requirements and then completed a master's degree in language education—a dream that had been deferred years before at the birth of my children.

Simultaneously my new position as the lone ESL teacher in our building meant that I began to emerge as a teacher leader in my high school. I took advantage of every opportunity to learn new skills, to travel, and to take on new roles that pushed my boundaries and opened identities within me. The productive overlap of professional development at school and studying critical perspectives in graduate school brought fresh provocations to my thinking and to my practice as my professional perspectives shifted and my worldview was being transformed.

Soon after completing the master's degree, a much-loved university professor created a way for me to pursue a doctoral degree without quitting my job. With almost no understanding of what a PhD is or what this decision would mean for me personally and professionally, I took the plunge.

THEORETICAL FRAMEWORK

In this chapter, I explore my ongoing evolution from high school teacher to university professor and connect that evolution to learning experiences that have created space and opportunity for transformative adult learning. The method of *currere* (Pinar, 1994) invites us to reflect on our pasts, to project ourselves forward into our hopes for the future, to evaluate our current commitments, thereby, to notice and name the relationships between these three steps. Pinar (1994) urges, "Juxtapose the three photographs: past, present, future. What are their complex, multi-dimensional interrelations? How is the future present in the past, the past in the future, and the present in both?" (p. 26). Examining the connections between one's past, present, and future weaves the common strands into the shape and direction of one's life, not only conceptually or in the abstract, but made visible through action. The point is to foster the kind of self-knowledge which leads to changes in the way people go about living their daily lives, to foster the ability to take action in your personal context, to encourage praxis. In a 2014 publication (Adams), I applied Pinar's (2004) four steps of *currere*, which Pinar dubs the regressive, the progressive, the analytical, and the synthetical (p. 35) to create a lens through which I:

- Examined my own past as a rich data source (the regressive)
- Looked toward the future, toward what is possible (the progressive)
- Took the opportunity to look backward to the past while examining the present (the analytical), and then

- Re-entered the present (the synthetical) (paraphrased from Pinar, 2004, p. 35).

Jack Mezirow's (1991) transformative adult learning theory also provides guidance for having a "complicated conversation" with myself as "an ongoing project of self-understanding in which one becomes mobilized for engaged pedagogical action" (Pinar, 2004, p. 37). Pedagogical action moves me toward a potentially new understanding of how and why non-traditional, older adults may be uniquely poised to successfully navigate the complex maze and rigors of academia as they continue to pursue transformative learning opportunities in midlife. In addition, an unexpected avenue for transformative adult learning opened in 2015 when I was invited to join a small group of people from all over the world to become Warriors for the Human Spirit with Dr. Margaret Wheatley.

To organize my thinking for the task in 2014, I created a table in which I sorted my journey into Mezirow's (2000) 10 phases of transformative learning (p. 19) (see Table 1.1). As my journey in academia now further unfolds, the process of seeking tenure and promotion has provided a serendipitous time to check myself with a new question: Is what I am what I hoped to become? Once again, here I employ Mezirow's (2000, p. 22) 10 phases of transformative learning to map my steps:

1. A disorienting dilemma
2. Self-examination
3. A critical assessment of assumptions
4. Recognition of a connection between one's discontent and the process of transformation
5. Exploration of options for new roles, relationships, and action
6. Planning a course of action
7. Acquiring knowledge and skills for implementing one's plan
8. Provisional trying of new roles
9. Building competence and self-confidence in new roles and relationships
10. A reintegration into one's life based on conditions dictated by one's new perspective

This new table provides shape for the ongoing "complicated conversation" (Pinar, 2004) I am having with myself. Here I walk a metaphorical labyrinth of the regressive, the progressive, the analytical, and then re-enter the present through the synthetical to see if I am indeed what I am becoming in spite of, or perhaps because of, the opportunities and pitfalls inherent in academia.

WALKING MEZIROW'S 10 STEPS

A Disorienting Dilemma

Disorienting dilemmas can be big, life-altering events like the end of my marriage, or they can be subtle moments in which the ground beneath our feet rumbles and threatens our balance. In this case, my disorienting event is composed of a life-altering event, my separation and eventual divorce, followed by a series of seemingly small moments that gradually revealed a pattern that made me squirm. This pattern emerged in my work as a teacher educator, in which my primary role is to teach education courses for undergraduates who are preparing to become middle and high school teachers. However, in addition to my teaching, I frequently serve as a consultant in K–12 settings. I take this work seriously since I know from my own high school teaching days how much I counted on external consultants and advocates to speak truth to power in ways I was not at liberty to do.

Saying aloud something many are thinking, but are not willing to say, is risky. You do not always know whether you will be thanked for your honesty. Even if the moment seems to pass without incident, there can be consequences later. In these moments, I sometimes feel like the young child from the well-known fable in which everyone can clearly see the emperor is stark naked (Andersen, 1837) as he tries to convince the crowd he is wearing the latest finery. In the story, the child's cry emboldens the crowd to laugh; in the real world, speaking my truth sometimes silences the group at the table. Suddenly it is not the emperor who is exposed and standing alone; it is me. Afterward a few individuals might quietly thank me for saying what everyone was thinking; sometimes I am uninvited from the next meeting or even pushed out of the project.

Self-Examination

The fallout from my attempts to speak my truth to perceived power rarely feels good, even when there seem to be no negative consequences. If I am thanked, I still feel frustrated that others have left the dirty work to me. If I am ostracized, I feel hurt, angry, and threatened. I also feel resentment toward those who knew the truth and remained silent, but kept their seat at the table.

A Critical Assessment of Assumptions

What dynamics have I assumed to be at work in these situations? When I sense power differentials between people at the table, I begin to worry about who has power over others. I wonder if everyone is safe to speak frankly and to contribute their best thinking to the work. If I think some are being silenced, I feel a sense of obligation to speak up. I assume that if I do not speak, perhaps no one will, and as a result, I fear a poor decision will get made with serious repercussions for silenced stakeholders. I generally assume that I am at the table to make a real contribution to the work when in fact I might just be there so someone can check a box that indicates external stakeholders have participated in a process. Too often my heart rate increases, my voice gets louder, my rate of speech increases, my vocabulary complexity ratchets up, my hands get animated, and my body leans into a combative stance, revealing my subconscious belief that a fight is at hand and I must win it by being smart, knowledgeable, and fearless.

Recognition of a Connection Between One's Discontent and the Process of Transformation

Afterward, even if I "win," I do not feel victorious. In fact, I feel self-conscious, embarrassed, and exhausted. If I have just burned a bridge, I feel humiliated and fearful. I worry about the long-term implications of my actions. I sometimes feel used and betrayed by those who secretly agreed with me but were willing to let me take the heat alone.

When I am able to reflect on these experiences, afterward I have often sought out the person or persons with whom I engaged in these battles to apologize for my behavior and to attempt a reconciliation. Some have welcomed my overtures while others have rebuffed me. A few have curtly informed me they "don't do reconciliation." Even when I have achieved some sort of reconciliation, afterward I have often wished fervently that I had avoided the mess altogether.

Courageously speaking my truth and wisely refraining from speaking too much truth required a new set of skills from me. My first step in learning was to carefully observe individuals who exhibited wisdom, ethical responses, and diplomacy under difficult circumstances to see what I could learn from them.

Exploration of Options for New Roles, Relationships, and Action

As I was wrestling with managing myself, some community leaders in my neighborhood became aware that a struggling neighborhood elementary school was in danger of being assigned to a charter operator with no public engagement with families or neighborhood stakeholders. Hastily a task force composed of community developers, leaders from nonprofit agencies, local church leaders, and leaders from the neighborhood multiservice center gathered to consider the available options for this school. I was invited to join this group in light of my multiple identities: I am a resident in the neighborhood, a member of a church actively engaged with neighborhood issues, executive board president of a community development corporation, a former teacher in the district, a parent of children who had graduated from the district, and a teacher educator. Joining was a no-brainer for me: I felt a strong responsibility to provide a K–12 educator's perspective, to bring best curriculum and pedagogy practices to the group's work, and to ensure that the neighborhood's families had a role in shaping a new vision for their school. My personal and professional identities, ethics, and commitments were on full display every step of the way.

Being a member of this task force meant spending many hours meeting with district leaders who had not anticipated any objection to their plans to turn the school over to a charter operator. It also meant meeting with representatives of a powerful local charter advocacy group whose stated mission is to dissolve the existing school district into separate schools operating somewhat independently while being loosely affiliated to share essential services (ESL and special education certified personnel, building maintenance, transportation, food, purchasing, etc.).

In these meetings, I wrestled inwardly, agonizing over whether to speak or to remain silent. The chair of the task force preferred diplomacy, but like most members of the task force, he sometimes did not fully understand educational terms or processes under discussion. Anxiety welled up as I listened to polite discussions that could have serious implications for teachers, students, and families.

I also felt an ethical obligation to reveal my own commitments to public education, especially when we met with district leaders and representatives of the charter advocacy group. Ironically, interfering with the casual insertion of a charter operator into the local school required the task force to petition the district for permission to take over the school ourselves through a pathway created by the superintendent with the support of the same advocacy group. This pathway is euphemistically known as "innovation" status and mirrors the ways charter schools operate. Ultimately, I chose to speak quietly with these individuals after the meeting to express my dismay at the plight of this school. My statement was, "I am completely opposed to the district chartering schools and diminishing the ties between schools. I also strongly disagree with the charter advocacy group's mission to support this effort. However, I love my neighborhood, and I care deeply what happens to this school, so I am a member of this task force and am working toward innovation status for this school, even though I do not believe in this approach." It would have been much easier and safer to smile politely and say nothing, yet that would have made me feel complicit with the advocacy group's agenda. Each time I made this statement, I consciously worked to keep my voice calm, my body soft, and my tone sincere, yet polite. In each case, my statement was met with apparent courtesy and stated appreciation for my honesty, but over time I realized the task force chair sometimes excluded me from meetings with district leaders and/or the charter advocacy group's representatives. Those old feelings of frustration, hurt, and humiliation returned.

Planning a Course of Action

Learning to speak truth to power by myself was not yielding the changes I needed, so I was intrigued by an e-mail invitation I received in 2015 from author and organizational specialist Dr. Margaret Wheatley to join her project, *Warriors for the Human Spirit*. My experiences have included multiple week-long trainings, monthly video calls with my cohort mates, reading and discussing related books, learning the daily practice of sitting meditation, and making connections between what I am learning and my professional practice. My initial commitment was for 1 full year, but ongoing opportunities to learn and grow have kept me involved now for more than 3 years. To say this commitment is challenging is an understatement, but I am grateful for what I am learning.

My professional work has long been shaped and influenced deeply by Wheatley's books, particularly *Turning to One Another: Simple Conversations to Restore Hope to the Future* (2002). So, when I received this invitation, I jumped at the chance. Meg Wheatley's teachings and her book *Who Do We Choose to Be? Facing Reality, Claiming Leadership, Restoring Sanity* (2017) have resonated deeply within me as I consider the current state of school reform in this moment and my role in advocating for students, families, and teachers amidst these reforms.

ACQUIRING KNOWLEDGE AND SKILLS FOR IMPLEMENTING ONE'S PLAN

Entering into Warrior training allowed me to experience new learning, including:

- participating in regular online meetings with a teacher and with others from my cohort;
- completing three distinct week-long retreats followed by ongoing trainings during the year; and
- studying traditional and contemporary approaches to spiritual disciplines.

It is Wheatley's (2017) question, "Who do we choose to be?" that reminds me that my behaviors and responses are choices. If behaviors are indeed choices, I needed to learn how to make better ones. Through my Warrior training, I am learning a daily practice of sitting meditation and to notice thoughts, feelings, and reactions within myself as they arise. This noticing is meant to be curious and friendly with myself, rather than punitive or shameful. A yearlong engagement with Warrior teachers and with my cohort mates gave me the opportunity to notice how often I respond with anger and aggression to situations like those I described earlier. I began to wonder what would happen if I listened longer before speaking. I also began to notice my own physical indications that I am getting anxious, angry, or frustrated in meetings.

Provisional Trying of New Roles

Anxious feelings still revealed themselves in my body, but now I noticed them earlier, before they ran away with me. I generated a short list of strategies to help me maintain composure. These include making time for a short meditation break before entering meetings; keeping my hands and body busy with notetaking; processing my thinking in writing rather than speaking; closely monitoring my breath and my heart rate; remembering to take deep breaths; and drafting my questions or comments first in writing before I speak aloud. I also have requested private feedback from trusted colleagues after meetings regarding my communication and demeanor.

Building Competence and Self-Confidence in New Roles and Relationships

While I am still quite verbal, as a result of my strategies, I am speaking less in meetings and choose more carefully what I will say and how I will say it. I still sometimes hear the heat in my voice, but now I notice my own aggression more quickly and am better equipped to rein it in. Simply stating the depth of my feelings and commitments frames my energy as passion, rather than signaling to others that I am on the attack.

A Reintegration Into One's Life on The Basis of Conditions Dictated by One's New Perspective

When I am in my best frame of mind, I remember that nothing productive ever results from violence, manipulation, coercion, or aggression. If I am going to be a person who believes truth can be spoken without aggression, then that is who I need to start *being* now.

I want to be a collaborator and a positive contributor in the work of the task force and in my role as a teacher educator. I want to be known as someone who has high expectations and gives honest feedback, yet who is also compassionate and supportive. Currently many of my students do perceive me in this way, but some mistake my passion and high expectations for judgment, or even more painfully, some have believed I do not like them—the last thing I want to model for prospective educators.

My roles as a teacher educator and as a task force member require me to take a stand for what I believe is right and to advocate for students, teachers, families, and schools. This work is too important to allow my passions and frustrations to run away with me. I must acknowledge my fears of how I will be perceived and perhaps punished for my beliefs, but I cannot let fear of failure paralyze me from acting. The reality is I have no control over how others choose to perceive me, but I can choose how and when I express myself.

I am aware that I will still sometimes forget myself in the midst of a conversation that matters to me, but my new practices and my emerging identity as a Warrior empower me to notice my responses, to be friendly and curious with myself about these behaviors, and to channel them into peaceful, productive responses.

To summarize, here is the table of Mezirow's 10 Phases of Transformative Learning (2000, p. 19) listed with my life events and actions that correspond to each phase.

Table 1.1

Mezirow's 10 Phases of Transformative Learning (2000, p. 19) With New Events and Actions

Mezirow's 10 Phases of Transformative Learning	Life Events and Actions that Correspond to the 10 Phases of Learning
1. A disorienting dilemma	Acting as an agent of advocacy within and beyond the academy brings both rewards and consequences professionally. Speaking truth to power feels like my duty, yet makes me a target for unwanted attention.
2. Self-examination	I remember my commitment to keeping a foot in the K–12 world and to not getting trapped in the ivory tower, but that compliant teacher still longs to avoid negative backlash and wants to please.

(Table continued on next page)

Table 1.1 (Continued)

Mezirow's 10 Phases of Transformative Learning (2000, p. 19) With New Events and Actions

Mezirow's 10 Phases of Transformative Learning	Life Events and Actions that Correspond to the 10 Phases of Learning
3. A critical assessment of assumptions	Advocacy moves me into an aggressive stance. In the moment, this seems reasonable, persuasive, and necessary. Fighting fire with fire or countering power with power appears logical.
4. Recognition of a connection between one's discontent and the process of transformation	Academia seems to reward aggression. But I suspect the truth is counterintuitive: Adding aggression is ultimately destructive, not how I want to be and act in the world.
5. Exploration of options for new roles, relationships, and action	Helping to re-open a neighborhood school aligns me with my community, but publicly puts me at odds with a powerful organization.
6. Planning a course of action	I wonder: What is advocacy without aggression? I commit to a year of Warrior study
7. Acquiring knowledge and skills for implementing one's plan	Committing to a daily sitting meditation, to regular meetings with a teacher and my cohort, to completing three week-long retreats followed by trainings; and to studying approaches to spiritual disciplines provided new learning and skills.
8. Provisional trying of new roles	I begin to tell others about my study and to say that I am a Warrior for the Human Spirit until I can without much discomfort. I develop strategies for managing myself better in stressful situations.
9. Building competence and self-confidence in new roles and relationships	Meditation practice and working with a teacher help me notice my body tensing for aggression. I learn to soften myself sooner and to control myself in stressful conditions. I am talking less when tempted to respond with aggression
10. A reintegration into one's life based of conditions dictated by one's new perspective	New skills and habits of mind bear fruit in my personal and professional life. When I choose to speak, it is a conscious decision and with a clear recognition and acceptance of possible consequences.

CONCLUSION

When I began my Warrior journey, I found it difficult to refer to myself as a Warrior without laughing with embarrassment. Who am I to proclaim myself a Warrior? But unlike soldiers who train for war and who must take up weapons, a Warrior for the Human Spirit is working toward wholeness and well-being for all members of the community. We face reality, claim our leadership, and join hands to collaborate with others who also seek to be of service. We train ourselves to see the truth of the conditions around us and face those conditions with courage and with non-violence.

A Warrior's gentle, generous, and humane responses to challenging conditions can change the discourse (Eubanks et al., 1997) as we engage with those who seem to be working at cross purposes against us. Warriors listen to understand. We slow down our reactions and choose our responses, especially when the situation is tense. We choose to believe in the goodness of others even as we begin to see glimpses of goodness in ourselves. We resist categorizing others as enemies because that quickly ratchets up the violence and is counterproductive. We do not dig in and cling to old traditions, but are awake and open to what is possible at this time. We work to bring what is needed to fruition.

What I have just described is still aspirational for me. I fall quickly into old patterns of frustration, anger, and distrust, especially when I am weary or not taking good care of myself. But my new daily practices and my trusted Warrior companions keep me grounded. My Warrior identity reminds me of who I choose to be, so I am learning to calm myself, take a deep breath, and slow down my thinking so that I can choose wise action. Warriors have passions, like everyone, but we learn to master and channel those passions, rather than be captive to them. Warriors create generative space and build capacity for collegiality, for learning from and with one another. We turn our energies and efforts toward refreshing and supporting our communities. A Warrior for the Human Spirit is who I choose to be in this moment and who I intend to become.

Working through Pinar's (2004) "complicated conversation" with myself explores the path of my own past as a rich source for understanding (the regressive). I have looked toward the future, toward what is possible (the progressive) and realized who I choose to be in that imagined future. I have looked backward to the past while examining the present (the analytical) to understand my patterns of response and behavior, and to identify new learning necessary for who I will be in the future. Finally, I have re-entered the present (the synthetical) with a newly shaped identity and with new practices for developing and maintaining this identity.

Mezirow's (2000) 10 Phases of Transformative Learning provide a lens for analyzing the steps of my journey on this Warrior path and for checking myself against my new identity and my clarified intentions as a Warrior. I am learning it is possible to take up disorienting events in our lives as learning opportunities, rather than hiding from them or avoiding them. In choosing to embrace disruptions and changes as opportunities rather than threats, I have learned how to live into a new future as a single person and have found fresh, authentic ways to be of service to my personal and professional communities. Walking into the newly established neighborhood school and seeing the fruits of our collective hopes and dreams come to life is immensely rewarding.

The end of my marriage was certainly hard on all my family, but many years later, my kids and I are still fiercely committed to one another; we are learning to share life in new ways with my ex-husband, too. We have celebrated graduations (including my own!), weddings, the birth of my first grandchild, and together we grieve the painful death of my dear daughter-in-law. My life is certainly not the future I planned, but responding as a Warrior, understanding disorientation (Mezirow, 2000) as an opportunity for growth, and applying the *currere* (Pinar, 2004) process makes life events meaningful and fruitful rather than random and threatening. My response to dilemma and its learning potential reveals the truth that I am indeed what I am becoming. With courage, this process will continue to unfold for me as I am attentive and stay open to continued new learning.

REFERENCES

Adams, S. R. (2014). Currere, unexpected journeys, and unplanned destinations in academia. *The Brock Education Journal*, 4–10. http://brock.scholarsportal.info/journals/brocked/home/article/view/445

Andersen, H. (1837). The emperor's new clothes. In *The little mermaid*. C.A. Reitzel.

Chödrön, P. (2016). *When things fall apart: Heartfelt advice for hard times* (20th Anniversary Edition). Shambhala.

Eubanks, E., Parish, R., & Smith, D. (1997). Changing the discourse in schools. In P. M. Hall (Ed.), *Race, ethnicity, and multiculturalism: Policy and practice* (pp. 151–168). Garland.

Mezirow, J. (1991). *Transformative dimensions of adult learning*. Jossey-Bass.

Mezirow, J. (2000). Learning to think like an adult: Core concepts of transformation theory. In Jack Mezirow & Associates (Ed.), *Learning as transformation: Critical perspectives on a theory in progress* (pp. 3–34). Jossey-Bass.

Pinar, W. (2004). *What is curriculum theory?* Lawrence Erlbaum.

Wheatley, M. (2002). *Turning to one another: Simple conversations to restore hope to the future*. Berrett-Koehler.

Wheatley, M. (2017). *Who do we choose to be? Facing reality, claiming leadership, restoring sanity*. Berrett-Koehler.

CHAPTER 2

BEHIND THE BLACKBOARD

Voices of Migrant Teachers

Maria Aurora Bernardo
Archdiocese of Wellington, New Zealand

Diana Lea Baranovich
University of Malaya

Maria Khristina Manueli
Methodist E-Academy

SO MUCH YET SO LITTLE

The internationalization of education, significantly driven by globalization, has enabled the transmigration of educators in many parts of the world. This has been going on for the last two decades, consequently, increasing the mobility and migration of teachers mostly from North America, Europe and some parts of Asia and the Pacific (Bense, 2016). However, despite such indication, there is a considerable dearth of literature that explores the

Narratives on Becoming: Identity and Lifelong Learning, pp. 15–31
Copyright © 2021 by Information Age Publishing
All rights of reproduction in any form reserved.

experiences of international educators. The little available research focuses on the experiences of Western-born and English-speaking teachers, with some mention of the struggles in enculturation and discrimination (Bense, 2016; Bernardo & Almonte-Acosta, 2014; Bernardo & Malakolunthu, 2013). In this study, we use our personal stories to shed light on these experiences.

We reflect on our stories from the prism of identity formation and lifelong learning. We argue that migration is in itself a form of lifelong learning; and we locate ourselves as its both facilitators and beneficiaries. Furthermore, we postulate that our professional identities as educators are transformed and strengthened by the migration experience.

Drawing From Our Stories

We employ autoethnography, as a method, to guide the conceptualization process, where we can harness our personal experiences through the process of reflective writing and conversation (Bernardo, Butcher, & Howard, 2013). We derive primary data from our autobiographical accounts. We use autobiographical reasoning in analyzing the data as it is useful in forming a cohesive identification and understanding of identity development, particularly in periods of change and crisis (Habermas & Köber, 2015). Our initial concern is that we may remember an event inaccurately with the passage of time and that our perspectives of ourselves in that period have evolved. Thus, we need to emphasize that our narratives are not so much historical evidence, but references from which we try to establish the continuity of our consciousness between the person we were then and who we are now. Essentially, our recollections are a means by which we explain how past events have shaped our present understanding of ourselves (Pasupathi, 2015).

We divided the research design into three phases that involved individual and collective reflections. The first phase was a private undertaking, where we each revisited our migration journey, with a focus on our collective experience, that is, teaching in a university in Malaysia. This approach respects the privacy of each author and directs the reflection process towards the aims of this chapter. We then shared the reflection with the others for unpacking and analysis. A second reflection analyzed our individual journeys through the lens of our roles as educators—the changes and challenges. We did this to give more focus to our recollection because it ramified to other aspects of our lives, which are not within the study's purview. In the third phase, we synthesized the salient points of our reflection into seven *realizations* (the word "theme" may seem a better academic language, but intuitively it did not quite capture our visceral translation of what emerged in our reflection journey).

Who We Are

Under autoethnography, the authors are the primary participants. The authors/participants come from different contexts: Maya (Bernardo) is a Filipino Catholic currently working as an adult educator in the Catholic diocese in New Zealand; Diana (Baranovich) is an American-Muslim working in Malaysia, and Tina (Manueli) is a Filipino, who worked and studied in Malaysia, and is now working in a Methodist adult religious organization in Germany. Part of the study will investigate the dynamics of discrimination, which offhand can be gleaned from the experiences of Maya and Tina as nationals from a developing country working in a relatively more economically developed country such as Malaysia. This then will be balanced by Diana who comes from a developed country, working in a comparatively lesser developed country. Maya and Tina are both Christians from different faith traditions, whereas Diana is a Muslim. Maya is single; Tina is a mother of two and married to a German national; and Diana is a mother of two adults, a grandmother, and married to an American. The authors come from different fields: Maya is an educator and manager, Diana is both an educator and a psychologist, and Tina is a linguist. The authors met at a university in Malaysia where they were all employed as visiting lecturers. When the three went separate ways, with Maya and Tina leaving Malaysia, they kept the connection by writing collaboratively on topics that can bring the lenses of their fields into dialogue.

As a matter of ethical research practice, we will not reveal the name of the university in Malaysia and instead refer to it as a "Malaysian university." The authors worked as visiting academics in the same Malaysian university.

Malaysia—A Land of Color and Complexity

The experiences of Maya, Diana and Tina all happened in Malaysia. To understand their story, it is important to explain the Malaysian context.

Malaysia is a federation of 13 states and 3 territories. Malaysia is also a multiethnic and multireligious country. The three dominant races are Malay, Chinese, and Indian. There are also several thousand expatriates from all over the world living and working in Malaysia, predominantly based in Kuala Lumpur. Approximately half of the population is ethnically Malay, known as the *Bumiputras*, which means the "original people." Islam is the established religion of the state, and the government system is closely modeled on the Westminster parliamentary system coupled with the legal system based on common law (World Population Review, 2018). Muslims of Malaysia do have to follow the Sharia Law of Islam in matters of marriage and family. The head of state is the King, while the head of government is the prime minister.

Internationalization of Malaysian Higher Education

Higher education in Malaysia is part of the national strategic plan known as *Wawasan* 2020 (Vision 2020). Its primary aim is to make Institutions of Higher of Learning (IHL) or universities to be world-class in standing. The success indicator of its achievement is to have most of its IHLs be on the list of top 100 universities in the world, and at least one of its universities lands among the 50 best universities in the Times Higher Education Supplement (THES) ranking by 2020 (Ramli et al., 2013). Among its main thrusts are to intensify internationalization, and to increase IHLs' global competitiveness by attracting more international students and recruiting international lecturers (Ahmad et al., 2012). This plan resulted in the more than 50% increase of international students and 20% increase in the hiring of international academic staff, mostly hired in private IHLs (Samuel et al., 2017; Symaco & Wan, 2017).

IDENTITY FORMATION AND LIFELONG LEARNING

Both identity formation and lifelong learning are concepts that scholars are still grappling to understand. Thus, there is no universal definition of these concepts across different disciplines such as education, psychology, and sociology. These concepts are multidimensional, with varying levels of analysis and manifestations and interacting with other phenomena (Cotè, 2015). Azmitia (2014) pointed out that identity is best conceptualized as an intersection of gender, ethnicity, and social class. In the case of lifelong learning, although the term has been used in different contexts, its definition remains unclear (Aspin & Chapman, 2007; Maclachlan & Osborne, 2009). However, when these concepts are gleaned from the standpoint of a lived experience rather than an academic discourse, identity formation and lifelong learning are symbiotic, and in fact, indivisible. Hence, for the purposes of this chapter, we clarify that we are focusing on the formation of our professional identities as lecturers who taught in a foreign country (Malaysia). Accordingly, we view ourselves as facilitators of lifelong learning, as well as postulating that our migration experience is also a lifelong learning practice that strengthens our professional identities as educators.

Identity Formation

The authors' view of identity formation as migrant educators resonates with the work of Erikson when he defined identity as a "subjective sense of invigorating sameness and continuity" (1968, as cited in Way & Rogers, 2015). His psychosocial identity formation theory posits a seventh stage in which the middle-aged adult strives to create and nurture people and contribute to positive changes for the betterment of society (Erickson, 1980). This stage is driven by the need to define and deliver our professional legacies. Similarly, we derive insights from other identity theories such as Marcia's identity statuses (1993, as cited in Worrell, 2015), which consist of *moratorium, achievement, foreclosure, and diffusion*. The *moratorium* status refers to a stage when an individual (or migrant) who is actively exploring identity alternatives but has yet committed to an identity. Identity *achievement* is the status in which an individual/migrant could articulate an identity they can commit to. *Foreclosure* is the condition in which the migrant committed to an identity without exploration. Finally, *diffusion* refers to individuals who have neither explored nor committed to an identity (Worrell, 2015).

However, within these typologies of identity formation are dynamics that require justification beyond the field of psychology. We believe that identity is not just a complex construct but also a phenomenon that can only be explained by an amalgamation of different theoretical perspectives (Cotè, 2015). We have been made aware of the role of the cultural scripts that shape our thinking about others and our view of ourselves as women, as belonging to an ethnic group, and as followers of a faith tradition, among others. These factors often intersect in the way we perceive and rationalise the effect of migration on our professional identity.

Lifelong Learning

Traditionally, lifelong learning has been ascribed to education (or learning) that happens after formal schooling, often interchangeably referred to using words such as adult education, careers education, and continuing education. However, lifelong learning as a construct suffers from conceptual ambiguity, one that is in search of definitional clarity (Aspin & Chapman, 2007; Maclachlan & Osborne, 2009). Bagnall (as cited in Aspin & Chapmann, 2007) stated that there are four functions of lifelong learning: (1) the preparation of individuals for the management of their adult lives; (2) the distribution of education throughout an individual's lifespan; (3) the educative function of the whole of one's life experience; and (4) the identification of education with the whole of life. We are adopting Maclachlan and Osborne's (2009) definition of lifelong learning as the "structured, purposeful learning throughout the lifespan, from cradle to grave, and by lifetime, we include all the activities, formal and informal, through work and through leisure that adults are involved in on a day-to-day basis."

The contribution of this essay to lifelong learning is illuminating the effect of the educator's experience as its facilitator, within the context of globalization. The authors suggest that for international educators to be effective facilitators or translators of lifelong learning, their experience as foreigners should be taken into consideration. Given the discussed definition, the experience of migration is lifelong learning in itself. Hence, international educators are both facilitators and participants of lifelong learning.

CULTURE

Worrell (2015) argued that "culture" could be used interchangeably with racial and ethnic identity. We adopt the same view when we refer to the culture in the Malaysian university and our own cultures of origin. Culture presents meanings, practices, and shared narratives about historical experiences, symbols, and worldviews that are passed down through enculturation and changed over time as children, adolescents, and adults develop personal relationships and adapt to their changing environments (Azmitia, 2015).

This brings about an important delimitation to our chapter, as we focus on the university culture without generalizing it to the Malaysian culture.

OUR STORIES

Reconnecting With the Past

We came to Malaysia under different circumstances, but we seem to converge to a common reason—the need for professional change and growth. Maya has been a university administrator and lecturer in a university in the Philippines for almost 18 years. Diana has recently finished her doctoral studies and would like to teach in the university and try her hand in publishing; she was also driven by the call to help Asian students learn more creatively. Tina received a doctoral studies scholarship to study in Malaysia. When in Malaysia, we each encountered different struggles, which we narrate in our personal voices below. We chose a specific story that underpins the complexity of our reflections.

Cultural Clashes—The Silent Battle

Maya

I was teaching a postgraduate class in educational leadership. One of my students have difficulty speaking English; I saw that in the first few days of class. He sat there looking awed by the cacophony of discussion, which I encourage in all my classes. One time, he visited me in my office, with his young wife. He told me two things that left me flabbergasted—first, that I am the first female teacher he ever had. Second, his house helpers in the Middle East are Filipino women. I did not reply to those comments and proceeded to ask him the purpose of his visit. What I could not tell him is that his words were a total shock for me, especially when he proceeded to appeal that I "help" him pass his course, which does not mean giving him tutorial support but giving him more consideration in marking his paper. So, I told him, he must work like the rest of the students. He looked down-cast; I did not sense any indignation on his part; he was not a violent or even an arrogant man, I could see. He just wanted to see if he could find a way out of a crisis, in ways perhaps that he has been used to and based on his knowledge of women and of my people. He left and never bothered me again. My semester with him ended uneventfully. He had perfect atten-dance and I made sure I gave him a chance to share his thoughts with the class. In other words, I made him earn his grade. He showed up for the written exams and was among the last to leave. He was evidently trying his best to pass, and so I passed him. It was not a high mark, but it was appro priate to the results of his exams and the effort he put into the class. I just hope in the short time we were together I had given him a positive image of a woman and of a Filipino as a teacher.

Diana

No single story stands out but rather a general feeling of putting up with the slow pace by which things are done, like finalizing my work contract. The Malaysians have little sense of urgency, which gets on my nerves some-times, especially when something needs to be done immediately. Another point of struggle is trying to understand their intention. Often it is hard to get a clear answer-even if it is a simple yes or no.

I needed to ask the questions repeatedly and in different ways, exploring ways of getting answers. Sometimes, it has to get to a point that I have to show how upset I am by literally storming out and getting my own answers, before I could actually get a response. This sudden aggressive outburst does not sit well with me, but I must admit however, that there are times that I felt close to lashing out.

Tina

When I came to Malaysia to do my PhD studies, I already had knowledge of the country, its culture, and its language, being a Malay language teacher back in the Philippines. It was not my first time there, as I have been there a few times. More or less, I can say that I was already "ready" to live in Malaysia. While doing my studies, I was hired as a visiting lecturer, and then later on promoted as a senior lecturer. Despite having full knowledge of the language and the culture, there were small cultural misunderstandings, particularly of how the locals view me. Some of them view Filipino women based on the Filipino soap operas they watch or their interaction with Filipino overseas workers. Their impression varies from being lewd to being soft-spoken to being liberated. They have this misconception that you can do almost everything without being held accountable (by your religion), such as by your choice of clothes (e.g., short skirts or sleeveless blouses). As much as I act professionally and wear appropriate clothes whenever I teach or work, some students still see me in a different light. They see me as liberated, attractive, and sexy. I continue to act as professional as I can and did not address this issue so much. Nevertheless, the Malaysian students' respect and admiration towards their mentors, most especially those who could speak their language, is notable.

The Invisible Whip—Institutional Bullying

Maya

I experienced some form of bullying from fellow academics or colleagues as well. The most explicit memory was attending a faculty meeting where all the lecturers from the faculty were present. The meeting was held in Bahasa. Foreign lecturers were given an earpiece where someone translates the proceedings to English. There was this portion when the translator went silent. Apparently, there was some heated discussion going on. I pretended to go along and look clueless but what I can gather is that they were criticizing the foreign lecturers for being lazy and not wanting to do anything beyond what they feel they are contracted to do. At the time of that meeting, I had learned Bahasa well enough to understand it but not so much to speak it. The local female lecturer beside me nudged me and asked, "Do you understand what was said?" I lied and said "No." I verified my suspicion of what transpired through another local lecturer, and I was right. I felt that was cultural bullying, like hitting us in the face blindfolded. I also remember having to fill in forms written in Bahasa with no translations in my first few weeks of work and being expected to hand them over in a day, regardless if I understood them or not. I felt these treatments were made to discourage me, which only motivated me to cope as fast as I could.

Diana

Indeed, one of the frustrating aspects of being at the university is the envy of the locals. I have come to know over the past several years that they have grown to feel threatened by me: the rapport and influence that I have with the students, and my community connections. The real nail in the coffin was when I received my associate professorship. At that point, a few senior members of the counselling department, which is one of the departments where I teach and supervise master's and research students, banded together to keep students away from me, and try to suppress my exposure—to no avail, however. These few people, under the leadership of a certain ringleader, tried to convince my students to change to Malaysian supervisors because I am an American and do not understand the Malaysian culture. They also tried to convince the department head not to allow me to teach marriage and family counseling course, which I had been teaching for 4 years, because I do not understand the context of the Malaysian family unit. Furthermore, they made a case that my American psychotherapy qualification and certification disqualifies me from teaching counselling courses in Malaysia since only Malaysian certified counsellors can teach these courses. They even tried to say that this was a law. I consulted a lawyer regarding this matter and found out that it was not (a law). This is all very ironic because I was originally hired to teach counselling courses and had taught nearly every counseling course for 5 years before this became an issue. The ringleader was even very happy to have me in the department at that time and would say that I was "heaven sent." But when I became more popular with students and in demand with outside counselling agencies and professional organizations, the ringleader did not like the idea of him or the other local counselors being upstaged by a foreigner.

The issue was even raised up to the vice chancellor until my department head, the dean of the faculty, the ringleader and I were called for a meeting. The vice chancellor confirmed that there is no such law in Malaysia, and that anyone with an overseas counseling qualification can teach these courses in Malaysia. The vice chancellor asked if I was qualified and they both assured him that I was and have done an excellent job in the last 5 years. The vice chancellor said it was a closed case and I continued to teach counselling courses as well as supervise counseling students without any more problems.

Becoming a Global Educator

Maya

Its impact became discernible a little later and perhaps when I worked in Australia and later moved to New Zealand. I could say that that experience made me more courageous as a woman. I know that if I can take care of and protect myself in that setting, I can protect myself in less traditional contexts. Also, I know I can operate and engage meaningfully in a more liberal context. It also affirmed me as a teacher, that as I go through the challenges of migration—the judgement over my background, qualities of myself I cannot or will not choose to change (e.g., being a Catholic), being a woman and Asian. With these odds stacked against me, I discovered that being a good teacher is my stronghold and my tool to break down the walls around me. It will not be a smooth start, but if I do it with integrity and passion, I will be respected and appreciated. I can rely on my competence as a teacher to challenge the discrimination of others and even my own insecurity. My research is also taking that shape. If I publish, it is an arsenal I can show to people whom I feel will look down on my third world PhD and me. My publications remind me that I am globally competent.

Diana

I have learned within the classroom setting to unite diverse people, who would not unite on their own accord. I have done this by randomly putting students in small groups and changing the groups every time. Personality wise, I have learned to speak up for myself more, stick up for myself more, not to take reciprocity for granted, and not to hope for much teamwork overall. Now, there are some exceptions for certain people. Overall, I have grown even more comfortable with myself as a professional. There is much work that still needs to be done in Malaysia where education and mental health are concerned. I tend not to look at the overall big picture because that gets far too overwhelming. So, at the end of the day, if I can sit back and honestly say that a student, a client, a supervisee, a colleague, a superior, or a friend is better off because he or she has crossed my path than if he or she had not crossed my path—my job has been done.

Tina

Professionally, working in Malaysia opened many opportunities that I could not have back in the Philippines. It gave me the opportunity to participate in and organise conferences and workshops, as well as share my work locally and abroad. It gave me opportunities to do research in various aspects of my discipline. It helped me create a network of fellow researchers and professors within and outside of Malaysia. It also honed my skills in doing research as well as in teaching. It made me more creative, patient, and compromising in dealing with the administration, fellow faculty members and staff, and students. It also gave me a kind of power I never had in terms of presenting myself in various academic and diplomatic situations. Being a citizen of a third-world country makes you feel less valued, but because of your own personal and professional qualities, it gives you a kind of validation and importance.

Only recently have I come to realize how I felt "liberated" and how much my perspective as a global educator became wider after I moved out of Malaysia. The experiences I had there helped me shape the kind of researcher, teacher, and administrator I am today. My experiences there gave me an edge in marketing myself as a global academic in a very competitive environment here in Europe. In summary, I can say that teaching in Malaysia helped me become a better teacher, researcher, and most of all, a better human being.

Realizations

The results of our reflective exercise were a revelation to us, particularly when we compared each other's reflections and realized that our views of a situation are not general and may be unique to us. It was also important to guard ourselves against either romanticizing or dramatizing our journeys, and the honest conversations helped in putting that into perspective.

We synthesized our reflection into seven realizations.

Realization 1: We All Feel the Call to be Migrant Educators

The three of us instinctively knew that to grow further as educators, we needed to get out of geographical origins. Motivations could vary from more significant opportunities for professional development, to the need for a greater challenge, to simply following our intuition. This was regardless of whether we came from a developing country like the Philippines or a developed country like the United States.

Realization 2: Is It Discrimination, Envy, or Prejudice?—It Is in the Eye of the Beholder

The experience of discrimination did not come out strongly in our study. The treatment we received as foreign lecturers varied with the culture of the faculties where we belong and were mediated by our ability to speak the local language. Maya felt discriminated, Diana felt envied, and Tina felt stereotyped.

An interesting finding for us was to see how we ascribe different words and meanings to what might be a similar treatment. For example, both Maya and Diana belong to the same faculty. Maya felt discriminated; Diana felt she was envied. Maya may be coming from her cultural script of coming from a colonized country (thus, looked down upon by those who are more powerful; in this case, that could be being a powerless foreigner). Diana, on the other hand, did not feel discriminated but envied, which may be a product of coming from a country which has never been colonized (in fact, was a colonizer). Discrimination and envy are two different things, and yet it was used to describe a somehow similar situation. Tina, in contrast, claimed to have not experienced either discrimination or envy. However, she believed what she experienced is prejudice from all races—prejudice on her being a woman coming from a more liberal society from Malay and Muslim women; prejudice of Westerners and Western-educated Asians against Asians for being perceived as intellectually inferior, lazy, or naive; and the self-prejudice to believe that this is the reality. She observed that Westerners and Western-educated are bolder in making demands and in expressing their disgust over university policies and systems.

Realization 3: Mediators to Assimilation

Strongly connected to the second realization is to know that Tina did not feel discriminated against at all. We then realized Maya and Diana's experiences were isolated to their faculty. It seems that Tina's faculty is more inclusive compared to Diana and Maya's. Another factor is that Tina as a linguist speaks Malay fluently, which made it easier for her to fit into the environment. Another way of looking at it, as compared to Maya and Diana's experiences, is it is hard to undermine Tina because she would have quickly picked it up.

Realization 4: Cultural Adjustment Goes Both Ways

We also realized that the adjustment goes both ways: for the students and us. This deepens in complexity if the students themselves are foreigners. This realization goes with Maya's experience as a female and Filipino interacting with a male student from the Middle East. The role of religion also factors in when Maya and Tina must adjust their expectations of the students' performance because most of them are fasting. This also includes understanding students and colleagues who are in polygamous marriages. Although these family dynamics did not show in the teacher-learning interactions, our own sociocultural scripts of what makes up a "proper" family and how we judge men who are not monogamous, are among those stereotypes that hover at the back of our heads. In these precarious dynamics, we find our students often guiding us on how to engage with the host-country environment.

Realization 5: Using a Gendered-Lens was Inevitable

We do see a gendered lens in the way we view our experiences. By this we mean a feminist lens; how a patriarchal society such as in Malaysia view women in general. This pertains to Maya's experience of having to prove herself as a female teacher beyond the stereotype impression of Filipino women as domestic helpers and of women in general, in strongly patriarchal societies such as those in the Middle-East as well as the stereotyped view of American women, with regard to Diana. These experiences as well as other experiences beyond the university life that touched on our sense of safety and adhering to social scripts of women in a Muslim society affected our view of our power within this milieu and our behavior within and beyond the classroom and the university.

Realization 6: Our Professional Identities Are Our Sanctuary Identity

An important realization for us was that our professional identities along with the beliefs of our competency to teach well in any context becomes our psychological sanctuary against the incessant crisis of adjusting to a foreign culture. We realized that we could not control people's stereotype about where we come from but being a good teacher can elevate our status from being a stranger and a minority to someone with a respectable status.

Realization 7: Migration Has a Positive Effect on Our Professional Identities

Migration, in our experience, has a positive effect on our professional identities, by clarifying our strengths and motivating us to better our craft. It has made us more resilient, resourceful, and independent. We learned how to take care of ourselves, manage our relationships, and protect our reputations. We were motivated to be and do better. It has also taught us how to teach better in a multicultural classroom and to teach inclusivity within the classroom setting.

REFLECTIONS, QUESTIONS, QUESTS

From our reflections, it was hard to relate to Marcia's (1993) identity statuses since there was no shift in our professions as academics. Hence, there was no impetus to explore options deliberately for our professional identities. In fact, the change of context expanded our ability to engage with students from different cultures and deepen our sense of mission as educators. Our experiences find more affinity with the field of intercultural studies, particularly the integrative theory that proposes that prolonged exposure to one culture develops intercultural personhood that can effectively interface with one's original culture. An intercultural personhood emerges when one has fully accepted their own cultural distinctiveness and accepts the distinctiveness of others (Kim, 2015). This sophisticated self-other orientation is a long process, and one which can only happen if one is willing to be transformed by the migration experience.

Berzonsky (as cited in Szabo & Ward, 2015) mentioned that there are different identity styles, which determines one's ability to engage with a foreign culture. The identity styles can be informational, normative, or diffuse avoidance. Informational identity style is open to alternatives, seeking and evaluating relevant information in their environment. Normative identity style, on the other hand, is obstinate with worldviews and intolerant of ambiguity. Lastly, those with diffuse-avoidance style will strategically avoid self-relevant feedback and make tentative decisions on how they would like to engage with the new environment. We reckon (and this may be our bias) that we adopt an informational identity style, and for some time, used diffuse avoidance. One indicator that we are growing an intercultural personhood is the decreasing compulsion to compare one's culture against another, and the use of non-judgmental language instead of assuming we know better.

Stress is definitely a prominent part of our experience, and most of it is from the communication. Hence, we learned to integrate by maintaining the cultural identity of our ethnic origins and being open to the cultural identities of people from other ethnicities that we get in touch with, as a way of acculturation (van Oudenhoven & Benet-Martínez, 2015). The study also proposes that professional identity, as educators, can be a sanctuary identity that can provide emotional or psychological protection against the many crises that undermine a sense of self-worth.

Our reflection also brought us to clearly see the gender-lens, in our case, the feminist lens we bring into our view of ourselves as migrants and in our professional identity as educators. Fivush and Zaman (2015) claimed that this is inevitable, as the social construction of our identities is interwoven with our gender. For example, a feeling of safety and powerfulness in a foreign environment (much less a patriarchal society) are all shaped by cultural scripts. This was obvious to Maya but not to Diana. This feeling wanes with years of exposure as Tina looks back in hindsight. These gendered lenses are malleable and can be reshaped with more significant exposure to different environments, as Maya found when she began working in other countries such as Australia and New Zealand, and as Tina found after she migrated to Germany.

The results unveil the effect of migration on the professional identity formation of the educators. International lecturers who have developed intercultural personhood can act as cultural mediators (Bense, 2016), who could bridge cultures, foster inclusivity, and develop intercultural competence. Thus, migration has a positive effect on both the lecturers and their students.

We believe that the experience of teaching in a foreign context is a form of lifelong learning. The aims of lifelong learning are: (1) to spur economic development and progress (Barr & Griffiths, 2007); (2) to support personal development and fulfilment; and (3) to encourage social inclusiveness and democratic understanding and activity (Chapman & Astin, as cited in Aspin & Chapman, 2007), which all resonates with the benefits we feel we have gained from our international experiences. We can also see how the educator is instrumental in mediating and energizing the achievement of these aims.

Within the context of international education, the educator is both a beneficiary and an agent of lifelong learning. Intercultural competence along with the ability to translate this into pedagogy are crucial skills for international educators. Accordingly, this conclusion calls for the examination of lifelong learning not just as a tool for achieving students' learning outcomes, but also as a by-product of the professional identity and practice of the teacher.

REFERENCES

Ahmad, A. R., Farley, A., & Naidoo, M. (2012). An examination of the implementation of federal government strategic plans in Malaysian public universities. *International Journal of Business and Social Science, 3*(15), 290–301. http://ijbssnet.com/journals/Vol_3_No_15_August_2012/33.pdf

Aspin, D. N., & Chapman, D. J. D. (2007). Lifelong learning: Concepts and conceptions. In D. Aspin (Ed.), *Philosophical perspectives on lifelong learning* (pp. 19–38). Springer.

Azmitia, M. (2014). Reflections on the cultural lenses of identity development. In K. C. McLean & M. Syed (Eds.), *The Oxford handbook of identity development* (pp. 286–296). Oxford University Press. https://doi.org/10.1093/oxfordhb/9780199936564.013.033

Barr, J., & Griffiths, M. (2007). The nature of knowledge and lifelong learning. In D. Aspin (Ed.), *Philosophical perspectives on lifelong learning* (pp. 189–210). Springer.

Bernardo, M., Butcher, J., & Howard, P. (2013). The leadership of engagement between university and community: Conceptualising leadership in community engagement in higher education. *International Journal for Educational Leadership, 17*(1), 103–122. https://doi.org/10.1080/13603124.2012.761354

Bernardo, M. A. C., & Almonte-Acosta, S. (2014). A closer look at internationalism in international education in the Philippines: A journey towards authenticity. In I. Silova & D. Hobson (Eds.), *Globalizing minds: Rhetoric and realities in international schools*. Information Age Publishing.

Bernardo, M. A. C., & Malakolunthu, S. (2012). Culturally inclusive behaviors of Filipino teachers in international schools in the Philippines: Perspectives of international education in a developing country. *International Journal for Educational Development*. http://dx.doi.org/10.1016/j.ijedudev.2012.05.055

Bense, K. (2016). International teacher mobility and migration: A review and synthesis of the current empirical research and literature. *Educational Research Review, 17*, 37–49. https://doi.org/10.1016/j.edurev.2015.12.001

Côté, J. (2015). Identity-formation research from a critical perspective: Is a social science developing. In K. McLean & M. Syed (Eds.). *The Oxford handbook of identity development*. Oxford University Press. https://doi.org/10.1093/oxfordhb/9780199936564.013.015

Erickson, E. (1980). *Identity and the life cycle*. Norton.

Habermas, T., & Köber, C. (2015). Autobiographical reasoning is constitutive for narrative identity: The role of the life story in personal continuity. In K. McLean & M. Syed (Eds.), *The Oxford handbook of identity development*. Oxford University Press. https://doi.org/10.1093/oxfordhb/9780199936564.013.010

Kim, Y. Y. (2015). Finding a "home" beyond culture: The emergence of intercultural personhood in the globalizing world. *International Journal of Intercultural Relations, 46*, 3–12. http://dxdoi.org./10.1016/j.ijntrl.2015.03.018

Maclachlan, K., & Osborne, M. (2009). Lifelong learning, development, knowledge and identity. *Compare: A Journal of Comparative and International Education, 39*(5), 575–583. https://doi.org/10.1080/03057920903138506

Marcia, J. (1993). *Ego identity: A handbook for psychosocial research*. Springer Verlag.

Pasupathi, M. (2015). Autobiographical reasoning and my discontent: Alternative paths from narrative to identity. In K. C. McLean & M. Syed (Eds.), *The Oxford handbook of identity development* (pp. 166–181). Oxford University Press. https://doi.org/10.1093/oxfordhb/9780199936564.013.002

Ramli, N., Zainol, Z. A., Aziz, J. A., Ali, H. M., Hassim, J., Hussein, W. M. H. W., Markom, R., Dahalan, W. S. A. W., & Yaakob, N. I. (2013). The concept of research university: The implementation in the context of Malaysian university system. *Asian Social Science, 9*(5), 307–317. https://doi.org/10.5539/ass.v9n5p307

Samuel, M., Tee, M. Y., & Symaco, L. P. (Eds.). (2017). *Education in Malaysia: Developments and challenges*. Springer.

Symaco, L. P., & Da Wan, C. (2017). Development of higher education in Malaysia: Issues and challenges. In M. Samuel, M. Y. Tee, & L. P. Symaco (Eds.), *Education in Malaysia: Developments and challenges* (pp. 53–66). Springer.

Szabo, A., & Ward, C. (2015). Identity development during cultural transition: The role of social-cognitive identity process. *International Journal of Intercultural Relations, 46*, 13–25. http://dxdoi.org/10.1016/j.ijitrel.2015.03.019

van Oudenhoven, J. P., & Benet-Martínez, V. (2015). In search of a cultural home: From acculturation to frame-switching and intercultural competencies.

International Journal of Intercultural Relations, 46, 47–54. http://dx.doi.org/10.1016/j.ijntrel.2015.03.022

Way, N., & Rogers, O. (2015). [T]hey say black men won't make it, but I know I'm gonna make it: Ethnic and racial identity development in the context of cultural stereotypes. In K. C. McLean & M. Syed (Eds.), *The Oxford handbook of identity development*. Oxford University Press. https://doi.org/10.1093/oxfordhb/9780199936564.013.032

World Population Review. (2018). *Malaysia population 2018*. http://worldpopulationreview.com/countries/malaysia-population/

Worrell, F. C. (2015). Culture as race/ethnicity. In K. C. McLean & M. Syed (Eds.), *The Oxford handbook of identity development* (pp. 249–268). Oxford University Press. https://doi.org/10.1093/oxfordhb/9780199936564.013.029

CHAPTER 3

FOUR DAUGHTERS, ONE MOTHER

Stories of Revising Identities

Gail Simpson Cahill
Lesley University

This chapter holds up a mirror to a family of five women, a mother and her four daughters, who range in age from 22 to 60 years old. The investigation centers on the lived experiences in a female-centric/female dominated home. The stories are an autoethnography written by the mother, which uses self-reflection, personal narrative, and writing to explore each woman's individual experiences within the family and in society (Chang, 2016). Based on first-person narratives that tell stories over time and in close tandem with meaningful life events, this is a case study of a female family unit. These narratives, according to narrative psychologists, are driving factors in a person's behavior and appear to be fundamental to how people work out who they are and who they may become (McAdams, as cited in Benedict, 2007).

———————————

Narratives on Becoming: Identity and Lifelong Learning, pp. 33–46
Copyright © 2021 by Information Age Publishing
All rights of reproduction in any form reserved.

Each participant was interviewed and asked three open-ended questions. The first question was descriptive and asked the respondent to share personal and professional stories that she would like others to know about her. The second question asked the respondent to share pivotal moments that had an impact on or changed how she currently thinks or acts. The third question asked each respondent to imagine herself in 10 years. Responses were primarily oral, although, subsequent to the interviews, some participants chose to provide additional written information. The author then analyzed the narratives for common themes.

THE FAMILY

The Mother: Mae

Mae was born into a working-class family. Her mother was a homemaker, and her father worked in a government job. Neither parent graduated from college, but Mae never doubted that all her siblings would (and did) attend college, as Mae notes, "It was a given." She is the fourth of five children, once described by a psychologist friend as having "the take-charge, organized tendencies of an oldest child but the engaging personality of a middle child." Education and service were two important themes in her household.

THE DAUGHTERS: ELIZABETH, MARY, LEIGH, AND TAYLOR

Elizabeth

Elizabeth was born to Mae and Austin after 7 years of marriage. She is the oldest girl and the only real "ginger," as she puts it, in the family. "When I was born, no one expected a redhead; in fact, one of my grandmothers kept holding me up to a window to check if my hair was still red!" Elizabeth describes herself as "a secret jock, a single mother of an 11-year-old daughter who likes to dance and organize things."

Mary

Mary was born 14 months after Elizabeth. "I am Elizabeth's Irish twin, as I have been called." Mary describes herself as "quiet" and laughs when she recalls that, growing up, her older sister Elizabeth "did all the talking for me." Mary's sisters concur that she is the "calm amongst us." Mary reports that many of her memories center around sports. "I loved going out on the field/court with my teammates to play a game." Mary recalls constantly having some sort of ball in her hands.

Leigh

Leigh was born 4 years after Mary and 5 years after Elizabeth. She describes herself as "hardworking and a defender of others." As far back as she can remember, she loved art and reading. She kept many drawing notebooks and was always at the bookstore for "one book or another." Leigh thought her older sisters were "the coolest."

Taylor

Taylor is the youngest of the four sisters. There is a 12-year gap between Taylor and Elizabeth, 11 years between Taylor and Mary, and 7 years between Leigh and Taylor. She describes her relationship with her siblings as "weird initially, because they were so much older; it felt like I had four mothers instead of one." Taylor has always had many friends, many with whom she remains involved today, as a result of the camaraderie developed when she was playing sports. However, she often wished for one best friend. She now realizes that she has three best friends in her sisters.

THE STORIES

The stories of these five women reveal a small window into feminine identity development based on lived experiences. The stories highlight many common themes that cut across several generations of women. They are stories that bring to life family dynamics and values, relationships between and among family members, negative body image, intimate partner violence, individual struggles, resiliency, and career and professional development. The stories also expose pivotal moments in each woman's life that affected how she thought or acted. The stories are their words, based on their memories and interpretations. They are stories of revising identities.

Family Unit Dynamics and Values

The most prominent theme in all the stories is the dynamics of the family unit comprised of grandparents, parents, and sisters. Each of the daughters has vivid memories of time spent with their grandparents. They have many memories of their mother's parents, Nana and Grandpa. They did not have many memories of their father's mother, however, because she died the same year that Leigh was born. They have the most stories about "Daddo," their father's father, because he lived the longest of all their grandparents.

Elizabeth describes Daddo as, "tall and handsome," a "gentle giant." She recalls "Friday night pizza" at his house, and her favorite pizza remains "grilled chicken and red pepper." Her other "Grandpa" loved to "cheat" at checkers just to see whether she was paying attention. Her "Nana" smelled of ivory soap, gave them baths in the kitchen sink, carried a seemingly endless supply of lemon drops in her pocketbook, and put everything in Tupperware. "She had the cleanest house I have ever seen.... I think I have her gene."

Mary has many similar recollections of her grandparents. "I got to know Daddo more than my other grandparents because he lived the longest." One of her favorite memories is "checking up on him" when her aunt and uncle were away. "I would go over on my lunch break and bring him a McDonald's shake because it was his favorite." Mary paused in conversation and became tearful when she recalls Daddo's death. "Daddo was drifting, his eyes were closed, but when my husband read the note my father wrote about how special a father he was, Daddo smiled. I knew he heard the words. I was glad that I was there with him. Right after I left, he died."

Mary was in high school when her grandmother, who had Alzheimer's, moved into her house. "It wasn't easy for my family, but my mom and dad made it seem effortless." Mary added: "One of my favorite times with my grandmother was when I tucked her into bed at night, and she asked if I would wake her up the next morning to have breakfast.... I always said "yes," to which she smiled and gave me a kiss. She asked this same question every night."

Leigh loved Wednesdays with her mother's parents. "I loved walking the pond with them and trying to spot all the wildlife." Leigh recalls every Sunday, "going to church and then visiting my grandparents' house." Taylor, the youngest, has fewer memories because, "all but Daddo died when I was young." Taylor thinks it was "funny that Daddo cooked an egg for his dog, Ebony, and gave him candy corn sometimes." One vivid memory for Taylor is her father's eulogy of Daddo. This made an impression on Taylor because she had never heard her father speak about emotions, as "he was always so quiet." She still remembers one line from the eulogy: "The day that my mother died, a piece of my father died with her." Taylor's Aunt Pam heard the eulogy, knew that she was dying, and asked her father to deliver her eulogy. Taylor felt very close to her aunt, and, with tears, she stated that her father delivered her aunt's eulogy 1 year ago.

All four daughters recall family events. The oldest daughter, Elizabeth, relates many adventures with her family. She still enjoys her family's tradition of "two weeks in New Hampshire" each summer. Her favorite trip was "going across country," remembering, in particular, swimming in a rooftop pool in New Orleans. All daughters love that their family hosts Christmas each year and that their mother completes the "hunt," a tradition of following clues on index cards to find the first gift. As Elizabeth notes, "We love how she writes poems and funny things about each of us." Like her sisters, Leigh loves her "two weeks in New Hampshire," especially the preparation. "We would go to BJs and stock up on snacks; my favorite was the 'Airheads.'" She, too, speaks at length about the cross-country trip. "My mother made a special place in the van for me to color, read, and sleep." She laughs when she recalls her father's reading of plaques: Everywhere we went, he had to read every plaque ... the Alamo, the Hermitage ... my sisters would roll their eyes, but I loved it and would read along with him.... I guess maybe that's why I majored in history in college, like him.

Mother-Daughter Relationship

The mother-daughter relationship is also highlighted in each of the daughter's stories. Elizabeth credits her mother's "belief in her" and "support of her daughter" as two important reasons she finished her bachelor's degree in business. One favorite memory for Mary was working with her mother for 7 years. "I remember the days we would drive to work together. We had so many great conversations. It was just so much fun getting to know my mom more. I miss those days!" Leigh reflects on her mother's home and work schedule: "My mother is my greatest source of feminism.... My mother worked many hours at several jobs, went to school a lot, but still took care of us ... and loved us to the moon and back." Taylor attended the same elementary school at which her mother was an administrator. She shares fond memories of driving with her mother to school during her elementary years. "I remember singing in the car and reciting my multiplication tables." Each day, Taylor would venture into her mother's office for a snack and inevitably bring a friend with her because "she was a nice principal so everyone wanted to come with me."

Father-Daughter Relationship

The father's presence in the family unit is captured by the mother and all four daughters. Mae describes her husband as her "best friend" and "greatest support" who encourages her, "to do what makes me happy."

Elizabeth fondly describes her father as someone like her. "We don't talk much about our emotions." Mary describes her father as a "man of few words" and recalls one particular time, around her wedding, when her father told her how proud he was of her. Mary remembers going into her room that night and crying. "There were so many more instances when he was proud of me in my life without saying the words, but just hearing them, it was so special because, you know, he is a quiet guy that doesn't express his emotions much."

The Parents

Leigh characterizes her parents as partners, a team that works but not in a "stereotypic" way, describing that although her father works outside the home, he spends, "more hours driving us places, cooking, and cleaning." Taylor remembers his driving her to school "without ever complaining, and because he worked at night, we all knew he didn't get much sleep." He drove her "both ways in middle school.... I loved rocking out with him.... Our favorite tune was 'Silver Thunderbird.' He coached my basketball team, too, [and] he was a great coach!"

Leigh believes that her parents' partnership highlights that "men and women are equal." She further remarks that her father is a strong defender for the positive treatment of women. Leigh recalls being told one day that the music she was listening to was "very disparaging towards women, and [she] should not support it." Leigh remarks, "What other father says that?" and then adds, "None that I have met." Leigh explains that she never grew up believing that "[she] couldn't do something because [she] was a girl."

Sister Relationships

The sister-to-sister bond is also a recurring theme in the stories. Elizabeth notes that she has many friends, but, ultimately, "It is my sisters that are my best friends." Her daughter, Ava, is credited with bringing her even closer to her sisters. "I can express things through her; she's kind of an outlet.... I can involve [my sisters] through her ... I love them so much, and we get closer all the time." Mary "looked up to [her] older sister but was jealous of her beauty." Mary sees herself as protective of her younger sister, Leigh, and was sad that she "once cut her hair." Taylor is 11 years Mary's junior. "I was her night nanny.... She was my little buddy growing up. I loved having someone to take care of." Leigh recalls how her oldest sister, Elizabeth, would "rub [her] back" when she cried about some of the "mean things that happened to [her] in 7th grade." Mary would just "hug [her] and make [her] laugh." Taylor jokes that she grew up with "four mothers instead of one," but as she has grown older, she has become, "very close to each of them, they are my best friends."

Family Values

Mae notes that two of her family's values were education and giving. According to Mae, her father's education was cut short by "WWII and a growing family. I think this made him [her father] more adamant that all my siblings should receive a higher education, which we all [five siblings] did." Mae's mother, however, believed that education was very important, but "equally important was giving to others." Mae relates many stories about volunteering in church as a Sunday school teacher and bringing meals to families. "It seemed as though at least once a month my mother was delivering meals to a family.... 'We can always throw in a few more potatoes' was one of her favorite expressions."

Each daughter confirms that education is an important value, but as Leigh notes, "We were expected to help others." Church-related activities and helping grandparents are two of the frequently highlighted activities. Elizabeth further notes that "even her daughter [Ava]" is involved in "Best Buddies" at school and laughs that "another generation" of service has begun.

Challenging Life Experiences

Negative body image is a theme woven into some of the stories. Mae's story infuses two generations of women, herself, and her mother.

> I was always pretty popular as a kid in elementary school. My grades were great. I was pretty outgoing ... [but] that changed in middle school when I became extremely self-conscious. I really don't know what happened. . . . I was always very skinny and often teased about this.... My mother told me that she was also teased about being thin when she was young.... I think that made me feel pretty bad.... I don't know, it's like I was a balloon, and all the air went out of me.

Elizabeth shares a particularly deep hurt that centered on body image. She candidly writes about her struggles with an eating disorder:

> For nearly six years, I battled an eating disorder that was my friend, my safety net, and my identity. By starving, purging, and exercising away my inner self-hate, worries, and struggles, I thought I was opening myself up

to loving others more fully; thus, by losing weight, people would like me and accept me. After all, this is what TV and magazines told me. I started counting calories and working out every day. Slowly my body began to change. People started to notice my physical change and say things like, "Wow, you look good," or "Did you lose weight?" The more attention I received, the more calories I cut out of my diet; thin was the key to being loved.

One isolated story, yet poignant theme that "influenced her behavior," was Leigh's involvement with intimate partner violence. Leigh reports that her first male relationship was "abusive." She believes that she was very "vulnerable" because she thought that all men were like her father, "quiet, loving to all, and extremely respectful towards women." Leigh likens her first relationship to the "stereotypical teenage movie," as he broke down her self-esteem, "little by little" and "tried to isolate [her] from friends." The first time they had sex, she told him to stop, but he told her to "shut up," and "she cried until he was finished." Eventually, the relationship ended, with her parents' help, but not without causing scars. "I was mad at men, I believed they were all scum.... I treated men like objects because that's how I was treated."

Mary and Taylor also relate stories that contained a disorienting dilemma, or a time when they experienced an event that caused them to become unbalanced (Mälkki, 2010). Mary experienced a physical dilemma. In high school, she played on three varsity sports teams as a freshman. Unfortunately, Mary's ankles hampered her playing. "Hurting my ankles impacted my life." Mary had to wear ankle braces when she played. "I hated the nicknames like Rainbow Bright and Leg. I put on a smile and laughed, but inside I was angry."

Taylor's disorienting dilemma was psychological. The often-talked-about "senior slide" in high school was more dramatic for Taylor. She was hospitalized and diagnosed with obsessive compulsive disorder (OCD), depression, and anxiety:

> Learning about my imperfections was hard, especially since I am a perfectionist. Learning what triggered my diagnoses and [triggered] me was hard. However, these diagnoses have led to some of the best moments of my life. I never thought I would love myself, but I now live my life with passion, and I am learning to appreciate who I am for what I am, instead of what I am not.

Resiliency

All five narratives also relate stories with themes of resiliency that transformed and revised the respondents' identities into stronger emotional selves. Mae started high school a much quieter version of herself. "I was quiet. I was placed in the highest grouping of students academically. I was with the same kids in every class, and I was bored." In response, Mae decided to do something that changed her high school experience. "During my high school years, cheerleading was very popular." Mae and 200 of her female classmates tried out for three spots on the cheerleading team. Mae was chosen, and by her senior year, she was a co-captain. "It was nice to meet lots of people and have something to do every day besides schoolwork. High school ended on a positive note for me."

The life changer for Elizabeth was becoming a mother. "Once I became a mother, it stopped being about me and became being about her. I finished school and have much more confidence in my abilities." Mary found her solace in sports and to this day, many of her best friends remain "the girls [she] met playing ball in high school and college. Sports got me through high school."

Today, Leigh advocates for herself and others "I will not put up with [abuse] these days, and if anyone I know or meet is in an abusive relationship, I will be the first to offer support." Her strength, she believes, developed from family and friends' love and support, "going to an all girls' high school," and therapy. Her healing took time, but, eventually, Leigh realized that she "didn't deserve to be treated so badly." Her choice of college majors, history, and art history, she believes, heightened her "awareness of discrimination towards women throughout history." Leigh speaks at length about the Guerilla Girls, a group of female artists who expose "the hypocrisy of women in the arts and advocate for intersectional feminism … support human rights for all." Leigh believes that art also "helped [her to] heal."

Taylor's hospitalization experience, she believes, "basically smacked me in the face with what I wanted to do in the future, become a counselor." As a recent college graduate, Taylor shares what she considers "the greatest impact on [her] in college," the *Girlhood Project*. The project is a mentoring program that brings together middle school adolescent girls and undergraduate women students for activities and discussions. The college students plan each session. About the *Girlhood Project*, Taylor states, it was a "community inside of college … a safe place to be me … instilled greater confidence in my abilities, helped me see my body through a lens other than the media, and showed me that my thoughts and opinions were valid, and I could share them."

Professional Development and Career Choices

The professional development/career choices were revised and continue to be revised for each respondent. Mae envisioned herself teaching, being a wife, and, later, a mother. She did not foresee herself being an administrator. During her 9th year of teaching, however, Mae was asked to apply for her first administrative job. At the same time, Mae was informed that she needed certification as an administrator, which meant more coursework, despite already having earned two graduate degrees. Mae entered the local university, but, after several courses, she was "shut out" from taking any other courses until she chose a degree track. "I met with my advisor. He said that I should get my doctorate. I was stunned. A doctorate? No one in my family had ever received a doctorate. A month later, I was enrolled in a doctorate program in educational leadership."

Over the next 20 years, Mae became an adjunct faculty at local colleges and held several administrative roles; however, over time, her longing for the classroom became more pronounced. "My roots were in teaching, and I began to think about ending my career in a teaching role." Eventually, Mae was selected as a professor at a small private university. "I was sad to leave my dear colleagues, but I was excited about my new adventure."

Elizabeth laughs when she talks about career choices. "I really had no idea what I wanted to do. I was a liberal arts major until one professor told me I couldn't go wrong with a business degree. My least favorite subject was finance, and, yet, here I am today working as a financial analyst." Elizabeth hopes to eventually move into a managerial/leadership role and complete an advanced degree.

Mary graduated from college with a degree in criminology. "I wanted to be a police officer." Her professional goals changed, however, after working in security and realizing that she "hated to shoot a gun." Mary hopes her future includes good health, two children, her own classroom, and the possibility of teaching "a college class or two." She may, however, end up on a totally different career path. "I am interested in so many things. Who knows? I plan to keep on working with an eye to growing myself in my career."

Leigh also holds many hopes for the future. When she graduated from college, her career goal was to work in an art museum. Then, a teacher friend said that her school needed a para-educator, so Leigh applied. "I needed full-time work and insurance." She was selected for the job. "Never, in a million years, did I ever think I would like teaching … [but] I love it!" Today, Leigh dreams of continued teaching, getting "[her] master's, maybe a doctorate, and having a kid."

Taylor majored in psychology in college because she was unsure of a career path and "figured that it was a safe choice for no matter what [she] did." Taylor is in graduate school and now hopes to eventually get a "Ph.D. and have [her] own counseling practice. I should have known I would land on counseling because when I was in elementary school, every year I was chosen to be a friend in someone's school counseling group!" Her family is also very important to Taylor. "I want my family to be proud of me; they are the biggest driving force in my life." Taylor wants to travel, explore, and grow, "I want to learn new things that excite me."

DISCUSSION

This chapter provides a glimpse into the lived experiences of five women, whose stories often shine a spotlight on the research on women's development. The women revised their personal and professional identities over time, some in more pronounced ways than others. The mother always wanted to teach, yet her journey was interrupted for 25 years when she held administrative positions. Elizabeth, the oldest, was unsure of a career, chose business, and now works as a financial analyst, a career that she never anticipated. Mary wanted to be a police officer but now teaches. Leigh always wanted to work in an art museum, yet, like Mary, seems to have found her passion in the schools. Taylor chose psychology as a major because she believed "it would help [her] in any job." Taylor now realizes that counseling is her passion. In essence, the "becoming" and the "to become" for these five women may be defined as the sum of their personalities, experiences, and education.

The stories transcend the generational cohorts (Baby Boomer, Generation X, and Millennials) represented. The most joyful events shared by all five women centered on stories of family relationships during gatherings such as "Friday night pizza," "walking the pond," and the "Christmas hunt." The daughters' stories capture many special moments with their parents and grandparents, including vacations, mystery rides, and sporting events. They also identify at least one disorienting dilemma that transformed their personal lives: Elizabeth's eating disorder, Mary's injuries, Leigh's intimate dating violence experience, and Taylor's hospitalization (Clark, 2008).

Two of the most pronounced concerns of women reported in the literature are body image and intimate partner violence. The stories of struggling self-esteem related to body image were captured across three generations: grandmother, mother, and daughters. The grandmother and mother were reportedly "ashamed" of their less than "full figures." Elizabeth and Taylor talk about the influences of the media, in particular, on how women should look and dress (Jackson et al., 2013). Elizabeth developed an eating disorder, from which approximately 20 million women today suffer in the United States (Wade et al., 2011). Leigh disclosed her history of intimate dating violence, an experience that between 44% and 88% of females experience during adolescence and young adulthood (Bonomi et al., 2012).

The stories touched upon the mother-daughter bond—a bond that has a strong influence on a woman's development (Cwikel, 2016; Fingerman, 2001; Singh, 2013). In fact, one researcher referred to this relationship as the "literal mother of all relationships" (Tannen, as cited in Cwikel, 2016, p. 263). The daughters all spoke fondly of their father's constant support, which has been found to influence the positive, lifelong health and development of women (Alleyne-Green et al., 2016). The mother, too, notes her husband's support of her career, which can be considered a shift in social norms and gender relations as compared to earlier generations (Kasen et al., 2006). The bond between and among the daughters, however, seems especially strong and is highlighted throughout all the daughters' stories. Researchers have found that such a bond, which spans birth order and ages, often protects adolescent girls from feelings of loneliness and fearfulness (Padilla-Walker et al., 2010).

The stories also highlighted several additional positive influences on each woman's evolving identities. In addition to the support of family and friends, counseling is seen as an important source of positive influence to the development of self. Elizabeth states that counseling and family support "literally saved [her] life," and counseling helps Leigh to become a "stronger person" who is now able to help "other kids with their challenges" and Taylor to discover her "specialness" and her "future career." Mary and Taylor note their participation in athletic teams as fostering positive self-esteem through the lasting friendships they developed. In this regard, MacPherson et al. (2016) and Rauscher and Cooky (2016) note that peer groups of female athletes can have positive effects on women's identity development.

Taylor discussed a form of support that a growing number of studies have documented as beneficial to healthy female development, her participation in coursework that combines feminist pedagogy with practice, specifically the *Girlhood Project*. Taylor has "no doubt" that her participation positively influenced her self-esteem and confidence as well as that of the middle schoolers who participated on a weekly basis. Research has shown that groups and activities that foster dialogue and develop collaborative relationships among girls have positive results (Gonick, 2004; Jackson et al., 2013; McIntyre et al., 2007).

Journeys are never smooth but, rather, are filled with both peaks and valleys. The journeys of these five women are no different. Theirs are stories of joys and sorrows that highlight the significance of family, friends, counselors, and female support groups. The personal and professional stories of these five women are still unfolding, and, as their journeys evolve, their narratives will no doubt continue to revise their identities. As the youngest among the women stated, "I want to continue changing and growing forever."

REFERENCES

Alleyne-Green, B., Grinnell-Davis, C., Clark, T. T., Quinn, C. R., & Cryer-Coupet, Q. R. (2016). Father involvement, dating violence, and sexual risk behaviors among a national sample of adolescent females. *Journal of Interpersonal Violence*, *31*(5), 810–830. https://doi.org/10.1177/0886260514556762

Benedict, C. (2007, May 22). This is your life (and how you tell it). *New York Times*. https://www.nytimes.com/2007/05/22/health/psychology/22narr.html

Bonomi, A. E., Anderson, M. L., Nemeth, J., Bartle-Haring, S., Buettner, C., & Schipper, D. (2012). Dating violence victimization across the teen years: Abuse frequency, number of abusive partners, and age at first occurrence. *BMC Public Health*, *12*(1), 637. https://doi.org/10.1186/1471-2458-12-637

Chang, H. (2016). *Autoethnography as method*. Routledge.

Clark, M. (2008). Celebrating disorienting dilemmas: Reflections from the rear-view mirror. *Adult Learning*, *19*, 47–49. https://doi.org/0.1177/104515950801900310

Cwikel, J. (2016). Development and evaluation of the Adult Daughter-Mother Relationship Questionnaire (ADMRQ). *Family Journal*, *24*(3), 263–272. https://doi.org/10.1177/1066480716648701

Fingerman, K. L. (2001). *Aging mothers and their adult daughters: A study in mixed emotions*. Springer.

Gonick, M. (2004). Old plots and new identities: Ambivalent femininities in late modernity. *Discourse: Studies in the Cultural Politics of Education*, *25*(2), 189–209. https://doi.org/10.1080/01596300410001692148

Jackson, S., Vares, T., & Gill, R. (2013). "The whole playboy mansion image": Girls' fashioning and fashioned selves within a postfeminist culture. *Feminism & Psychology*, *23*(2), 143–162. https://doi.org/10.1177/0959353511433790

Kasen, S., Chen, H., Sneed, J., Crawford, T., & Cohen, P. (2006). Social role and birth cohort influences on gender-linked personality traits in women: A 20-year longitudinal analysis. *Journal of Personality and Social Psychology*, *5*, 944–958. https://doi.org/10.1037/0022-3514.91.5.944

MacPherson, E., Kerr, G., & Stirling, A. (2016). The influence of peer groups in organized sport on female adolescents' identity development. *Psychology of Sport & Exercise*, *23*, 73–81. https://doi.org/10.1016/j.psychsport.2015.10.002

McIntyre, A., Chatzopoulos, N., Politi, A., & Roz, J. (2007). Participatory action research: Collective reflections on gender, culture, and language. *Teaching and Teacher Education*, *23*, 748–756. https://doi.org/10.1016/j.tate.2006.12.025

Mälkki, K. (2010). Building on Mezirow's theory of transformative learning: Theorizing the challenges to reflection. *Journal of Transformative Education*, *8*(1), 42–62. https://doi.org/10.1177/1541344611403315

Padilla-Walker, L. M., Harper, J. M., Jensen, & Alexander C. (2010). Self-regulation as a mediator between sibling relationship quality and early adolescents' positive and negative outcomes. *Journal of Family Psychology*, *24*(4), 419–428. https://doi.org/10.1037/a0020387

Rauscher, L., & Cooky, C. (2016). ready for anything the world gives her? A critical look at sports-based positive youth development for girls. *Sex Roles*, *74*(7–8), 288–298. https://doi.org/10.1007/s11199-014-0400-x

Singh, J. (2013). Mother-daughter relationships in fasting, feasting. In M. S. Thirumalai (Ed.), *Language in India* (pp. 428–417). Maharshi Dayanand University.

Wade, T. D., Keski-Rahkonen, A., & Hudson, J. (2011). Epidemiology of eating disorders. In M. Tsuang & M. Tohen (Eds.), *Textbook in psychiatric epidemiology* (3rd ed., pp. 343–360). Wiley.

CHAPTER 4

NEGOTIATING THE TRANSITION FROM HIGH SCHOOL TO COLLEGE

Two Narrative Accounts

Patrick Flynn
University of Maine at Farmington

Gabrielle Comeau
Old Dominion University, Norfolk, Virginia

INTRODUCTION

College-bound high school seniors carry emotional, self-image, social, and academic baggage with them when they transition to the first college year. Transitioning students who come from families with a long history of college attendance, degree attainment, and professional careers bring the expectation that they will continue the tradition of postsecondary success.

Narratives on Becoming: Identity and Lifelong Learning, pp. 47–58

Upper middle-class American White male students who come from such families are uniquely equipped for success given the long history of White male privilege firmly established in American culture. However, women have outnumbered men in college applications and enrollment for the last 40 years (Carbonaro et al., 2011; Riegle-Crumb, 2010; Rocheleau, 2016), which has increased the expectation that female high school seniors will attend postsecondary institutions as a matter of course. Meanwhile, the experience for male students has become increasingly more fraught with self-doubt and disengagement (Turner, 2016). In short, the pressure to succeed and "fit in" at a college or university at age 18 has made the transition year more difficult for both males and females over the last two generations.

By 2010, college enrollment in the United States had reached nearly 70% of postsecondary students, up from 16% in four generations (Arnett, 2015). Most new students meander through college attempting to answer the question they asked when they began considering the merits of a post-secondary education: "What kind of job would really fit me best, given my abilities and interests?" (Arnett, 2015, p. 145). A second set of questions, implied by the first but often more dearly felt by emerging adults leaving home for the first time, include: What kind of life am I capable of? What kind of life can I make based on my values, my desires, and my hopes? The following narratives reflect on each of these questions.

These two narratives are not offered as exemplars that can be generalized to the experience of similarly situated current students, but instead as contributions to a larger discussion of the first-year experience (FYE). Gabrielle Comeau's narrative is very recent and recounts experiences that continue to shape her postsecondary educational career. Patrick Flynn's undergraduate experience ended in 1990, and his narrative is the product of nearly 30 years of reflection. Patrick's FYE as an upper middle-class white male student at an Ivy League liberal arts institution (Cornell University, 1986-1987) is qualitatively different from Gaby's FYE in 2015 at Central Maine Community College. Gaby is White and her family is in the middle class. Her first choice was a highly selective 4-year liberal arts college, Roger Williams University in Bristol, Rhode Island. As the narratives show, however, the many points of connection between Gaby's and Patrick's reflections suggest common experiences.

The authors met at Poland Regional High School in Poland, Maine, in 2012. Gaby was a freshman and Patrick was the school's assistant principal. We developed a connection through Gaby's work with the Student Ambassadors, a cocurricular activity that Patrick supervised. In our FYEs reflected upon here, we discuss many shared experiences: coping with the emotional conflicts that arise from leaving home and joining a new community; reevaluating and reestablishing self-image; breaking some social connections and (re)making others; and transferring academic skills and talents from one setting and set of expectations to the next level.

METHODOLOGY

We chose qualitative, narrative method as our methodology to provide the reader with a nuanced understanding of our FYEs. The key to narrative methodology "is the use of stories as data, and more specifically, first-person accounts of experience told in story form having a beginning, middle, and end" (Merriam, 2009, p. 32). The purpose of narrative inquiry is to make sense of a person's life as lived, creating "meaning and significance with respect to the research topic" (Clandinin & Connelly, 2000, p. 42). We were interested in using narrative to engage in a conversation regarding the FYE by identifying our own shared elements, separated by 30 years but still familiar to us both.

Our experiences constituted a moment of crisis that led to a shift in our self-perception. Neither of us was able to achieve separation-individuation, the capacity to view transition without anxiety or the expectation of rejection (Mattanah et al., 2004, p. 213; Turner, 1991). We determined that narrative was the most effective way to convey our affective experience of the first year of college. I (Patrick) invited Gaby to collaborate after learning about her FYE. Setting the two stories side-by-side offered the opportunity to make meaning through comparison. Throughout the project, Gaby and I drafted language, shared it with each other, provided comments and suggestions, and incorporated each other's recommendations into revisions.

FIRST NARRATIVE: GABRIELLE COMEAU, HIGH SCHOOL CLASS OF 2015

Gaby has lived in western Maine her entire life and graduated from a small rural high school. She has completed her second year at Central Maine Community College and is planning on transferring to the University of New England to study Pharmacy.

My stress started sophomore year of high school. My high school really pushed going to college and picking a major before you even got accepted. Like every sophomore to go through that school, I had to do a presentation on this topic. The presentation had to be between 10 to 15 minutes in front of a panel of judges; the judges included one freshman, one junior, and two teachers. The topic was a career that we wanted to pursue when we grew up, and I did my presentation on becoming a pastry chef because I enjoyed baking. However, in the process of preparing the presentation, I realized that was better as a hobby than a career for me. I looked into different colleges I could attend, where I could possibly live, where I could get a job, etc. Doing this presentation got me thinking about what I really wanted from my life and what I wanted in a college.

I kept thinking about what I wanted to be when I grew up, and I eventually settled on social work. What helped solidify this decision was the fact that I had so many people telling me that they could see me being a great social worker. I was fueled off of other people's opinions. In high school I was pretty impressionable. Even though I knew what was best for me, I wanted to fit in and do what everyone else wanted me to do. During my junior year I got the opportunity to go on a college touring road trip called The Gran Tourismo hosted by the high school. We visited six different schools in Massachusetts and Rhode Island: Wheaton College, University of Rhode Island, Bryant University, Roger Williams University, Salve Regina University, and Johnson & Wales University. This trip was my first time ever touring a college, and also the first time I set foot on Roger Williams University (RWU) campus. The minute we got to RWU, I fell in love with it. The campus is in Bristol, Rhode Island, an adorable port town that I wanted so desperately to be a part of.

As soon as I got into senior year I was completely overwhelmed. In a very short amount of time my whole life as I knew it was going to change. I was pushed to apply to college by the school and my family, even though I was unsure about where I wanted to go or even if that's what I wanted. I kept thinking about RWU and how much I loved it, but I knew it was expensive. Although I was unsure, I decided to go for it and apply. We were urged to apply for one safe school, one reach school, and one school that was about our level. The reach school was one that was a little out of our range in terms of expectations, grades, extracurriculars, sports, price, distance from home; it was anything that would challenge us. I applied for four schools: Roger Williams University, Bryant University, University of Rhode Island, and University of New England. My reach schools were Roger Williams University and the University of Rhode Island; my safety school was Bryant University, and my just-right school was the University of New England. I felt pressured and rushed, like I hadn't explored all my options, but I knew I was making a lot of people happy and I wasn't "wasting my brain" by joining the military or by going right into the work force. More than anyone, my grandparents were the biggest influences and my motivation to go to college. They encouraged me to make a better future for myself through education.

When I started to get my acceptance letters I was overjoyed; I got accepted to all the schools I applied to with very generous offers, but I was most excited about my acceptance letter from Roger Williams. They offered me a scholarship that would pay for half my tuition per year and a job as a math tutor. Both the scholarship and the job offer, as well as a beautiful campus with great food swayed my decision away from University of New England. I sent in my deposit and started to get things in place for orientation and move in day. I anxiously waited all summer to go back to the campus, and when it came time to leave for orientation, I could not get out of the house fast enough. My parents and I were on the road for about 4 or 5 hours, navigated through Boston traffic, got lost on campus for an hour, and then stood in line for my name tag and group assignment. Our group assignments were based on our majors. Since my major was social work, I was paired up with the psychology and sociology group.

I spent all day with my group, traveled around campus, ate lunch with them, and made friends. I realized that most of my group members were native to Rhode Island and were already very familiar with the campus and student life. The other students informed me that RWU was a pretty popular school, and many of the people on campus liked to party. When I was young my parents told me stories about the parties they went to when they were younger. They scared me away from drugs and alcohol, so at this point in my life I had no interest in starting to party. While we were touring, I found out that part of the orientation was staying overnight in the dorms. Somehow I missed that information in the materials sent home and did not come with an overnight bag. It would be my first and only night I spent at Roger Williams.

I was terrified; I felt so alone and trapped. We were staying in older dorms; they were plain, dirty, cold, and dark. I didn't know what to think; all I knew was that I didn't want to be there anymore. I called my parents where they were at the hotel and told them I didn't want to stay there anymore. I went home the next day in tears because everything I had wanted and dreamed was going down the drain. When I got home we started the process of dropping me out of school. As soon as I dropped out of Roger Williams I felt unbelievably relieved. I felt like I had dropped a huge weight from my shoulders, but then it became quickly overwhelming. I felt the pressure of having to be doing something after high school and I started to panic. I thought of so many things and countless options. I wanted to go to college because I didn't want to let my parents down, but I felt like I needed a break from school. I thought about taking a year off from school and working, so I could save up some money. But I also thought about joining the military because they would help pay for my education. But after some talking, my mom suggested I look into Central Maine Community College because that's where she attended college and graduated with two degrees. I didn't think I had any other reasonable options my parents would approve of, so I decided to look into it. I called the college and they were still accepting late students, so I sent in my application and was accepted almost immediately.

After my application was accepted, they rushed to get me in. I took my Accuplacer tests for English and writing, and within the day I had signed up for my classes and had already bought my books. I only planned on staying at Central Maine Community College for a semester or two when I first applied, just long enough to figure out what I wanted to do. But I finished a second year at the community college in May 2017 and had a chance to reevaluate my wants and goals. I changed my major and got on track to graduate by 2019 with two associate degrees.

Looking back, I think one of the biggest reasons I got so nervous about going to Roger Williams was that it was so far from home. I have a very close relationship with my family and friends, so I had a hard time convincing myself that moving far away would be a good thing. Through the years I've watched as my friends transferred schools, dropped out, or changed majors, and I saw how much my best friend struggled when she moved away from home for school. She was never really able to cope with the distance, and about halfway through the first semester of sophomore year, she dropped out. What I'm trying to get at is that you don't truly know yourself until you're put in a foreign place and told to do your best. When you're young you don't really understand how different your life will be once you leave home and start over.

SECOND NARRATIVE:
PATRICK FLYNN, HIGH SCHOOL CLASS OF 1986

Patrick is a high school administrator at a small rural high school in Western Maine. He has taught in two high schools outside of Chicago, Illinois, one of them suburban and upper-middle class and the other rural and lower-middle class. He received a PhD in Adult Learning and Development from Lesley University in 2019.

My academic success through the eighth grade in my hometown of Kildeer, Illinois, dominated my self-image and in large part cemented my ambition to attend a highly selective college or university. I accelerated through primary school with work differentiated for me and, occasionally, a few other students at each grade level. I entered sixth grade at the junior high school in the honors track and graduated at the top of the class in eighth grade. My speech at graduation focused on the transferability of the skills and knowledge we attained in junior high through the rest of our lives, with an emphasis on the transitory nature of education itself. My message was that even though everything changes, we can always depend on the basics acquired through study and practice to come to our aid when we need them.

My social skills through grade eight also developed quickly and deeply. I entered adolescence at age 11 and immediately established my identity as heterosexual and in need of romantic connection. By grade eight, I had "fallen in love" with two different girls. I engaged in roughly 20 romantic relationships before graduating high school. I had made private plans to spend the rest of my life with two of these girls and was emotionally crushed when both relationships ended, one of them in the eleventh grade and the other in my first year of college.

The decision to apply to colleges and then to attend Cornell University ran parallel with the need for romantic ties, but neither informed the other in any meaningful way. I assumed that my relationship with my high school girlfriend would continue and we would end up together after she graduated from college 5 years later. I assumed that our connection was strong enough to withstand the distance, which was the only variable I saw changing after I graduated high school. I imagined her hanging out with the same friends she had made in her first three years of high school and did not imagine the hole left by the graduating seniors (not just me, but many others who had been long-time friends of hers and mine). I did not imagine that she would struggle with my departure any more or less than I would, which meant that I assumed she would cope as I would and we would therefore maintain our connection through occasional phone calls and near-daily letters. I noticed but was not concerned by the gradual drop-off in the frequency of her responses to my regular six or seven letters a week.

My social life in high school kept me confident and comfortable with myself. I had never considered myself "popular," but my role as yearbook editor senior year helped me realize that for years I had ignored cliques and divisive labels (or been oblivious to them) and established friendships with a wide variety of students. My close friends were members of the upper-middle class, middle class, lower-middle class; they were athletes and/or musicians and theater performers; they were male and female; they were Christian, agnostic, Jewish, and Hindu; they were from my town or from the two others that fed our school system. We went to rock concerts, occasionally drank alcohol, engaged in some minor neighborhood vandalism, and talked and listened to music for hours and hours. We worked part-time jobs, watched each other play soccer and run track, and played pick-up games of basketball and softball. In the early 1980s, before we had our driver's licenses, we rode our bikes to each other's houses and spent whole days on the weekend and during the summer in the surrounding woods or "downtown" in the two suburbs near us that had town centers. Once we had cars, we went on joyrides and crossed state lines just to feel transgressive. In short, my social life in secondary school was well-adjusted and emotionally satisfying. I gave no thought to maintaining any of the connections I had established in secondary school as I moved on to college, except for the relationship with my high school girlfriend, which I fully expected to continue through our postsecondary careers and into adulthood. I remember believing that the relationship with her would sustain me. I do not remember at any point thinking about making friends at college.

Not surprisingly, it took months for me to establish any kind of superficial social connection at Cornell. I chose a single for my dorm assignment and was relieved when campus housing granted my request. I moved in quickly, a day before most other students (out-of-state students had some leeway not available to in-state students), and promptly shut my door when my mother left. I attended but did not actively participate in a few of the orientation activities that Cornell offered before classes began; I skipped most of them. I took the campus tour and was required to take part in the dorm ice-breakers on one of the first nights we were there. I listened to music on headphones so that no one would have to hear the kind of music I liked, and I ate at odd times to avoid the crowds or seeing others from my dorm. I walked to and from class and rarely explored the rest of campus or Ithaca for the first 2 or 3 months.

By the end of October, I had heard from a mutual friend still in high school that my girlfriend had started dating a 12th-grade friend, someone whose name had started coming up more often in her increasingly less frequent letters. I panicked but did not acknowledge our relationship was over for at least another year. By November, I had applied to Indiana University as a transfer student, largely because my closest friend from high school was attending IU and was begging me to come to Bloomington. I see this now as an attempt to reconnect and as a tacit admission that whatever social capital I had earned in high school had completely dissipated.

After that first semester at Cornell, however, and after I had made the decision to transfer, I began to hang out with my suitemates more often. I developed friendships and even made an enemy. I started a brief and superficial relationship with a female student and was propositioned a few times by a bisexual male student. There was one awkward night of pornographic movies staged for five or six of us guys by the student who propositioned me, and one disconcerting night where we (male and female) sat in a circle in a dorm room and passed a hash pipe under black light. I passed on both the proposition and the pipe. Despite my casual experience with alcohol in high school, I refused offers in that first year and even went so far as to label myself an alcoholic to stop people from continuing to ask me to partake. However, even with this trepidation, two friendships I established in second semester were strong enough to last into my mid-20s. It was as if, once I decided to leave Cornell, the pressure was off and I was able to open up to people. I did not regret leaving, however, and I remember a surge of adrenaline as I packed on the last day and the radio serendipitously played Phil Collins's pop hit "Take Me Home." Whenever I hear the song now, I still see the blank wall of my empty single dorm room, with the window to the left, the door to the right, and the bed behind me .

During that year at Cornell, my academic life took a decidedly negative and lonely turn. I realized quickly that much of the feeling of success I experienced for the first 13 years of school came from my ability to impress people who already believed I was different from them. My early love of reading and my verbal and math skills set me apart from others but in the same mold as my older brother, 2 years ahead of me, in whose wake I coasted for my entire school career. At Cornell, not only did no one know who I was, no one seemed to care what I thought. My first meeting for a course called "Folk Tales and the Romantic Imagination" set the tone. This was a seminar limited to eighteen students drawn from all years. The class started at 9:05 A.M., and by 9:00 on this first day, the room was full. We sat around a table for fifteen minutes waiting for the instructor before one "student" announced she thought it was time to start class. She was the graduate student instructor, something none of us undergraduates had realized until she spoke. I remember thinking, if my "professor" was so intimidated by the course, how could I possibly be effective? I did not speak in any of my classes unless the instructor called on me, which they rarely did. I settled into the comfortable anonymity of long lectures and silent assessments.

I had finished sixth in my class in high school. I earned no grade less than a B in any class. In contrast, in that first semester at Cornell, I earned two Cs and only one A. I withdrew from a class for nonattendance. I made no attempt to visit any professor until the end of the first semester as finals approached and I panicked, thinking that if I did not become "more than a number" to my instructors, I would lose whatever advantage I had recently heard might accrue from the effort. I earned better grades second semester and entered Indiana University with a mildly impressive transcript.

As I moved through the material and the assignments at Cornell, I gradually depended more on my innate curiosity as a guide. I bought classical and jazz CDs in Ithaca on solo trips into town. I checked out canonical books from the Cornell library, titles I had heard of but knew little about. I engaged in political conversation with my suitemates and watched the anti-apartheid demonstrations in the quad. My mind slowly reemerged and once again helped me form an image of myself as someone who was intelligent, thoughtful, and capable of contributing to serious conversations. Then I left in May and enrolled at Indiana University in August.

Over the course of my FYE and into my second FYE at Indiana, my self-image underwent significant revision. The process felt external, shaped by my environment rather than any purpose of my own. In that Cornell year, I was stubborn, unwilling to seek society, friendship, or any other comfort that might replace the feeling I had in my hometown of Kildeer, Illinois, as an adolescent. At the time, I could not conceive of it, but now it is clear that at some level I considered my achievements in high school as terminal. They defined me and led me to believe that the self I created there would simply continue in a new location with new fans and a new purpose. My original purpose, however, had never been defined in high school. I had no clear vision of life during or after college. College itself became the new terminus. During the summer before my first year, I continued the feeling that I was valuable and worthy of praise. When the validation and praise did not immediately come at Cornell, I began to believe that I had been forgotten by the world. I had left home without leaving it behind—the self I created in high school came with me and stayed, stuck, as I failed to negotiate a new self. I saw glimpses of my (new) self in interactions with others who were meeting me for the first time, and I was not impressed. They knew nothing behind what I presented to them, and I had screened off the depth and breadth that defined me in high school. I felt abandoned. My new self hesitated and retreated. I slowly began to recognize that I had no reputation and no laurels, which frightened me into paralysis.

At no point at Cornell, and not until my junior year at IU (when I decided to attend law school after graduation), did I feel as if college were an opportunity to prepare for a career, or make solid friendships. Instead, I defined myself by the reactions others had to me. I fumbled through social relationships, never getting close to anyone but my new Indiana girlfriend, whom I would marry in 2000. Even my childhood friend, who became my roommate (being with him was the reason I chose Indiana), ceased to hold my attention and became irritating because he had found new friends who showed no interest in me outside of time with him. Drinking, eating ridiculous amounts of food, and watching endless sports defined my connection to him and to new friends, all originally his. At first I blamed my high school girlfriend for holding me back, but in fact I was empty and afraid of who I wasn't and who I would never become (the person I was in high school, who was supposed to be the person I would always be).

This, as far as I can tell, was the start of the imposter syndrome, which remained with me deep into adulthood, through my time practicing law (1993–1995); working as an editor in publishing houses (1995–1998); and a year earning a Master of Arts degree in English Literature (1997–1998). I found my footing and my calling when I began teaching high school students in 1999.

CONCLUSION

The value of narrative in qualitative research comes from its ability to share experience that cannot be captured in other modes. While not sufficient to generalize, reading our stories together suggests the difficulty emerging adults face when trying to recenter after leaving secondary school

(Tanner, 2006). Both of us felt a profound sense of personal loss when we left home, and neither of us was able to immediately adapt the considerable intellectual and emotional resources we developed during childhood and adolescence to use in our new environments. We lacked purpose and felt as if we had betrayed the selves we had created before enrolling in college. The good news is that we each adapted eventually to a new set of expectations for ourselves and redefined our perceptions of success.

Our adaptations were made possible in part through our development, characterized by identity formation, in response to the negative FYEs. Schwartz et al., (2005), citing Erikson's 1968 work, proposed that identity formation is most coherent when the individual possesses a greater degree of agency, defined by Schwartz et al. (2005) as:

> a sense of responsibility for one's life course, the belief that one is in control of one's decisions and is responsible for their outcomes, and the confidence that one will be able to overcome obstacles that impede one's progress along one's chosen life course. (p. 207)

Students who have a more developed identity (i.e., a greater degree of agency) also possess greater degrees of self-confidence and efficacy.

The "optimal sense of identity ... is experienced merely as a sense of psychosocial well-being ... [characterized by] a feeling of being at home in one's body, a sense of 'knowing where one is going,' and an inner assuredness of anticipated recognition from those who count" (Erikson, 1968, p. 165). Gaby's academic success at Central Maine Community College led to a greater sense of personal agency, as did Patrick's formation of a strong social network at Indiana University. Each of us redirected our energy toward a new goal, a process that resulted directly from the perceived failure of our FYE.

Status was important to each of us as we considered postsecondary education. We were unable, however, to translate status into a satisfying FYE. Both of us were supported and celebrated by our immediate families, but we lacked the internal confidence in our ability to recenter (Tanner, 2006) in our new college environments. We surprised ourselves in our first conversation about coauthoring when we discovered that Patrick's feelings about his first year, although mediated by thirty years and a succession of professional and personal "adulting" (McClay, 2015) experiences, did not differ qualitatively from Gaby's feelings about her first year. Both of us sensed that the selves we had created through a series of childhood successes both social and academic were not suited to the new postsecondary culture. However, after the FYE, we cut paths through new institutions, new towns, and new emotional landscapes. The FYE played a crucial role in helping us arrive at new understandings of ourselves and our identities.

REFERENCES

Arnett, J. J. (2015). *Emerging adulthood: The winding road from the late teens through the twenties* (2nd ed.) [Kindle Fire version]. www.amazon.com.

Carbonaro, W., Ellison, B. J., & Covay, E. (2011). Gender inequalities in the college pipeline. *Social Science Research, 40*(1), 120–135. https://www-sciencedirect-com.ezproxyles.flo.org/journal/social-science-research/vol/40/issue/1

Clandinin, D. J., & Connelly, F. M. (2000). *Narrative inquiry: Experience and story in qualitative research*. Jossey-Bass.

Erikson, E. (1968). *Identity: Youth and crisis*. W. W. Norton.

Mattanah, J. F., Hancock, G. R., & Brand, B. L. (2004). Parental attachment, separation-individuation, and college student adjustment: A structural equation analysis of mediation effects. *Journal of Counseling Psychology, 51*(2), 213–225. https://doi.org/ 10.1037/0022-0167.51.2.213

McClay, B. D. (2015). Are we there yet? *Hedgehog Review, 17* (2), 10–11. https://hedgehogreview.com/

Merriam, S. (2009). *Qualitative research: A guide to design and implementation*. Jossey-Bass.

Riegle-Crumb, C. (2010). More girls go to college: Exploring the social and academic factors behind the female postsecondary advantage among Hispanic and white students. *Research in Higher Education, 51*, 573–593. https://doi.org/ 10.1007/s1116201091690

Rocheleau, M. (2016, March 28). On campus, women outnumber men more than ever. *The Boston Globe*. https://www.bostonglobe.com/metro/2016/03/28/look-how-women-outnumber-men-college-campuses-nationwide/YROqwfCPSlKPtSMAzpWloK/story.html

Schwartz, S. J., Cote, J. E., & Arnett, J. J. (2005). Identity and agency in emerging adulthood: Two development routes in the individualization process. *Youth & Society, 37*(2), 201–229. https://doi.org/10.1177/0044118x05275965

Tanner, J. (2006). Recentering during emerging adulthood: A critical turning point in life span human development. In J. J. Arnett & J. Tanner (Eds.), *Emerging adults in America: Coming of age in the 21st century* (1st ed., pp. 21–55). American Psychological Society.

Turner, P. (2016). Supporting freshman males during their first year of college. *College Student Journal, 50*(1), 86–94. https://www.projectinnovation.com/college-student-journal.html

CHAPTER 5

CONFESSIONS OF A TRANSPLANTED MIND

"Second Street" Stories of Transgressing, Transforming, and Integrating

Allyson Eamer
Ontario Tech University

INTRODUCTION

We, in the West, are living in an era in which identity politics have launched an ever-growing number of social movements. Stories of self-determination dominate our news cycles and newsfeeds. Those of us who are aware of our privilege are scrambling to prove ourselves worthy allies, and to signal aspects of our life stories that distance us from the colonizers, the racists, and the misogynists. We do this so that we can claim, however tenuously, some sensitivity or personal experience with respect to being disadvantaged. The reality, of course, is that none of us is singularly victim or oppressor. Intersectionality theory explains that our identities comprise

Narratives on Becoming: Identity and Lifelong Learning, pp. 59–73
Copyright © 2021 by Information Age Publishing
All rights of reproduction in any form reserved.

all our different social locations, with one/some being more salient within a specific power structure. As Hankivsky (2014) explained, "Human lives cannot be explained by taking into account single categories, such as gender, race, and socio-economic status. People's lives are multi-dimensional and complex" (p. 3).

The markers and (dis)advantages associated with social class are as complex and contested as any other components of identity, but class mobility may afford a uniquely expeditious means of reinventing oneself. What follows is a personal narrative that deals with my own identity as an academic from the working class. It is the story of the disconnect between my blue collar, anti-intellectual roots, and my current reality as a scholar. It is my attempt to hold these dialectical tensions while navigating my way to a cohesive identity. It represents my effort to deconstruct what it means to be a life-long learner, and how higher education affords access to power structures.

Education has long been considered a *ticket out* of humble origins, along with professional sports, entrepreneurship, and entertainment celebrity (Collins et al., 2014; Eitzen, 2001; Sternheimer, 2011). Those individuals for whom these avenues have successfully afforded social class mobility undoubtedly tell stories about having always known they were special or different. Perhaps our need for a cohesive identity is so strong that we actively rewrite, suppress, or forget elements of our early lives to ensure a better fit with our current version of ourselves. But what does that reinvention cost us? For scholars with working class roots, the tension is present daily as we write, read, and speak in ways that members of our family of origin do not. As bell hooks (1994) put it, "Demands that individuals, from class backgrounds deemed undesirable, surrender all vestiges of their past create psychic turmoil" (p. 182). Using the autoethnographic method, I attempt in this chapter to present my process of working through that "psychic turmoil."

The Autoethnographic Method

Cole and Knowles (2001) referred to the autoethnography as a form of research in which the self is used as a vantage point from which to explore broader sociocultural elements. Arising in response to traditional social research that valued objectivity, ethnography asserted that all social research is informed by, and interpreted through, the sociocultural lens of both the researcher and the participant. That being the case, autoethnography, in which the researcher uses his/her own life as the source of data for exploring social contexts/patterns/forces, is unabashedly subjective.

Herein, I use my memories of life experiences to explore my own class mobility. I relied heavily, at the outset, on the words of other working-class individuals (both fictional and real) to uncover the language with which to speak about my roots. I read the masterful works of Alice Munro (1998), Margaret Laurence (1974), John Guare (1994), and Charles Dickens (1860/1962) as they told the stories of their working-class characters: Rose, Morag, Paul, and Pip, respectively. I chose these particular works of fiction because the characters (all of whom experience being transplanted out of their working-class lives) have unsettled me over the years by prompting me to revisit their private pain again and again.

In addition to rereading the stories of fictional people, I was also compelled to seek out stories of working-class academics. I hungrily read the essays in *This Fine Place So Far from Home* (Dews & Law, 1995) and *Strangers in Paradise* (Ryan & Sackrey, 1996), feeling tremendous connection to the writers and revelling in the familiarity of their themes. Through their stories, I was exposed to descriptions which triggered memories of my own, and I was prompted to interrogate those memories through a critical theory lens. I kept in mind that both what we remember and what we forget can provide insight into the psychosocial claims that shape our interpretation of our lives, with *forgettings* serving to smooth over contradictions and discrepancies (Haraway, 1988; Haug, 1987).

Social Class

Convention holds that social class encompasses economic resources. Research seems to indicate that North Americans believe a more even distribution of wealth is desirable (Norton & Ariely, 2013), with the 2011 Occupy Movement in both the United States and Canada attesting to a moral awakening with respect to economic disparity. Yet in spite of the widespread protests, extreme income inequality remains a global reality. bell hooks (1994) explained, however, that social class incorporates markers other than economic ones: "It only took me a short while to understand that class was more than just a question of money, that it shaped values, attitudes, social relations, and the biases that informed the way knowledge would be given and received" (p. 178). Charlip (1995) juxtaposed drinking beer and watching televised sports with drinking wine and watching PBS. Fussell (1983) speculated that one's definition of social class depends upon one's own social position. He suggested that those at the bottom equate social class with money, while those in the middle incorporate education and occupation, and those at the top claim taste, values, and style are important markers. If social class, then, is an indeterminate grouping of people based on a variety of contested factors, how can we know if we have achieved class mobility? If furthering one's education is considered to be an effective strategy for class mobility, is the concomitant increased income more salient evidence of the transition than the types of books on one's shelves? These are some of the questions which prompted this autoethnography.

FINDING KINDRED SPIRITS IN LITERARY FICTION AND ACADEMIC LITERATURE

Notwithstanding the aforementioned tendency to ascribe one's current identity markers to lifelong propensities, I will attribute my inclination to seek kindred spirits in the printed word to a childhood spent immersed in books. I attended a small K–8 school consisting of children with working class parents. Although test results indicated that I was reading eight grade levels above my own, my parents would not have insisted on gifted programming, nor would they have even known such an option existed. When the teachers no longer knew what to do with me, I was sent to help the Special Education teacher with her students. Years later, as an elementary school teacher myself, I would marvel at the lack of initiative that allowed my teachers to let me languish as *teacher's helper* for so long.

I learned early to value the way in which books broadened my world through the vicarious navigation of life experiences, geographic terrains, and emotional landscapes. From Winston Churchill's capture in South Africa and Esther Hautzig's exile in Siberia, to the Soul Brothers and Sister Lou navigating Southside racism, crime, and police brutality, I read compulsively, making almost no distinction between fiction and non-fiction. Thus, when embarking on this autoethnography, it was natural, I suppose, that I defaulted to other people's stories. As a researcher, I was compelled to scour the academic discourse on class mobility and was delighted to learn there were others like me, who routinely felt like interlopers—who worked in academia but had family trees with few/no high school diplomas. I felt emboldened by the companionship of fictional and real-life comrades.

From other people's stories, I learned that upward mobility seems to necessitate an external transformation as substantiation for one's claim on middle-upper class membership. This was evident in both fiction and in academic literature. From fiction, I noted: "'This is the way you must speak. Hear my accent. Hear my voice. Never say you're going horse-back riding. You say you're going riding. And don't say couch. Say sofa'" (Guare, 1994, p. 76). From academic literature, I read: "I started buying and listening to Joni Mitchell and jazz records. I had never heard of a bagel and cream cheese.... I just ate, listened and kept quiet" (Lang, 1995, p. 171).

In academic circles, I worry that my education has not transformed me *enough*, and that my impatience with jargon and dense language gives me away as an intellectual lightweight. I alternate between a fierce pride in my ability to serve as an agent of subversion and a fierce embarrassment when certain epistemological debates are lost on me. Like Lang (1995) described, I learned to observe, listen, and keep quiet until I could participate safely and pass as *native-born*.

MY STORY/IES

Until I undertook graduate studies, in my 30s, the life stories I shared publicly were framed by gender, religion, language, and the social capital associated with attractiveness, extroversion, and athletic ability. I would tell of being the introverted younger sibling of a beautiful outgoing sister, of my academic achievements, and of my family's involvement in the church in the small Ontario city where I was raised. I would speak of the absence of independent female role models, my friendships with Francophone children, and my aptitude for learning languages. What my stories did not contain were themes of social class.

The Balancing Act

For many middle-class people with working class roots, a precarious balance must be maintained between the public and private domains. While I was a graduate student, references to some of the people in my neighborhood would have been portrayals of colorful characters, rather than as real people whose lives overlapped intimately with mine for many years. Any tales in which I was marked by my working-class membership always included an epilogue that validated my parents' values and choices.

When revisiting childhood memories of my community, I became deeply sensitized to the importance of the geographical boundaries that established class distinctions amongst the children I went to school with (see Figure 5.1). The critical intersection was at Robertson Avenue and Second Street. Second Street divided the haves from the have-nots. Those children who crossed Second Street at Robertson Avenue with the crossing guard were privileged. Living north of Second Street meant living in a single-family dwelling (not a duplex, townhouse, or trailer). It meant having a mother who worked in an office and a father who wore a white shirt to work. Those who lived south of Second Street were significantly less well off. Those dwellings, it seemed to us then, housed teenaged boys who had run-ins with the police, and people who spent a lot of time on their front porches. My family lived directly on Second Street, neither north nor south of the dividing line, not sufficiently well-off to be considered middle class, but not part of the *other crowd* either. It seems I have walked that middle line all my life and that Second Street has become something of a metaphor for the ambiguity of my own class membership.

Figure 5.1

The Neighborhood

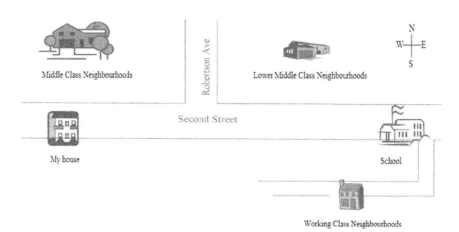

I lived on Second Street on the bottom floor of a duplex, the daughter of a factory worker and a dry-cleaning attendant. My house was one of about 20 in a strip of houses that stretched along Second Street from the elementary school at one end to a car dealership at the other. My earliest friends included children who had regular visits from social workers, and who wore socks on their hands for mittens in the winter. Their homes were where my earliest sleepovers and birthday parties took place. By the age of six, I understood that some fathers drank alcohol while seated inside parked cars in the driveway, and some mothers had male friends who spent the night and left early in the morning.

Partway through grade school, something marvellous happened. A girl with East European heritage arrived at my elementary school. I cultivated her friendship, wanting desperately to be associated with her different-ness. One evening when I'd been invited to stay for dinner, I witnessed a bewildering discussion between my new friend and her mother. They were debating whether "lace over *blue* linen" was the best choice for the dining room table on that particular evening. In my house there was only a kitchen table, and it was permanently covered with a plastic tablecloth. That may have been my first awareness of class difference.

My strong academic performance in high school earned me a place in a prestigious postsecondary institution and, as a result, I learned that a higher social class had afforded my dorm-mates many advantages. I learned, for example, that if freed from the need to spend summers earning money for tuition, one could travel through Europe accumulating stories as fascinating as anything I'd ever read about.

In my first year of university, I exhilarated in the sense of freedom that comes with dormitory living away from watchful parental eyes. Eager to participate in the social life of my dormitory house, I frequently contributed a bottle of wine to parties. I can still recall the wave of shame when a fellow student who lived on my floor asked why I always bought such cheap wine. I confess that, due to the sting of his words, I still occasionally get a knot in my stomach when ordering wine in a restaurant. It was at university that I learned that almost all previously acquired knowledge associated with the acts of eating and drinking could not be applied to the rest of my life.

Teaching and Shape Shifting

In my 20s, I became an elementary school teacher, a choice Norquay (2000) referred to as "long the preserve of upwardly mobile working-class women" (p. 52). To pass as a legitimate member of the middle class, I began experimenting with how to present myself in my new world. Over the next decade or so, I constructed various versions of myself, and landed on two that served me well for a time: the rebel (my earliest incarnation) and the chameleon (which I considered more enlightened). As a rebel, I could present myself as someone reluctant to claim membership in any particular class. I could enjoy the shock value of telling tales about the old neighborhood to people with considerable class privilege, while simultaneously enjoying their tacit acknowledgement that I had *bettered* myself. Alice Munro's character Rose in *The Beggar Maid* employed this tactic too: "Years later she would learn how to use it. She would be able to amuse or intimidate right-thinking people at dinner parties with glimpses of her early home" (Munro, 1998, p. 179). Conversely, I could enjoy the satisfaction of knowing that my big-city stories of rubbing elbows with important people would be shared within my family with at least a grudging respect. My rebel identity, however, never quite aligned with my predisposition to people-pleasing and conformity, and over time, I transitioned into my chameleon identity.

As a chameleon, I was capable of moving back and forth between two worlds, appearing to belong exclusively to whichever one I was inhabiting at a given moment. I did learn, though, that it required considerable effort to stifle whichever part of me was out of synch with the setting I was in.

Eventually, I came to resent refraining from using the *big words* that would have perfectly expressed an idea or concept, knowing that I would sound pretentious in the old neighborhood. Similarly, I was tired of feeling alienated by the middle-class conversations in the staffrooms of the elementary schools where I taught. I would realize in time that adopting the chameleon identity came at a personal cost.

Doctoral Studies

My graduate studies, begun in my thirties, forced me to come to terms with the indisputable truth that higher education tapped into something integral to my being. By then, I was a single mother, teaching full time and taking the train into the city to pursue an advanced degree in the evenings. By all measures, I ought to have buckled at the financial stresses and competing demands on my time. Instead, I felt energized in ways that I had not experienced in my undergraduate studies. A transformation had taken place, and I had achieved a state of readiness that rendered me indefatigable while single-parenting, and simultaneously writing report cards, lesson plans, and graduate papers.

To my surprise, my doctoral studies transformed me in a way that alienated me from my teaching colleagues just as my working-class heritage had done previously. I soon sensed that a reference to the ideas and concepts I was encountering in my studies was construed as judgement upon their choice not to pursue an advanced degree. My motivation for being in my colleagues' classrooms had become suspect, even though my job description and the school board's integrated service model required it. My chameleon skills were being stretched considerably as they were called upon now to allow me to function in three contexts: academia, my elementary school workplace, and my family of origin. I found myself nodding mutely in most interactions, wary of revealing my ignorance, my ambition, or my intellect, depending on the context. Within a matter of a few years, I was seeking a full-time academic position at a nearby university, and saying goodbye to my elementary school career.

On my frequent visits home to the old neighborhood, I can still easily find much to talk about with relatives and childhood friends: parenting, marriage, divorce, relationships. I can easily avoid mentioning my publications, my graduate student supervisions, and my conference presentations. I can express genuine interest in their jobs and achievements, knowing they will not likely inquire about mine, or that if they do, a one-sentence answer is usually in order: "I used to teach children and now I teach adults."

While I was perhaps neither a legitimate rebel nor a successful chameleon, I believe that there existed in me, from an early age, a sense of protectiveness with respect to my family's values, a protectiveness that would compel me to try to integrate the version of me whom I relied on as a scholar with the one who grew up on Second Street.

THEORIZING CLASS MOBILITY

In G. A. Cohen's analysis of choices available to the proletarian (one whose capacity for labour represents his/her only commodity), the Marxist political philosopher proposed an allegory consisting of ten working class people locked in a room (Cohen, 1983). He suggested that if a single key was within reach of each of the ten individuals, and could be used by one person only to open the door, a variety of responses would be elicited. Some, he suggested, may have no wish to leave. Others may be unhappy living in the room but lack the ambition to reach for the key. Still others may worry about the battle that would ensue if everyone reached for the key at the same time. Cohen (1883) used the allegory to consider how *crowded exits* limit individual freedom with respect to class mobility.

To understand my own class mobility and its implications, I chose to draw on the fictional and real-life stories of working-class individuals who had *found a way out*. While rereading the fictional stories, I began to spot patterns, and I theorized that the working-class characters seemed to adopt one of four general stances with respect to class mobility. Next, I considered the stories written by academics with working class backgrounds to see if these same four stances would apply in real-life accounts. Indeed they did, and a typology emerged consisting of (1) The Resigned: individuals who were resigned to their working class existence and had no aspirations for upward mobility, (2) The Willfully Oblivious: individuals who viewed/presented themselves as having agency and social capital in their own right and were oblivious to class limitations, (3) The Contemptuous: those who were contemptuous of the entitlement of the upper class and who justified their contempt with evidence of hypocrisy; and (4) The Escapers: individuals who aggressively sought the means to achieve class mobility and leave behind their lower-class markings.

Weaving my own four theoretical categories into Cohen's locked room allegory, I imagined that of the ten, some would be the ones whom I have called "The Resigned." They would maintain that contentment comes from accepting one's life inside the room. Some would be "Willfully Oblivious" and would not concede that there were compelling advantages to living on the other side of the door. There would also be, among the 10, "The Contemptuous"—people who felt disdain for those on the outside. There might also be "Escapers" who would attempt to seize the key, even at the expense of the others, convinced that whatever lay beyond the locked door of the room was both desirable and accessible.

Table 5.1

Typology

Classification	Fictional Characters	Working Class Academics
1) The Resigned individuals who are resigned to their working-class existence and have no aspirations for upward mobility	"I'm wrong in these clothes. I'm wrong out of the forge, the kitchen or off th'meshes. You won't find half so much fault in me if you think of me in my forge dress with my hammer in my hand or even my pipe. You won't find half so much fault in me if supposing if you should ever wish to see me you come and put your head in at the forge window and see Joe the blacksmith there at the old anvil in the old burnt apron sticking to the old work." ~Joe Gargery in *Great Expectations* (Dickens, 1860/1962, p. 226).	"My parents preferred to live in a working-class neighbourhood of Sacramento, California, even though my father's income as a plumber would have made it possible to purchase a home in a suburban setting. Dad said that he was more comfortable in Rio Linda, among 'his kind of people'." ~Dwight Lang, Professor of Sociology, Son of a Plumber and a Homemaker (Lang, 1995, p. 160)
2) The Willfully Oblivious individuals who view/ present themselves as having agency and social capital in their own right and are oblivious to class limitations	"Rose knew Billy Pope would go back to work tomorrow with stories of the millionaire, or millionaire's son, and that all these stories would focus on his— Billy Pope's—forthright and unintimidated behaviour in this situation. 'We just set him down and give him sausages, don't make no difference to us what he comes from!'" ~Billy Pope in *The Beggar Maid* (Munro, 1998, p. 177)	"[My mother] often said to me, 'You can't eat books; you can't marry books. What are you going to do with all those books?' When [my father] saw me reading, he fretted about my future. 'Pegueros,' he'd say, 'I worry about you. You have no ambition; all you want to do is read.'" ~Rosa Pegueros, Assistant Professor, Latin American History and Women's Studies, Daughter of a Truck Driver and a Sewing Machine Operator (Pegueros, 1995, p. 90)

(Table continued on next page)

Table 5.1 (Continued)

Typology

Classification	Fictional Characters	Working Class Academics
3) The Contemptuous individuals who are contemptuous of the entitlement of the upper class and who justify their contempt with evidence of hypocrisy	"The ones who eat only out of tins. The ones who have to wrap the rye bottles in old newspapers to try to hide the fact that there are so goddamn many of them. The ones who have fourteen thousand pill bottles the week, now ... I tell you girl, they're close as clams and twice as brainless. I see what they throw out and I don't care a shit, but they think I do so that's why they cannot look at me." ~Christie in *The Diviners* (Laurence, 1974, p. 48)	"In the tales told by my father and the men he bartered with, the 'stupid rich bastards' almost always 'got it' in the end, outwitted by the poor little guy. I learned that the stupid rich bastards always underestimated us, always thought we were as dumb as we were poor, always mistook our silence for ignorance, our shabby clothes and rusted cars for lack of ambition or enterprise. And so they got taken, and sharing stories about winning these small battles made us feel better about losing the war." ~Laurel Johnson Black, Associate English Professor, Daughter of a Junkman and a Crossing Guard (Black, 1995, pp. 15–16)
4) The Escapers individuals who aggressively seek the means to achieve class mobility and leave behind their lower-class markings	"Can you believe it? Paul learned all that in three months. Three months! Who would have thought it? ...Paul looked at those names and said I am Columbus. I am Magellan. I will sail into this new world." ~Ouisa speaking about Paul in *Six Degrees of Separation* (Guare, 1994, p. 81)	"I promise myself: I will never have to work in that paper mill; I will never experience the intellectual isolation of a man like my father, who reads avidly but finds no one among the roaring machinery to discuss his thoughts with." ~Heather J. Hicks, Assistant Professor of English, Daughter of a Paper Mill Worker and a Homemaker (Hicks, 1995, p. 158)

CONCLUSION

So then, how do I figure into all of this? Who am I within Cohen's locked room and my own typology? In exploring my memories, I can say with relative certainty that as a young person, I did not feel discontent with my family's limited financial means. While I certainly knew that some of my classmates had higher standards of living, I don't remember class mobility as a goal that framed my worldview. It seems, then, that I spent many years like Dickens's Joe Gargery—as a resigned person. My departure for university was simply a natural continuation of school, at which I had always excelled. I understood that I would hold down part-time work while studying, and that I would return to my hometown each summer to work at as many jobs as I could manage. Furthermore, I understood that when my studies were complete, I would resume my life among family members and old friends, albeit with a framed degree to display on a wall in my parents' home.

As it happened, a series of life events, some happy, others not, resulted in my opting to go overseas to teach in China. Thirty years later, after an international marriage, two bouts of expatriate living in China, an unfulfilling career as an elementary school teacher, becoming a parent, getting divorced, earning graduate degrees, and spending over a decade in academia, I may have finally come to terms with my own class mobility.

I believe now that I constructed my rebel and chameleon identities so that I would not be forced to acknowledge that I was in fact an Escaper. To do so, I believed, would have been hurtful and disrespectful to my parents. It would have negated their efforts to provide a good life for their children. It would have broken with tradition … severing a link between myself and my progenitors, all of whom were farmers and labourers. Thus, I attempted to straddle the two worlds so as to avoid requiring my family and childhood friends to accept a transformed version of myself that I had not yet even fully embraced.

Given the complexity of life in this postmodern, global era, we can surely claim membership in a multitude of reference groups. As William Moses (1995) put it, "All thinking people have more than two souls" (p. 198). However, with respect to achieving an integrated class identity, I am not encouraged by the experiences of those whose stories I've been digesting. Alice Munro (1998) eloquently described the conflicting emotions of shame and loyalty experienced by her character Rose who "married well" and thus achieved class mobility: "Now that she was sure of getting away, a layer of loyalty and protectiveness was hardening around every memory she had, around the store and the town, the flat, somewhat scrubby unremarkable countryside" (p. 179).

Similarly, Renny Christopher (1995), an associate professor of English and daughter of a carpenter, described a split self, in which her two class identities are often at war with each other: "My old self doesn't respect my new self. My old self says I'm living a lazy, over-privileged life. My new self says, what more could I do? My old self says, you're not doing anything productive" (pp. 140, 150). Thus, it would appear that integrating and/or juggling multiple social class memberships can be a life-long task.

I have no fear that I am in danger of forgetting my working-class roots. My roots are in my speech, my frugality, my resistance to dense academic language, and in my work ethic. My fear instead is that I will never learn how to shake off my entrenched sense of inferiority, and that I will never stop feeling the urge to announce my class heritage right up front—like a confession that must be got out of the way, thereby denying others the chance to call me an impostor. I fear also that I will never become a successful hybrid—an embracer who proudly and smoothly travels between two worlds, rather than a rebel who resists membership in both, or a chameleon with an identity linked to the expectations of others.

I'd like to suggest that the term class mobility is a misnomer. Mobility implies a movement that takes one away from a place with the purpose of arriving at a different place. I object to this term for two reasons. Firstly, I am not convinced that the actions which enable one to claim membership in a higher class are necessarily purposeful. Without a doubt, some individuals have vowed to find a way out of a working-class existence, and actively sought the means to do so. However, I believe that there are also many "escapers," like myself, who stumbled across the boundary, having approached it unknowingly and circuitously over an extended period of time.

Secondly, I object to the implication in the term "class mobility" that one leaves one's original class behind upon gaining admission to a higher class. That is certainly not the experience of the comrades I've acquired through my reading. On the contrary, all of them describe a deep connectedness to their origins, and an awareness of how their class roots shape and frame their relationships, activities, and professional trajectories.

What really needs to be expressed here when considering class mobility is not the work of earning and maintaining a membership card, but the transformative work, afforded by higher education, that allows for the integrating of life scripts with overlapping and conflicting values and goals. These are the stories that need telling, not the tales of the bumpy road en route to a better life, but the stories of transgressing, transforming, and integrating … stories of the personal work required to reject duality; stories in which we recognize how education provides the language we need to conceptualize and talk about transformation; and stories in which we come to understand our agency in negotiating our own identities.

REFERENCES

Black, L. J. (1995). Stupid rich bastards. In C. L. B. Dews & C. L. Law (Eds.), *This fine place so far from home: Voices of academics from the working class* (pp. 13–25). Temple University Press.

Charlip, J. A. (1995). A real class act: Searching for identity in the "classless" society. In C. L. B. Dews & C. L. Law (Eds.), *This fine place so far from home: Voices of academics from the working class* (pp. 26–40). Temple University Press.

Christopher, R. (1995). A carpenter's daughter. In C. L. B. Dews & C. L. Law (Eds.), *This fine place So far from home: Voices of academics from the working class* (pp. 137–150). Temple University Press.

Cohen, G. A. (1983). The structure of proletarian unfreedom. *Philosophy & Public Affairs, 12*(1), 3–33.

Cole, A. L., & Knowles, J. G. (Eds.). (2001). *Lives in context. The art of life history research*. Altamira Press.

Collins, C., Ladd, J., Seider, M., & Yeskel, F. (Eds.) (2014). *Class lives: Stories from across our economic divide*. Cornell University Press.

Dews, C. L. B. & Law, C. L. (Eds.). (1995). *This fine place so far from home: Voices of academics from the working class*. Temple University Press.

Dickens, C. (1962). *Great Expectations*. Thomas Nelson and Sons. (Original work published 1860)

Eitzen, D. S. (2001). Upward mobility through sport? The myths and realities. In D. S. Eitzen (Ed.), *Sport in contemporary society: An anthology* (6th ed., pp. 256–63). Worth.

Fussell, P. (1983). *Class*. Ballantine.

Guare, J. (1994). *Six degrees of separation*. Random House.

Hankivsky, O. (2014). *Intersectionality 101*. The Institute for Intersectionality Research & Policy, Simon Fraser University.

Haraway, D. (1988). Situated knowledges: The science question and the privilege of partial perspective. *Feminist Studies, 14*(3), 575–599.

Haug, F. (Ed.). (1987). *Female sexualization: A collective work of memory*. Verso Press.

Hicks, H. J. (1995). Paper mills. In C. L. B. Dews & C. L. Law (Eds.), *This fine place so far from home: Voices of academics from the working class* (pp. 151–158). Temple University Press.

hooks, b. (1994). *Teaching to transgress: Education as the practice of freedom*. Routledge.

Lang, D. (1995). The social construction of a working class academic. In C. L. B. Dews & C. L. Law (Eds.), *This fine place so far from home: Voices of academics from the working class* (pp. 159–176). Temple University Press.

Laurence, M. (1974). *The Diviners*. Toronto, ON: McClelland & Stewart Inc.

Moses, W. J. (1995). Ambivalent maybe. In C. L. B. Dews & C. L. Law (Eds.), *This fine place so far from home: Voices of academics from the working class* (pp. 187–199). Temple University Press.

Munro, A. (1998). The beggar maid. In A. Munro (Ed.), *Selected stories* (pp. 154-189). Penguin Books.

Norquay, N. (2000). A most un-ordinary life. *Vitae Scholasticae, 19*(2), 51–63.

Norton, M., & Ariely, D. (2013). America's desire for less wealth inequality does not depend on how you ask them. *Judgement and Decision Making, 8*(3), 393–394.

Pegueros, R. M. (1995). Todos vuelven: From Potrero Hill to UCLA. In C. L. B. Dews & C. L. Law (Eds.), *This fine place so far from home: Voices of academics from the working class* (pp. 87–105). Temple University Press.

Ryan, J., & Sackrey, C. (Eds.). (1996). *Strangers in paradise*. University Press America.

Sternheimer, K. (2011). *Celebrity culture and the American dream: Stardom and social mobility*. Routledge.

CHAPTER 6

THE INTERSECTIONALITY OF RACE, GENDER, AND URBAN LEADERSHIP

Four School Leaders (Re)constructing Self and Identity

**Yesenia Fernández, Kitty M. Fortner,
Antonia Issa Lahera, and Anthony H. Normore**
California State University Dominguez Hills

INTRODUCTION

Narrative inquiry embraces narrative as both the method and phenomena of study. As Clandinin and Connelly (2000) put it, "People by nature lead storied lives and tell stories of those lives, whereas narrative researchers describe such lives, collect and tell stories of them, and write narratives of experience" (p. 2). The following is the narrative of our stories, the stories of how we became urban school leaders who, through a (re)construction

Narratives on Becoming: Identity and Lifelong Learning, pp. 75–91
Copyright © 2021 by Information Age Publishing
All rights of reproduction in any form reserved.

of self and identity, ultimately use our positions of power to advocate for just and equitable schools. These are our *testimonios*—literally translated as testimony which can be defined as "a narrative that conveys personal, political, and social realities. One's *testimonio* reveals an epistemology of truths and how one has come to understand them" (Delgado Bernal et al., 2012, p. 364). These narratives, though not all from the perspectives of persons of color, are all from perspectives of leaders who are frequently marginalized as a result of being advocates for justice and equity in spaces where that is often not accepted. These narratives are the testimony of our journeys, our (re)construction of self as social justice leaders in urban schools.

HOW A CHICANA BECAME A CHAMPION FOR EQUITY: YESENIA FERNÁNDEZ

My identity as an urban school leader developed as a result of multiple experiences in oppressive educational contexts, places where I was deemed an outsider and inferior because of my class, gender, and race. As a Chicana who grew up in poverty, I experienced first-hand the injustices our educational system can inflict upon students of color and low- income students. I was a high school student who was not allowed to take college preparatory coursework such as Advanced Placement (AP), simply because I had been an English learner in elementary school. When I was a teenager, I did not understand the implications of this door closing, the difficulties I would have getting into college and successfully navigating college as a result of the inferior education I received in the remedial academic track. Indeed, school officials often create gatekeeping mechanisms that result in unjust treatment of our youth, and it is this knowledge that I carried with me throughout my trajectory as an educator, this *conocimiento*, that ultimately fueled my desire to become a school leader. Influenced by Vygotsky and Freire, *conocimiento*, which translates to knowledge, in this case, "self-knowledge through reflexivity" (Mendez-Negrete, 2013, p. 227) is "a process that unfolds in the context of unearthing knowledge in relationship to the daily life we engage with others as we come to Self-knowledge" (Mendez-Negrete, 2013, p. 227).

Although I had been deemed inferior and without the valued knowledge to fit into the educational spaces I occupied, throughout my journey as a student and eventually an educator, I gained self-knowledge, a *conocimiento* of the knowledge I did have and the impact I could have on others. As Mendez-Negrete (2013) wrote, "engaging *conocimiento* as pedagogical praxis results in the re-stimulation of the trauma or entitlement that shapes who we are as persons" (p. 231). The trauma I experienced in an educational system not created for me became the lens through which I perceived my role as a teacher and eventually as an urban school leader. This lens defined the way I adapted to the tensions I faced as an educator. As a teacher, I recognized the same barriers acting upon my students; they were being tracked in remedial academic coursework and denied a voice, just as I had been. It was then that I decided it was only as a school administrator that I could change the experiences students had and ultimately, their trajectories.

My identity as a school administrator became tied to my unrelenting desire to mitigate inequities. I became a champion for equity and justice in our schools not because it was the noble and right thing to do—though it was—but because becoming a leader who advocated for equity and justice in our schools was part of my personal journey in constructing my identity as a Chicana. I felt responsible for insulating students from the experiences I had in public schools as a low-income person of color; my sociopolitical consciousness within the context of education was transformed. I saw my role as a school leader in the larger context of the school system and perceived my job as a moral imperative (Fullan, 2003). Learning how to be an advocate for equity in our schools from authors like Fullan (2003) was simultaneously occurring as my identity as a Chicana was evolving. Critical race theory (Ladson-Billings & Tate, 1995; Yosso, 2005) influenced this process. Solórzano and Bernal (2001) pointed out, "Critical race researchers acknowledge that educational institutions operate in contradictory ways with their potential to oppress and marginalize coexisting with their potential to emancipate and empower" (p. 313). This tension became my daily existence and how I approached my role as an urban school leader.

My goal as a high school administrator was to ensure that the educational spaces I occupied and led would empower our students of color, not marginalize them; that meant dismantling systems of oppression. I began by removing ability tracking mechanisms as an assistant principal. All students at the urban high school were placed in college preparatory courses by default. There were no minimum grade point average requirements or exams students needed to pass to be placed on the college preparatory track. Test scores and grade point average prerequisites serve to preclude students of color especially English Learners from college preparatory coursework and ultimately from higher education (Callahan & Shifrer, 2016; Fernandez, 2014). We also removed these prerequisites as requirements to enroll in AP courses. This was not an easy feat as I had many meetings and had to address the many concerns by teachers who said I was setting up students for failure and whose perceptions were that our students simply could not succeed in these courses. The battle, however, had a positive result as virtually every student took at least one AP course during the course of their high school career; this included English learners. The schools' graduation and completion of college preparatory coursework requirements for 4-year universities known as A-G coursework both improved and students were no longer relegated to the lowest rungs of academic coursework by default simply because they were students of color. I created policies which would have impacted my trajectory as a student when I was in high school to ensure equity on my campus.

The more time I spent in the field of education, the more my political ideology evolved informed by critical race theory; I became a more "militant" Chicana. My personal identity thus transformed as a result of the professional battles I was fighting trying to ensure an empowering school experience for students of color. The changes in my consciousness resulted in constantly (re)constructing my identity and ultimately led me to be an advocate and social justice leader. As a result of the challenges I faced as I had to convince others that it was important for all students to have a just education and not be marginalized as I had been, I learned to constantly adapt and be resilient in oppressive contexts. I saw myself in the students, and that knowledge became inextricable from my decision making, from my approach to conflict, from my resolute desire to remove barriers and advocate for just and.equitable urban schools even if others saw me as the "angry brown girl." I replicated the work I did at the high school level at the district level which led to national recognition by The College Board. In the end, I realized that I could make a difference in the lives of the students I served and that my identity as a social justice leader would propel me to guide other leaders in the same work, now as a university professor.

MY IDENTITY AS A LEADER FOR JUSTICE IN EDUCATION: KITTY FORTNER

I recall listening to the TED Talk by Chimamanda Ngozi Adichi (2009), "The Danger of a Single Story", and the wave of gratitude that I felt towards her for making it so clear. I had always understood my identity as a multifaceted construct and not a "Single Story." My motivations, influences, and experiences informed by my social, cultural, and political relationships are all part of my identity. My identity is dynamic and constantly evolving through discourse and interactions. Pearce et al. (2008) described how identity changes when we interact with our families, the environment, and with others. My identity includes what I do, what I believe, what I value, and who I will become (Helms, 1998).

One voice from my childhood that resonates most in my head is that of my grandmother. She taught me three important lessons that have become a part of how I identify myself. She taught me that God made people the way that they are and that we should embrace ourselves, learn to be "Okay" in our own skin. She also continually reminded me, "You don't have to like everyone's behavior, but you do have to love them." And finally, she said that God gave us two ears for a reason, and we have a responsibility to listen. I was raised in the heart of the South: Georgia, where a long tradition of fighting for civil and human rights persist; where acts of inclusion, equity, and opportunity continue to be elusive for certain minoritized and marginalized groups. Grandma influenced me to listen, to see, and to love people regardless of race, gender, ethnicity, sexual preference, socioeconomic status, or disability, and to be content in the person who I am and will become.

Moving along my path towards becoming a teacher, the voice of bell hooks was a motivating voice reminding me to pause and remember my roots. hooks (2003) uses the term "imperialist white supremacist capitalist patriarchy" to describe the power structure underlying the social system (p. 1). I am a Black, Native American woman who understands this system of domination and oppression that has labeled and minoritized me. I recall moving into my first apartment and going to college. The neighbor below didn't like Black people and she let me know in clear term: "We don't want any niggers or nigger lovers here." You see my roommate was White and the person helping us to move was White. And I recall the looks of fear and embarrassment on their faces. This is just one incident from my youth where this system created walls of inequity and exclusion. This was my awakening to the fact that my fight for inclusion included others. Reading Paulo Freire's (1970) *Pedagogy of the Oppressed,* Jonathan Kozol's (2005) *Savage Inequalities*, Kathleen Brown's (2004) "Leadership for Social Justice and Equity: Weaving a Transformative Framework and Pedagogy," George Theoharis's (2010) "Disrupting Injustice: Principals Narrate the Strategies They Use to Improve Their Schools and Advance Social Justice," and Tyrone Howard's (2010) *Why Race and Culture Matter in Schools: Closing the Achievement Gap in America's Classrooms* provided me with language to describe my leadership as leading for social justice.

My work as an educational leader in the heart of Santa Ana, California, where 93% of the students qualified for free or reduced price lunch, 82% were second language learners, 97% were minorities, and 75% of the parents were non-English speakers, is where I began identifying myself as a leader for social justice. Before this, I was responsible for myself, my family, and my friends. Now, there were 20+ students and their families, who I did not know, looking to me to help them navigate this system. My priority became providing students with a learning space that was supportive, just, and compassionate as well as helping their families to understand the education system.

Carolyn Shields (2009, 2013) described transformative leaders as leaders who need to balance both critique and promise; to effect deep and equitable changes; to deconstruct and reconstruct knowledge frameworks that generate inequity; to challenge inappropriate uses of power and privilege; to emphasize both individual achievement and the public good; to focus on liberation, democracy, equity, and justice; and finally, to demonstrate moral courage and activism. I challenge and dismantle inequities by emphasizing students' value as individuals and as participants in a global community. In my classroom, we had international pen pals and worked on ideas to better the lives of people's suffering (i.e., how to better inform and bring awareness to our community and the community of our pen pals about diabetes). I provide opportunities for student's voices to be heard. Each year students were required to present to their fellow students, the entire school, and to the community at large about something important to them. I also assist aspiring leaders to develop leadership dispositions as they start with their journey and identity as educators. At the university, I have taught in both the teacher preparation program and the educational leadership preparation programs. It is here where these students grapple with who they want to be as an educator. My belief, that all people have the capacity to solve their own problems, allows me to provide support and challenge them to look within themselves to determine what is important in the context of their work. Listening creates a supportive space to wrestle with and make the necessary growth to place equity at the forefront of their leadership practice.

At the university, I work with teachers who aspire to be urban school leaders (principals, directors, assistant-principals, etc.) in Los Angeles County, one of the most diverse areas in the United States. Principals set directions, develop people, and develop organizations (Leithwood et al., 2004). They play a vital role in building transformative school vision that promotes equity, diversity, and social justice (Kose, 2011); foster collaboration that leads to improved instructional practices (Balyer, 2012); and shape strong relationships among parents, communities, and educators (Ishimaru, 2012). Principals are the most important individuals on a school campus in terms of creating an equitable school culture and promoting positive social change (Santamaria & Santamaria, 2012).

In light of the world's chaos, principals must utilize leadership constructs that promote, recognize, unwrap, and cancel oppressive unjust school practices while instituting equitable, just, and culturally appropriate ones that transform schools into environments where all students can be successful (Shields, 2013). With changing fiscal environments; academic, cultural, and socioeconomic gaps separating learners; increased demands on accountability; community and stakeholder interests; changing demographics; new policies and mandates; the global setting in which we live; and difficult personnel issues, the role of the principal continues to change to meet a growing list of expectations (Lynch, 2012; Shields, 2004, 2013). Principals must be proactive agents of change using transformative leadership (Shields, 2013); be tenacious in their commitment to a social justice agenda (Furman, 2012; Theoharis, 2008); initiate inclusive and democratic practices within their schools (McKenzie et al., 2008); develop authentic relationships (Theoharis, 2007); critically self-reflect (Santamaria & Santamaria, 2012); and keep social justice pedagogy as a priority (Furman, 2012).

My work is to open doors for critical conversations, to help people learn what is important to them, how to listen, and how to value people. As an educator from K–12 to university, my classroom has been and continues to be a safe space for students to explore their own identities and learn to value the identities of others. As a principal, I invited parents, teachers, and students to openly voice their thoughts, creating an inclusive campus culture. Now at the university, I motivate aspiring school leaders to take a social justice stance and to lead for equity. My lifelong task is to transform schools and communities into spaces that are just and equitable. I lead for social justice by implementing protocols that: blur and erase the lines that separate us, open avenues for critical conversations around race, culture, gender, and social needs, and encourage others that their voice matters in this fight for civil and human rights. Dismantling walls that foster inequity through loving, listening, and valuing myself and others is how I advocate for social justice. This is the voice of my grandmother continuing to encourage me to be who God created me to be.

LEADING FOR ISSUES OF SOCIAL JUSTICE, FROM K–12 TO HIGHER EDUCATION: ANTONIA ISSA LAHERA

My narrative is written through the lens and experiences of a white woman and a professor of school leadership who currently works at an urban university located in metropolitan Los Angeles. To transform the lives of urban children in our schools, we need great teachers. Great teachers are fostered by school leaders. While the importance of the classroom teacher remains paramount, the role of the school leader has gained increasing focus thanks in part to work funded by the Wallace Foundation (Leithwood et al., 2004). My identity as an educator continues to be informed by my experiences as a teacher and now as a teacher of future leaders, I am guided by the knowledge that the impact of school leadership on student achievement is clear.

It is through the lens of preparing school leaders that I joined the California State University Dominguez Hills faculty in 2007. I have come to this very important place, CSUDH, to do critical work. My path here came through the K–12 public school system. My career began as a teacher, staff developer and site leader. My school sites spanned the grade levels and were situated in high poverty urban areas. Having grown up in the same system, what I experienced was both shocking and disturbing. The heavy emphasis on compliance, punishment, and blame lit a fire of action within me that burns still. Of deep concern was the preparation of teachers and leaders that were committed to transforming schools. My affinity for teaching, connection to research and scholarship, and belief in a duty to serve was fostered within the context of an urban classroom. In my first small fourth grade classroom, filled with African American, Cambodian, Mexican, and Vietnamese students who were entirely dependent on my skills, pedagogy, and practice, I quickly learned what I did not know. To provide the finest possible instruction for these school dependent children, the researcher in me was born. In my first classroom I learned to read, study, reflect, test, and trust in what researchers and theorists in the field of education were finding. The intersection of teaching, research, and service from that tiny classroom formed the foundation for all my work.

I looked to the university as the logical next step in the pipeline of improvement for marginalized schools. The public-school system in the United States has yet to fulfill the mission of academic achievement for all. Students in high needs communities continue to be served by both teachers and leaders without the experience or skills to transform dismal under-achievement. I chose CSUDH because of the population it serves and the goals and mission of the university. In alignment with my own personal and professional values system, the mission of CSUDH is to "provide education, scholarship and service that are, by design, accessible and transformative" (CSUDH History, Mission & Vision, n.d.a). In turn, the mission of the College of Education reads as (from Our Mission, Values & Goals, n.d.b):

> Through self-examination, collective learning, and research, we construct brave spaces that foster the holistic development of educators. Together, we challenge and dismantle systems of power and privilege in institutions of education. We re-imagine equitable responsive and just learning experiences for all learners, especially those from minoritized groups within our college and in our local schools. We are committed to advancing the following:
>
> - a justice focused agenda
> - the pursuit of equity
> - innovation in teaching and learning
> - rigorous and responsive research
> - collaboration with professional, local and
> - global communities, and student-centered partnerships
> - belief in the limitless potential of our work, each other, and those we serve

We are a college focused on re-imagining our schools and committed to advocacy. Similarly, the mission of the School Leadership Program reads:

> The School Leadership Program develops leaders with an adaptive mindset who use their heart and minds to engage courageously and humanistically create excellent learning environments. Using the lenses of critical pedagogy, generative dispositions, and habits of mind, leaders build and foster restorative school cultures that manifest learning, critical thinking, voice, debate, and collaboration. Creating systems that support the growth for all, with the moral commitment to the most under-served populations equity, justice and critical consciousness are ensured. With lenses of culture, dignity, social responsibility and informed citizenry, communities of activism thrive and transform. (School Leadership Program, n.d.)

The intersection of these two missions brings me to work every day and continues to (re)construct my identity as a professor of future school leaders focused on advocacy and ensuring equity in our schools.

I believe that every educational experience a student has should be transformative. It is my responsibility to create the most interactive, rigorous, and student empowered classrooms, so that educators who can create great learning experiences for their students will emerge. These dual missions demand that I create equitable learning experiences for every student here under my care and that I that engender great outcomes within my classrooms that emanate positive ideas, energy, and a plan for change. We are preparing the future leaders of our community's schools, and we need to do it properly, well, and now.

My current role is professor of school leadership; I simultaneously coordinate the school leadership programs and facilitate the leadership and management of federally funded multi-million dollar grants. Our School Leadership Program has set out to create a cadre of leaders to stem the tide of underperformance and turn around the entire K–12 system in our region. The School Leadership Program is an accelerated, hybrid program that is rigorous, connected, requires commitment, and changes lives. My responsibility is to ensure we can create the best possible school leadership preparation program for urban Los Angeles in both traditional public schools and charter public schools. I have worked on the design, implementation, supervision, and revision of each of our awarded grants. The current grant has us working in turnaround efforts with school leaders and their leadership teams in 30 of the most underperforming high schools in the county.

The highly charged political nature of schools has created an atmosphere of mistrust, toxic relationships, and lack of collaboration and growth. A central tenet of the work I do in the preparation of school leaders is to train them to stay focused on the work. All students and instructors take a deep introspective journey into their current values, behaviors, and practice through a series of assessments, 360-degree feedback tools, and self-reflection. Each person then develops a growth plan for improvement. At the same time, students are trained to focus and study the data they gather for decision making, create systems that support the conditions for improvement, and most importantly, make sure the work is not about them but stays focused on the work. I have spent my entire professional career living this manta of keeping the focus not about me, but about the work. This makes this particular exercise of highlighting my practice challenging.

The work has always been what is paramount, with my view of my role as one who must create the conditions for others to be fostered and grow to greatness. My principles and values have been grounded by the work of many. Theorists across disciplines, such as neuroscience and anthropology, hold ideas about teaching, learning, and creating spaces for students to grow at the edge of their development, along with a critical pedagogy that is grounded in hope. This philosophy includes a deep reflective practice and the need to be critically conscious about the work at hand (Freire, 2000). I have been a teacher for many years, and my practice and pedagogy continue to be refined. I collaborate often with instructors and coteach regularly and so my identity continues to be one of a teacher-leader.

I believe good teachers know research. My research agenda is centered in developing urban leaders who have a critical pedagogy grounded in hope. Using adaptive leadership (Heifetz & Linsky, 2002) and the framework developed in our program, I continue to study the intersection of our leadership preparation with the actual work of a school leader. Our preparation programs have been designed and continue to be modified as part of this research agenda. I focus on the power and importance of school culture. With the idea of a critical pedagogy emerging through leadership efforts to change the landscape of schools, I additionally remain focused on equity issues in all my research. The creation and fostering of leadership teams is a newly emerging component of this work. School leaders cannot alone do the work necessary in schools. Systems must be created to develop leadership in others so that when leaders leave, schools continue to thrive.

ADVOCATING FOR JUST AND EQUITABLE SCHOOLS, PERSONAL AND PROFESSIONAL NARRATIVE: ANTHONY H. NORMORE

Circumstances often propel individuals to become leaders. This narrative reflects the circumstances, journey, and voices that helped shape my understanding of leadership as a position, my leadership identity, and the intersections of race, gender, and urban leadership in that understanding. My narrative begins with a general sense of the pivotal roles of values. Values play a central role in my life. It is the essence of who I am as a human being and my professional life's work as a scholar-educator. My professional values act in sync with my personal values. I believe that human needs in life, as opposed to wants, appear to be few: food, water, shelter, and a sense of personal direction or purpose. I believe that people do not need more, at least to start, if their sense of direction or purpose is sufficiently strong. In this context, for me, having a sense of direction or purpose means having values that are concerned with decisions about right or wrong. As humans, we have the freedom of choice to decide what is right and what is wrong. However, decisions about right and wrong constitute only a subset of all the valuations I make. Above all else, my values represent the true essence of my spiritual "being"—my heart and soul and ability to decide what is good, true, just, and beautiful. My core values center on hope, love, respect, benevolence, good will and concern for the welfare of others, doing good deeds, trust, respect for self and all people, and an appreciation of the world in which I hold myself and others responsible.

My environment and experiences as a child, as a youth, and throughout my adulthood helped shape me to who I am today. I grew up in eastern Canada, and from an early age my parents, grandparents, and great grandparents taught my siblings and me the importance of extending our love to *all* people of the world, regardless of race, religion, nationality, or any other artificial distinction. For example, as children we thought that all families were the same in terms of access to community resources. Still, later in life, it was apparent to me that some families had less than others. Some of my friends were poor but I did not realize it. Racism was not as evident as poverty in my community. I grew up in a white rural community, where the only person of color was either the visiting nurse or doctor. Due to isolation of our community, people rarely moved, and therefore had minimal opportunity to experience knowing other races or ethnicities. What was understood was usually drawn from what we learned about other cultures in our prescribed school curriculum.

My upbringing focused on the importance of humility needed to live in peace and harmony with all persons; slander, greed, deceit, and arrogance had no place in the home or the community. Humility is a quality of being courteous and respectful of others. Acting with humility in any way does not deny our own self-worth. Rather, it affirms the inherent worth of all people. Another focus in my life—then and now— centers on honesty, integrity, and doing good deeds. I hold these as very important values that help me both personally and professionally to remain on a steady path.

One of the hallmarks of a stellar organization is when its culture is characterized by a shared belief that the organization contributes to the future health and livelihood of its members. It accomplishes this mission by integrating its activities into a set of values that act as bellwethers across communities and generations. My leadership work launches from a perspective that every interaction I have as a member of the education community must be consistent with my personal value system in supporting personal and professional growth, respect, integrity, compassion, competence, and responsibility. I strive for this growth and development in my daily interactions with others: in my role as teacher and mentor, in the seriousness that I give to my professional productivity as a scholar and researcher, in my duties as a member of various professional learning communities, and in my ability to integrate my professional skills into the important work of learning organizations locally and globally. I am currently a professor of school leadership. Since my years in education as a public school teacher, school site and district level leader, and a professor and department chair of educational leadership, it has been incumbent on me to encourage the individual talents of my students and colleagues. I have therefore facilitated the student skill development needed to succeed as professionals and scholars; devoted time to support the professional and personal development of graduate students by encouraging them to engage in the professional/academic community; and committed to long-term mentor-protégé relationships with students. Leadership is often thought to be an aptitude (Vygotsky, 1978, 2007), a skillset somehow developed through either watching great leaders at work, or somehow by reading accounts of success and drawing conclusions about what must have transpired. In most instances, this is due to a naïve belief that a single attribute creates the formula for success. In fact, there are lessons of history and thoughts of great minds from Aristotle to Aquinas from whom we can draw insight. There are frames of mind to consider leadership as work to adapt to change (e.g., Jean-Marie et al., 2009), and then to lead others through that change in a structured, systemic way (e.g., Fullan, 2003; Northouse, 2019).

Some believe that leadership can be taught (e.g., Northouse, 2019). If that is true, one of the core questions might be, "What do you teach?" One of the more common approaches is the study of great leaders. Others may focus on the traits and behaviors that successful leaders represent. In fact, leadership can be taught (Anderson et al., 2017); but emphasizing biographies, traits, and behaviors may not be the most fruitful path. Rather, the key to more effective leadership lies at the end of the path that begins with considering adaptive and authentic leadership as a way of thinking (Heifitz & Linsky, 2002). Based on research by Heifetz et al. (2009), common threads that weave throughout my own thinking in terms of effective leadership work across disciplines and include the "best interests" of the greater good; professional interests in gaining/sustaining the "trust" in systems; cultural awareness; reflective practice; professional and personal responsibility; and philosophy/value supporting equitable, equal, and excellent service for the collective public good.

I think of myself as an educator who facilitates learning opportunities rather than as a teacher of a subject. I believe that effective education does more than educate students—it also acts as a working model of civil society, and thereby helps to create, sustain, and improve our communities. Accordingly, I believe it is the responsibility of all educators at all levels to focus on educating and encouraging communities of students to develop into responsible, caring, and contributing citizens—building the future one student at a time at the local, regional, national, and global level. Effective education is inclusive, from the classroom to the board-room, because supporters of education believe that an inclusive education is best for students and for the community, and an inclusive democratic government for education is best for the community. Education must be barrier-free, values-driven, and respectful of every student, every worker, and every citizen.

My belief is that an effective educational system provides a quality education by guaranteeing that every child will have a place by making a habit to help, or at least to do no harm, to any child. My belief is governed by a democratic process that is open to every member of the community regardless of disadvantage or difference. As such, I believe it is my moral imperative to promote civil democracy in preference to any sectarian perspective as the basis for thriving communities; and to celebrate diversity by working with communities, colleagues, and students from different backgrounds, outlooks, and experiences. I believe in high-quality education for an ethnically and culturally diverse student population, equipping students with the capability to become productive citizens who continuously contribute to a global and rapidly changing society.

I embrace the adage "practice what you preach." Stating one thing and practicing another is not part of my daily interactions. I consider myself a servant leader, and a major role I play in graduate education is to assist learners in understanding their own learning and thinking processes, and to critically challenge taken-for-granted assumptions. For example, I focus on empowering my students in the classroom to take ownership for their own learning in the university classroom and in their school practice, to construct their personal and professional moral codes of behavior and examine how these codes are connected to their moral and social responsibilities as educators, educational leaders, public servants, and citizens, and to then search for solutions to enigmatic problems. While in graduate school, I was fortunate to receive a true "servant mentor" as my dissertation supervisor. Through his continued guidance and support I was able to feel much less overwhelmed, disoriented, and frustrated with the expectations graduate students often experience. My supervisor taught me the importance of creating a mentor-protégé relationship between professor and student. While helping me to adjust to the many nuances, idiosyncrasies, and unwritten codes of the institution, he provided me with leadership and mentoring characterized by coaching, guidance, assistance, advising, sharing, and sponsorship. This relationship has lasted over time and been marked by a substantial emotional commitment by both of us. The true mark of a mentor is seen when the protégé continues the legacy of the mentor who encourages students to "pay it forward."

Finally, in my role as an educator it is my responsibility to provide the guidance and sponsorship to my students by speaking or writing on their behalf, or simply "being" there on a spiritual level. I further believe that a professor should stand for the best that university life can exemplify—having a warm presence coupled with a deep personal integrity that spreads trust. A student should never need to worry about a professor's position on issues that affect human welfare—that a professor is there for people, for building and nurturing relationships, that the professor's word is true, and that the professor teaches all students by example and is ultimately guided by a strong sense of values, equity, and social justice.

CONCLUSION

As urban leaders and professors, the process of our identity formation went hand in hand with our evolution into leaders who advocate for equity and justice in urban schools. From our experiences in high school oppressed by inequitable policies, childhood experiences of racism, to teaching experiences with underserved populations and our own experiences with poverty, we learned we had a moral imperative to improve the lives of others through education. To do so, we learned and reflected and experienced a (re)construction of self and identity to become the social justice warriors we are today.

REFERENCES

Adichi, C. N. (2009). Summary: "The danger of a single story". https://english.umd.edu/research-innovation/journals/interpolations/fall-2018/summary-danger-single-story.

Anderson, H. J., Baur, J. E., Griffith, J. A., Buckley, M. R. (2017). What works for you may not work for (Gen) me: Limitations of present leadership theories for the new generation. *The Leadership Quarterly*, *28*(1), 245–260. http://dx.doi.org/10.1016/j.leaqua.2016.08.001

Balyer, A. (2012). Transformational leadership behaviors of school principals : A qualitative research based on teachers ' perceptions. *International Online Journal of Educational Sciences, 4*(3), 581–591.

Brown, K. M. (2004). Leadership for social justice and equity: Weaving a transformative framework and pedagogy. *Educational Administration Quarterly, 40*(1), 77–108. https://doi.org/10.1177/0013161x03259147

California State University, Dominguez Hills, History, Mission, Vision. (n.d.). https://www.csudh.edu/about/history-mission-vision/

California State University Dominguez Hills, College of Education, Our Mission, Values & Goals. (n.d.). https://www.csudh.edu/coe/about/mission/

California State University Dominguez Hills, School Leadership Program. (n.d.). https://www.csudh.edu/slp/

Callahan, R. M., & Shifrer, D. (2016). Equitable access for secondary English learner students: Course taking as evidence of EL program effectiveness. *Educational Administration Quarterly, 52*(3), 463–496.

Clandinin, D. J., & Connelly, F. M. (2000). *Narrative inquiry: Experience and story in qualitative research.* Jossey-Bass.

Delgado Bernal, D., Burciaga, R., & Flores Carmona, J. (2012). Chicana/Latina testimonios: Mapping the methodological, pedagogical, and political. *Equity & Excellence in Education, 45*(3), 363–372.

Fernandez, Y. (2014). *The" Socio-Academic" positioning of English learners in high school: Implications for policy and practice* (Doctoral dissertation). The Claremont Graduate University.

Freire, P. (2000). *Pedagogy of the oppressed* (30th anniversary edition). Continuum International Publishing Group.

Fullan, M. (Ed.). (2003). *The moral imperative of school leadership.* Corwin Press.

Furman, G. (2012). Social justice leadership as praxis: Developing capacities through preparation programs. *Educational Administration Quarterly, 48*(2), 191–229. http://doi.org/10.1177/0013161X11427394

Gonzalez, A., Lara, I., Prado, C., Lujan Rivera, S., & Rodriguez, C. (2015). Passing the sage: Our sacred testimonio as Curandera Scholar Activists in academia. *Chicana/Latina Studies: The Journal of Mujeres Activas en Letras y Cambio Social, 15*(1), 110–153.

Heifetz, R., Grashow, A., & Linsky, M. (2009). *The practice of adaptive leadership: Tools and tactics for changing your organization and the world.* Harvard Business School Press.

Heifitz, R., & Linksy, M. (2002). *Leadership on the line: Staying alive through the dangers of leading.* Harvard Business School Press.

Helms, J. V. (1998). Science—and me: Subject matter and identity in secondary school science teachers. *Journal of Research in Science Teaching, 35,* 811–834.

hooks, B. (2003). 5 'The oppositional gaze: Black female spectators. In R. Lewis & S. Mills (Eds.), *Feminist postcolonial theory* (pp. 219–233). https://doi.org/10.4324/9780203825235-17

Howard, T. C. (2010). *Why race and culture matter in schools closing the achievement gap in America's classrooms.* Teachers College Press.

Ishimaru, A. (2012). From heroes to organizers: Principals and education organizing in urban school reform. *Educational Administration Quarterly, 49*(1), 3–51. http://doi.org/10.1177/0013161X12448250

Jean-Marie, G., Normore, A. H., & Brooks, J. S. (2009). Leadership for social justice: Preparing 21st century school leaders for a new social order. *Journal of Research on Leadership Education, 4*(1), 1–31.

Kose, B. W. (2011). Developing a transformative school vision: Lessons from peernominated principals. *Education and Urban Society, 43*(2), 119–136. http://doi.org/10.1177/0013124510380231

Kozol, J. (2005, 2012). *Savage inequalities: Children in America's schools.* Broadway Paperbacks.

Ladson-Billings, G., & Tate, W. F. (1995). Toward a critical race theory of education. *Teachers College Record, 97*(1), 47–68. http://dx.doi.org/10.4324/9781315709796-2

Leithwood, K., Louis, K., Anderson, S., & Wahlstrom, K. (2004). *How leadership influences student learning: Review of research.* Commissioned by The Wallace Foundation and produced jointly by the Center for Applied Research and Educational Improvement, the University of Minnesota, and Ontario Institute for Leadership.

Lynch, M. (2012). A guide to effective school leadership theories. New York, NY: Routledge.

McKenzie, K. B., Christman, D. E., Hernandez, F., Fierro, E., Capper, C. A., Dantley, M., González, M. L., Cambron-McCabe, J., & Scheurich, J. J. (2008). From the field: A proposal for educating leaders for social justice. *Educational Administration Quarterly, 44*(1), 111–138. http://doi.org/10.1177/0013161X07309470

Mendez-Negrete, J. (2013). *Pedagogical conocimientos: Self and other in interaction.* National Association for Chicana and Chicano Studies Annual Conference. San Jose, California. (Paper 14). http://scholarworks.sjsu.edu/naccs/Tejas_Foco/Tejas/14

Northouse, P. G. (2019). *Leadership: Theory and practice.* SAGE.

Pearce, J., Down, B., & Moore, E. (2008). Social class, identity and the good' student: Negotiating university culture. *Australian Journal of Education, 52*(3), 257–271. http://doi.org/10.1177/000494410805200304

Santamaria, L. J., & Santamaria, A. P. (2012). *Applied critical leadership in education: Choosing change.* Routledge.

Shields, C. M. (2004). Dialogic leadership for social justice: Overcoming pathologies of silence. *Educational Administration Quarterly, 40*(1), 109–132. http://doi.org/10.1177/0013161X03258963

Shields, C. M. (2009). Transformative leadership: A call for difficult dialogue and courageous Action in Racialised Contexts. *ISEA, 37*(3), 53–68.

Shields, C. M. (2013). *Transformative leadership in education: Equitable change in an uncertain and complex world.* Routledge.

Solórzano, D. G., & Bernal, D. D. (2001). Examining transformational resistance through a critical race and LatCrit theory framework: Chicana and Chicano students in an urban context. *Urban Education, 36*(3), 308–342. http://dx.doi.org/10.1177/0042085901363002

Theoharis, G. (2007). Social justice educational leaders and resistance: Toward a theory of social justice leadership. *Educational Administration Quarterly, 43*(2), 221–258. http://doi.org/10.1177/0013161X06293717

Theoharis, G. (2008). Woven in deeply: Identity and leadership of urban social justice principals. *Education and Urban Society, 41*(1), 3–25. http://doi.org/10.1177/0013124508321372

Theoharis, G. (2010). Disrupting injustice: Principals narrate the strategies they use to improve their schools and advance social justice. *Teachers College Record, 112*(1), 331–373.

Vygotsky, L. (1978). *Mind in society: The development of higher psychological processes.* Harvard University Press

Vygotsky, L. (2007). *Social development theory.* Learning-Theories.com. http://www.learning-theories.com/vygotskys-social-learning-theory.html

Yosso, T. J. (2005). Whose culture has capital? A critical race theory discussion of community cultural wealth. *Race ethnicity and education, 8*(1), 69–91. http://dx.doi.org/10.4324/9781003005995-8

CHAPTER 7

"WHY WE MUST CONTINUE IN THE JOURNEY"

A Conversation Between Two Literacy Educators

Lorena Germán
Faculty, Headwaters School, Austin, Texas

R. Joseph Rodríguez
Faculty, St. Edward's University, Austin, TX

"[M]y life has been a story of the redeeming social and emotional value of public education. Education has been my defining moment, my mission, my goal, and my odyssey."

Sonia Nieto, *Brooklyn Dreams: My Life in Public Education* (2015, p. 4)

Narratives on Becoming: Identity and Lifelong Learning, pp. 93–107
Copyright © 2021 by Information Age Publishing
All rights of reproduction in any form reserved.

INTRODUCTION

The phrase "lifelong learner" can be overused with little interrogation of how it is enacted and maintained for a fulfilling, giving, and thrilling life for teachers and students. However, in recent years, an emphasis on the multiple literacies humans possess—from cradle to grave—further advance the concept of remaining a learner and thinker throughout one's life. In this chapter, we as two literacy educators present a conversation on the multiple beliefs, narratives, and perspectives we possess and how we use these to mediate our own identities in being and becoming lifelong learners among our students and teaching colleagues.

We share what informs our professional learning and pedagogies for a social justice lens directly connected to meaning-making across various literacies that include language arts and literature. We believe that all students can learn and succeed. This especially happens when teachers are aware of their own abilities, beliefs, biases, perceptions, and struggles to grow as professionals. It leads us to humane practices to begin and be sustained in our classrooms. We believe that a social justice lens must exist within our institutions where we teach. This lens should also be used in and beyond our own homes and communities.

In negotiating our identities in various settings, self-reflection requires making meaning of who we are and what we are becoming in the presence of more adults and students. This is how we realize we are still becoming and forming our personal and professional learning toward growth. That vulnerability and that honest journey are what we share with students and attempt to do daily for meaning-making across identities and literacies. Overall, our shared work challenges power dynamics and humanizes the classroom space. Moreover, we welcome all of our testimonies as we build community and socially responsible literacies.

The multiple identifications, or ally memberships, and identities in defining oneself that adult educators possess are also brought into the classroom. Through five identity-informed practices, we elaborate on the following in this chapter:

1. Adopting inclusive perspectives for teaching and learning,
2. Exploring connections across literary and social texts,
3. Forming one's selfhood with affirmation,
4. Negotiating identities across varied spaces, and
5. Reflecting on identities and their meanings.

Our conversation began in Summer 2017 via phone, electronic mail, and face-to-face meetings. We transcribed our notes, and ultimately we arrived at the five themes that connect our practice. We collected questions about our personal and professional lives that we include here.

Our conversations and interactions began organically and much like the organic intellectual Gramsci described who is engaged in diverse communities and with the people and their situational struggles in society (as cited in Hoare & Sperber, 2016). In this case, it means we are connected to our teaching colleagues, students, school staff, and families and how they make meaning and survive despite various odds in society. In conversation, we share how we enact the five practices in our own lives (identity-construction experience) and in our teaching for the formation and affirmation of our students and teaching colleagues.

Our identities began in distinct communities and brought us to diverse schooling and education communities. Lorena Germán was born in the Dominican Republic and raised in Massachusetts. She received a bachelor's degree in English from Emmanuel College and a master's in English literature from the Bread Loaf School of English at Middlebury College. In 2014, Lorena was recognized by the National Council of Teachers of English (NCTE) with an Early Career Educator of Color Leadership Award and in 2016 by the NCTE Latinx Caucus with the Excelencia in Teaching Scholarship. She is the cofounder of The Multicultural Classroom, an organization that supports teachers, administrators, and districts with culturally relevant and sustaining practices. Lorena is also Cofounder of #DisruptTexts, a grassroots movement to create a more inclusive and equitable language arts curricula that our students deserve. Currently, she teaches composition and literary analysis at Headwaters School, an independent secondary school in Austin, Texas.

R. Joseph Rodríguez is of Mexican descent and was born in Houston, Texas. He received a bachelor's degree from Kenyon College, a master's in English from the University of Texas at Austin, and doctorate in curriculum and instruction from the University of Connecticut. Joseph has taught English and Spanish language arts in a number of public schools, community colleges, and universities. His research interests include academic writing pedagogy, children's, and young adult literatures, and socially responsible biliteracies. Joseph is the coeditor of *English Journal*, a publication of the Secondary Section of NCTE. Currently, he is lecturer at St. Edward's University and teaches English language arts and reading in Austin, Texas.

Lorena and Joseph met when she received the NCTE Early Career Educator of Color Leadership Award in 2014. They met during a luncheon and realized they had many shared colleagues and friends and that they both lived in Austin, Texas. A friendship bloomed and critical consciousness took even greater forms. Since then, they have collaborated on various language and literacy projects that involve the advancing of multilingualism and multiculturalism in our curricula and instruction, reading and study of inclusive children's and young adult literary texts in the language arts classroom, and translating social justice and action into youth-led participatory action research. The invitation for collaboration research for this book chapter project brought us together as coauthors and solidifies our commitment to teachers who write with other teachers and beside their students.

INCLUSIVE PERSPECTIVES

Rodríguez: Inclusion can be seen as another buzzword in education, but I witness firsthand how instructional planning and learning outcomes influence our perspectives. We can adopt a global vision with an awareness of diversity in classrooms that serve students' immediate realities. We can introduce and maintain humane care and interest for our work in the profession. Inclusive perspectives encourage us to think of marginalized voices and underrepresented groups along with ways to support them in what we teach and learn together.

Germán: Inclusivity is what yields engagement and genuine learning. As we consider all of the selves present in the room, we strive to connect with them. Ideally, that brings everyone into the conversation and we, teachers included, are present.

Rodríguez: What can I do next that influences my growth as a teacher and learner? I ask myself this often to reflect on my practice and growth. As educators, we can guide instruction in many ways, but we also depend on students and our teaching colleagues to model how learning unfolds. Ambrose, Bridges, DiPietro, Lovett, and Norman (2010) noted,

> Learners may engage in a variety of metacognitive processes to monitor and control their learning—assessing the task at hand, evaluating their own strengths and weaknesses, planning their approach, applying and monitoring various strategies, and reflecting on the degree to which their current approach is working. (pp. 6–7)

What Ambrose and others described unfolds in our own teaching, and I want to know more from teachers who do this work.

Germán: Metacognitive thinking is integral to effective teaching and learning. In my classroom and in my work with colleagues, we spend time reflecting on our actions. We think about what we just did and how we did it as a way to get to know ourselves better, but also to know how to replicate success.

Two years ago, I taught a student who would use audio books or listen to someone read in order to complete the reading of the texts. In this case, we were reading a graphic novel. There were moments where he had not completed the written task, but had found a comfortable place in the corner of the room on the floor to continue the conversation connected to books and characters. In fact, he was ferociously reading a graphic novel on his own! He finished the book in class and was ecstatic. Immediately, he wanted to discuss his amazing achievement.

We spent some time reflecting on what he did as a reader, what his attitude was like as he read, what was different from past processes, what obstacles he overcame as a reader, and how he persisted with questions. That reflection led us to identifying his strengths and allowed him to realize his literacy powers and interests. This was transformative for him because it created positive and affirming self-talk, but more importantly a proven identity as a reader. These understandings were directly related to my experience reading and studying Beach, Johnston, and Stein's (2014) book *Identify-Focused ELA Teaching: A Curriculum Framework for Diverse Learners and Contexts*. The text argued that secondary ELA teaching should offer students examples for constructing their diverse and unique identities through the literature in our classrooms. In particular, students should experience inclusive practices by teachers in language arts and literary selections that are not monocultural or White American dominant. The approach the student adopted also holds true for educators. We reflect on our practice, and we think about ways to teach lessons better. We think about strategies to reach our students in more meaningful ways.

Rodríguez: Adopting inclusive perspectives for teaching and learning is at the heart of developing empathy. In fact, empathy is what allows young people and professional educators to connect to other humans across differences. As adult contributors to this society, our main goal with adolescents, preservice teachers, and professional colleagues is to prepare them for a future that is meaningful with civic responsibility and mindful practice.

Germán: Indeed. In an age in which social media and digital spaces are where many of us spend a lot of time, learning to connect to other humans across differences and distances is essential for our country's progress. It is essential for the future of our society. Teachers play an important role in facilitating these opportunities for empathy.

Regardless of the content area, be it math, science, or in English language arts classrooms, inclusive perspectives should be at the core of the approach to teaching. This work should happen meaningfully and in a mindful practice. However, many people are not always ready for the journey that this requires. This journey is challenging and multifaceted, because it requires the peeling of layers and the unlearning that teachers have believed and followed without self-questioning and change. Sometimes the beliefs and behaviors can be from the teacher's own preparation and teaching position. Life-long learning is individual and requires personal meaning-making.

CONNECTIONS ACROSS TEXTS

Rodríguez: Some texts can serve as counternarratives to the single telling about a people, event, memory, interaction, or historical period as Adichie (2009) explained and demonstrated via her TEDGlobal Talk. Single stories can be simply explained as a limited narrative that exists about a people group and leads to a bigoted, stereotypical perception of them out of fear. For example, a single narrative exists of many Latinxs in the U.S. as poor, struggling immigrants and far from achieving success. Often Latinxs are approached by non-Latinos with these misconceptions in mind. A majority of the people of Latinx descent are not immigrants, but native to the Americas and have had a relationship with the United States as it formed to the present.

Narratives that name and affirm often marginalized groups provide one attempt to recover their voices and contributions. Their human inventiveness merits attention in the arts and humanities that reaches students and professional colleagues. Also, as professionals, we must remain informed about the children's and young adult literature and research contributions that keep growing in our interdisciplinary fields. What are your thoughts on such narratives and texts?

Germán: Many texts serve as counternarratives. This connects to the idea of inclusive practices because welcoming these texts in the classroom is a way of sustaining culture and knowledge about people, communities, and voices historically marginalized, as Paris (2012) and Paris and Alim (2017) noted. These are communities that have been intentionally left out and treated inhumanely in education and social policies. The research reiterates the point about empathy as a necessary trait, but also makes me think about our life-long learning and journey. There is so much for us to dismantle in our understanding of what we believe as truth and what is possible through opportunity.

Rodríguez: Doesn't this mean that we have some responsibility in public and private education for securing "life, liberty, and the pursuit of happiness" for our students and educator colleagues, as stated in the Declaration of Independence (1776)? We can even now include The 1619 Project (Gyarkye, 2019) of *The New York Times Magazine* that challenges how we define the making of the United States and democracy in our republic (Gyarkye, 2019). How are these essential for lifelong learning though?

Germán: I think about these connections all the time: the ways that our current classrooms connect to history, contextualize the present, and hopefully improve the future. "What is it like for you, as you work with future teachers in your classroom? Do you engage in answers to that question?" I ask myself and my teacher colleagues.

Rodríguez: Which texts in particular influence us today?

Germán: There are so many texts that have impacted me in the past and others that are with me when I need to remember why I teach, when I need to press on. Two books I already mentioned are *Identify-Focused ELA Teaching* (Beach, Johnston, & Thein, 2015) and *Culturally Sustaining Pedagogies: Teaching and Learning for Justice in a Changing World* (Paris & Alim, 2017). There are also texts by Lisa Delpit (2006, 2012, 2019), David Kirkland (2013), and your recent publication *Enacting Adolescent Literacies across Communities: Latino/a Scribes and Their Rites* (Rodríguez, 2017). There are also parts of Malcolm X's (Haley & Malcolm X, 1964) autobiography that impact me in a deep way and some strong moments in the Bible that uplift me and shine light when moments feel dark.

Rodríguez: Sometimes when I enter ELA classrooms I miss seeing books or classroom libraries for students to select and enjoy. How can this be that we seek and value readers, but students do not experience books in their daily schooling or lesson plans in action in school libraries? Students must experience teachers reading books and writing narratives with them. I've seen you do this in your classroom and online with and beside your students.

We need to change how we invite our students to writing moments and experiences and to a reading life. So many of us can be involved in the reading and writing experience for students. Can meaning be gained from a text just by reading it alone, or would experience complement the transaction between reader and writer?

Germán: Yes, I explicitly teach my students to consider the political, historical, and social context of a work and how that adds meaning for the reader. I believe that while there can certainly be meaning gained from a text in its own right, human experience complements our conversations when we connect to the text. Additionally, as I continue in my journey as a reader and writer, I realize that the more I've experienced in life, the more I gain and can use to elicit meaning.

For example, there are texts that impact me now very differently since becoming a mother. There are books that I read and immediately think of how to teach them, but that wasn't the case before I became a teacher. The more I learn and the more I read, the more I write; I realize that these are all developing roles and practices. I don't know that I'll ever be done learning.

Selfhood With Affirmation

Rodríguez: Culturally responsive (Gay, 2018) and sustaining pedagogies (Paris, 2012; Paris & Alim, 2017) foment ways of knowing and speaking in the "practice of becoming." Freire (1968/2018) compounds these ideas by offering us the opportunity to connect both the word and the world and social justice lenses (p. 84). Together as educators and beside our students, we explore connections between texts and between ourselves and the text. We go beyond, too, and analyze the ways that texts are representations of authors and the positions those authors occupy. What about your social justice lens, Lorena?

Germán: No book or text is apolitical. That just does not exist in our world and lives. All authors carry a bit of themselves and their perspectives in what they publish. That is part of what makes authors unique and even successful. Therefore, texts allow us to see some of the world through the eyes of the author. That experience alone may or may not inspire empathy, but most certainly should lead us to think about our positions and those that intersect with more ideas and perspectives.

Moreover, a metacognitive experience occurs in the role of a reader, and reading stimulates metacognition for those who are engaged with texts and their world. The exploration within, around, and against a text is why I enjoy teaching and connecting with more educators and students. As a lifelong learner, as a woman, and as an immigrant, my identities play a role in the type of reader I am and can become. These identities intersect and awaken the politics of my being and body, informing what I read, how I read, what I write, and why I write it.

My students are also becoming aware of these identities and intersections of themselves. As educators, we need to consider how our identities play a role in what we do, how we work to remain learners, and why we must continue in the journey.

Rodríguez: Self-affirmation is essential in the gathering of voices with agency, as demonstrated in the literary works we teach. Some of these works include essays, novels, poems, stories, and songs. All are informed by human cultures and heritages native to the greater United States and our hemisphere and continent, the Américas.

Germán: Exactly. That journey of delving into oneself, figuring out why certain books stir us, and understanding why writing is a way of opening up the heart leads to self-awareness and self-affirmation. The student learner benefits from a coach and guide who can be the educator who listens, thinks, and cares. The agency that surges lives forward and to keep going is part of a long tradition in our human race.

We know about early history through science, yes, but also, and because of oral histories that merit more validation and inquiry. We know about ourselves, our heritages, and our past histories because people value community, self-affirmation, and voices. They passed on their learning to benefit communities and for the greater and common good. There is much more work to be done by adults (or perhaps "educators as adult learners") to support those who shall follow us.

Rodríguez: When did you first become acquainted with the concept of "lifelong learning" as an educator? Has this changed over time for you?

Germán: I first figured out I wasn't done learning when I thought I was! I've been an educator for over 10 years. Before the classroom, I spent years in non-profits, extracurricular programs, and others engaged in educational roles. When I became a classroom teacher, I realized I had so much more to learn, to read, to write, to create, to share, and to take in. I realized I would never stop learning and the humility I found in accepting that helped me.

My first lesson in being a lifelong learner was that learning didn't stop and it wasn't necessarily something you achieve. You might master a skill, but there are more skills and there are different ways of practicing a skill, so you don't even really master one. Thus, my second lesson was humility.

NEGOTIATING IDENTITIES

Rodríguez: When we look at the world around us and make those connections, sometimes we notice how the world does not affirm certain aspects of our identities and ways of being that include ethnicity, gender, race, and sexuality.

Germán: This is a troubling issue. Writers and educators influence change and can be a force for positive energy and impact. For instance, Thomas's *The Hate U Give* (2016) and Santiago's *Boricuas* (1995) anthology are two examples of texts that explicitly reflect and explore identities. Books that speak with and about marginalized people in this U.S. society. Those books end up being more than books, and become spaces of affirmation, of strengthening. Students write on their identities and reflect on their coming of age. As students, writers, and thinkers, we can address how the world dehumanizes many of us and the ways that we challenge what we face daily to cope, survive, and thrive.

Rodríguez: I am a member of many communities as a U.S. citizen who is of Mexican descent and identifies as gay, middle-aged, and middle class, among other identities. Sometimes these intersect, while other times I experience angst, bias, bigotry, indifference, prejudice, and contradiction. How do your identities appear in your teaching? How do you think your teaching colleagues and adolescent students experience their identities?

Germán: My intersecting identities play a central role in my teaching approach. Since I consider all of the communities of which I am a member, I emphasize diverse literature and a culturally sustaining approach to teaching and learning (Paris, 2012; Paris & Alim, 2017). Based on conversations with colleagues and my work to support other teachers, some conclusions I reached about how they experience their identities is that they are often based on ethnicity and gender.

My teaching colleagues of color are constantly considering their identities and how these impact who they are and how they interact with their students as teachers. This awareness curates their actions and approach to teaching, in many cases. These self-reflections and habits of mind are significant for lifelong learning. In fact, the reflection and habits are a deep and complicated conversation for many women teachers of color.

Moreover, my colleagues who are White Americans are sometimes questioning these ideas, but they have not fully or conclusively explored the ways that Whiteness impacts their teaching approaches. Students in my classes often comment how they have never found space in other classes and through their academics to explore their identities. They enjoy and seem to be fully engaged in the process of learning and becoming lifelong learners.

Rodríguez: Sometimes it feels like we are living in an age of the following identity-informed and context-based questions related to learning such as: "Why am I here? What is my purpose? Whose pain is greater? Which self-identification is most significant? How do I keep learning in the midst of change, challenges, and unpredictability? Who survives?" These questions appear often, especially as we endure and live in a Trump administration that is inhumane and even lawless with no accountability.

Germán: It does feel that way! I agree that the questions posted here may have existed forever. I mean, it's evident in literature, right? Texts from decades ago can often speak to these very questions present in 2020. In our current political and racial context and turmoil, the question of which self-identification to value the most is critically debated. There is the idea that we do not need to choose, because we all have equally important intersecting identities. There is also the possibility that ethnicity is often more significant than other identities. Because ethnicity is often most visible and the biggest determinant of inequity in the U.S. that often takes precedence over others.

Rodríguez: Would it be a hegemonic force that keeps us from deeper questioning and thinking for social justice, equity, and change?

Germán: Yes. In the United States today, the presence of White American supremacist cis hetero patriarchal cultural hegemony is strong and has dominated many movements and decades. While I have hope that non-beneficiaries can dismantle these conditions, it clearly takes more than just us. The culture of people in power as explored by Kirkland (2013) does not allow us to "search past the silences" sitting in front of us in the classroom seats with our students (p. 35). It also keeps us from critical questions about oppressive systems in place and in various educational settings, among others. As lifelong learners, it keeps us from going deep enough where we dismantle the ideologies present in our minds.

Rodríguez: I enter many spaces in a day. Upon reflection, I come to the realization that I am most at home in communities of joy, questioning, and trust. These communities I am thinking of are in the quest to leave the world better than how we found it and in which we grew up, with a heavy reliance on resilience.

Students have much to say to us in the schools, colleges, and universities where we teach and learn with them. In fact, students want to read, write, and express themselves in various forms and modes. We can and must invite them to write with us as we model through literature, our own narratives, and their stories of bravery, character, and courage.

Tell me about your imagination at work in the creative writing world in which negotiating identities may be unnecessary, but where one can be who one chooses to be without apology, blame, disregard, guilt, regret, and shame?

Germán: This world is fighting to live, right now, in my poetry. As a writer, I am still becoming free from the White gaze, from cultural hegemony. It is the place where I can be who I choose, as you stated: without apology, without blame, disregard, or judgment. As I am learning to imagine it, I am trying to share it with my students. That is a world where reality is filled with love, trust, joy, and honesty. There are still problems, but systemic oppression is not one of them when I work closely with my students.

REFLECTION

Rodríguez: The world of teaching can be in flux, yet we must remember that among our colleagues lie strength and difficulties for transformation in teaching and learning. Emdin (2017) argued,

> The kind of teacher you will become is directly related to the kind of teachers you associate with. Teaching is a profession where misery does more than just love company—it recruits, seduces, and romances it. Avoid people who are unhappy and disgruntled about the possibilities for transforming education. They are the enemy of the spirit of the teacher. (p. 208)

These words motivate me to keep going and to remain a learner in an age of turmoil and flux that includes alternative facts and opposition to democracy. Our spirit must stay alive and hopeful beside our students.

I admit there are places where I have worked that I had to escape from to keep sane and moving forward. The worst of times with an asphyxiating feeling can appear sometimes where we work, and we must make a way to keep going and to thrive. Ultimately, I realized that there are more teaching lives to lead. We must feed our mind and spirit as teachers and teacher educators. We must find rest, reflection time, and rejuvenation to keep going and stay healthy.

Germán: Emdin's point is key to maintaining the why you became a teacher at the forefront. In our work, it's so important to distinguish between critical viewpoints and complaining. The first is essential in becoming listeners and growing. Critical thinking also helps us to be problem solvers for good at our institutions. The complaining is also sometimes aimed at students and that can borderline into so many other issues. Being in those spaces and around those teachers isn't motivating and it isn't helpful for the work at hand.

I think about moments in previous teachers' lounges where I had to challenge comments made by teachers attacking students in their absence. Some of these were in the forms of jokes about their abilities, others were about constant disappointment about our institutions, and/or continuous critiques of their duties. Sharing concerns and raising issues is healthy, but never offering solutions and not presenting these concerns within a context of hope is demoralizing. Our feedback and frustrations, coupled with others' concerns and details, can yield potential change.

Opportunities for teacher leadership are important. The process of identifying a problem, brainstorming possible solutions, and stepping forth to lead that change is something we also want our learners to practice in community. We should be modeling it. It's a learning process, too. We may find our strengths in the process of becoming better and stronger among allies and learners.

Rodríguez: Our strengths are around us as we flank our teaching colleagues who believe in us. They are in our school buildings, across the country, and around the world. We are not alone in our literacy and social justice work; we are joined by many literacy teachers and scholars who believe in us and our students. We teach together; we must learn together, too. Sometimes I wonder if we are in agreement about what literacy means and that also means becoming power literate. Along the same lines, whose literacy matters in the work that we are doing and in the world of our teaching profession?

Germán: Everyone's literacy matters, yet I would say that those whose literacy is oppressed and neglected are in dire need of validation, celebration, and action. The literacy of children, of women, of LGBTQ writers, of working-class people, and of people of color are rarely recognized and deemed worthy in both academic and non-academic spaces.

In my work and my personal experiences, we are writing, reading, sharing, speaking, and being literate. We live literate lives in both digital and non-digital worlds, but these life practices may not always count in the classroom. When our words aren't in the classroom, we're erased.

Rodríguez: Some students may hold the perspective that learning is done after schooling is complete. Some educators may believe that learning is accomplished after earning advanced academic degrees and teaching credentials.

Germán: The minute someone becomes a teacher and needs to figure out how to teach one thing to 20 different learners at the same time, they quickly learn that those statements are not true.

Rodríguez: What is next for you, Lorena, as a lifelong learner?

Germán: I am learning more about how and why teachers step into this profession and finding ways to support each other. I am also planning on continuing to write more as a teacher-writer and to support my students in their student-writer roles. What's next for you, Joseph?

Rodríguez: Right now I am thrilled to be working with high school students who are pursuing their diplomas to pursue university studies. Also, I work with preservice teachers who will work with students of all age levels in our schools. It is an exciting time, and where I work there are many opportunities to influence change. The way forward is with hope and resilience and to effect change in the lives of students, educators, and families who seek to be treated fairly and with compassion.

Power as Educators

We must continue in the journey of becoming and being learners and teachers. We are all teachers. Whenever we give of ourselves, share our ideas, and contribute to larger social dialogues, we are teaching. As educators, we must see that in our students, too, regardless of age or continuum in their journey. We must see them as teachers, and that turns us into learners as we work beside them. There is a humility and respect required for us to re-envision ourselves as learners and consider those who sit before us as teachers. We are all learners. We are all here to learn from one another and to continue in this quest for growth.

Lorena often thinks about a student we will call Valeria whom she had in ninth grade. She had been deemed "bad" and "soon to drop out" by other educators, including the school administrators. In essence, she was no longer seen as a learner and certainly not a teacher. After the first several days of class, Lorena knew these descriptors were not seeing Valeria and her potential.

She noticed that granting Valeria opportunities to teach what she knew instead of being solely concerned about teaching her what she did not know was the way to gain her trust. Learning and teaching with Valeria became a powerful experience for Lorena. It was then, through that difficult year of undoing the schooling damage in her life, that Lorena realized what learning and teaching were really about and meant to be.

As educators, we all have power, literacies, and resources in varying degrees. We must intentionally leverage our power and work toward the collective good in learners' lives. Our aims to disrupt the cultural hegemony that hinders our freedom as well as to sustain the humility that allows us all to teach and learn must stay alive and strong.

Consider the messages of recent children's books that join the canon for literacy and social justice:

1. *Imagine!* (2018) by Raúl Colón
2. *Dreamers* (2018) by Yuyi Morales
3. *The Undefeated* (2019) by Kwame Alexander and Kadir Nelson
4. *Counting the Stars: The Story of Katherine Johnson, NASA Mathematician* (2019) by Lesa Cline-Ransome and Raúl Colón
5. *Woke: A Young Poet's Call to Justice* (2020) by Mahogany L. Browne, Elizabeth Acevedo, Olivia Gatwood, Theodore Taylor III, and Jason Reynolds

We are encouraged by all the teachers—and authors and illustrators of children's and young adult literature—who are also learners in the journey. We must also be encouraged by all the learners who persist as teachers beside us.

REFERENCES

Adichie, C. N. (2009). The danger of a single story. *TEDGlobal Talk*. www.ted.com/talks/chimamanda_ngozi_adichie_the_danger_of_a_single_story?language=en

Alexander, K., & Nelson, K. (2019). *The undefeated*. Versify, Houghton Mifflin Harcourt.

Ambrose, S., Bridges, M. W., DiPietro, M., Lovett, M. C., & Norman, M. K. (2010). *How learning works: Seven research-based principles for smart teaching*. Jossey-Bass.

Beach, R., Johnston, A., & Thein, A. H. (2015). *Identity-focused ELA teaching: A curriculum framework for diverse learners and contexts*. Routledge.

Browne, M. L., & Acevedo, E., Gatwood, O., Taylor, T., III, & Reynolds, J. (2020). *Woke: A young poet's call to justice*. Roaring Brook Press, Macmillan Children's.

Cline-Ransome, L., & Colón, R. *Counting the stars: The story of Katherine Johnson, NASA mathematician.* Simon and Schuster Books for Young People.

Colón, R. (2018). *Imagine!* Simon and Schuster Books for Young People.

Delpit, L. (2006). *Other people's children: Cultural conflict in the classroom.* The New Press.

Delpit, L. (2012). *'Multiplication is for White people': Raising expectations for other people's children.* The New Press.

Delpit, L. (Ed.). (2019). *Teaching when the world is on fire.* The New Press.

Emdin, C. (2017). *For White folks who teach in the hood … and the rest of y'all too: Reality pedagogy and urban education.* Beacon Press.

Freire, P. (2018). *Pedagogy of the oppressed* (50th anniversary edition). (M. B. Ramos, Trans.). Bloomsbury. (Original work published 1968)

Gay, G. (2018). *Culturally responsive teaching: Theory, research, and practice* (3rd ed.). Teachers College Press.

Gyarkye, L. (2019, Aug. 18). How the 1619 Project came together. *The New York Times Magazine.* https://www.nytimes.com/2019/08/18/reader-center/1619-project-slavery-jamestown.html

Haley, A., & A. S. Malcolm X. (1964). *The autobiography of Malcolm X: As told to Alex Haley.* Ballantine.

Hoare, G., & Sperber, N. (2016). *An introduction to Antonio Gramsci: His life, thought, and legacy.* Bloomsbury.

Kirkland, D. (2013). *A search past silence: The literacy of young black men.* Teachers College Press.

Morales, Y. (2018). *Dreamers.* Neal Porter Books, Holiday House.

Nieto, S. (2015). *Brooklyn dreams: My life in public education.* Harvard Education Press.

Paris, D. (2012). Culturally sustaining pedagogy: A needed change in stance, terminology, and practice. *Educational Researcher, 41*(3), 93–97. https://web.stanford.edu/class/linguist159/restricted/readings/Paris2012.pdf or https://journals.sagepub.com/doi/abs/10.3102/0013189x12441244

Paris, D., & Alim, H. S. (Eds.). (2017). *Culturally sustaining pedagogies: Teaching and learning for justice in a changing world.* Teachers College Press.

Rodríguez, R. J. (2017). *Enacting adolescent literacies across communities: Latino/a scribes and their rites.* Lexington Books, Rowman & Littlefield.

Santiago, R. (Ed.). (1995). *Boricuas: Influential Puerto Rican writings, an anthology.* One World, Random House Publishing Group.

Thomas, A. (2017). *The hate u give.* Balzer + Bray, HarperCollins.

CHAPTER 8

CAN A BAD APPLE
LOSE ITS ROT?

Sharon J. Hamilton
Indiana University School of Liberal Arts, Indianapolis

"What about that one? That little girl in the corner?"

"That's Karen Fleming. You wouldn't want her. We've decided that she's unadoptable. Borderline autistic, potentially sociopathic, uneducable, possibly trainable, will never hold a job, can't get along with anybody, child or adult. A real bad apple."

That is what my adoptive mother was told in 1948 when she asked why I was the only little girl in the Children's Aid Society (CAS) playroom that had not been put forward to her as a possible adoptee. That was my official identity and my declared (lack of) potential as a lifelong learner when I was 3 years old. My sense of self, reinforced daily by the matron, was that I was bad, a bad girl, born bad, and would stay bad.

Almost 70 years later, Louise Wetherbee Phelps (2017), Professor Emerita of Rhetoric at Syracuse University, in an essay exploring four different Canadian academics with cross-cultural histories, writes the following:

Narratives on Becoming: Identity and Lifelong Learning, pp. 109–119

Sharon J. Hamilton is a Canadian-born scholar and long-time teacher in
Canadian schools who, after getting a PhD from the University of London
(UK), moved to the United States for her university career.... Hamilton
broadened her initial interdisciplinary horizon (writing studies and literacy
education) to the scholarship of teaching and learning and its systematic
implementation at the institutional level, enabling the university (and
Hamilton) to take a pioneering role in national and international conversations about educational reform focused on enhancing and integrating
student learning.

This chapter tells the story of how uneducable and bad Karen Fleming
became Sharon Hamilton. My curriculum vitae identifies me as a Chancellor's
Professor Emerita of English with a PhD in language and literature from the
University of London, England, author and editor of several professional
publications and author of a literacy memoir (Hamilton, 1997), a play
(unpublished), and three novels written postretirement. My friends and
family know me as a retired teacher and professor, a mother, a partner,
and a person who enjoys concerts, theater, film, travel, and our two sheltie
puppies. I see myself as a better person than I was 70 years ago and yet,
from time to time, I still sense a whiff of the rotten core of that bad apple
within me.

Hannah Arendt writes that we excel in the company of others. A character in the play *Art* asks: "Are you who you think you are or are you who your
friends think you are?" This chapter will unfold dialogically between these
two ideas in five sections, each introduced by an epiphany about learning
and identity embedded in a brief anecdote.

SECTION 1: INTRODUCTION TO LITERACY

On the snow dappled Valentine's Day of 1948, I was driven away from the
Children's Aid Society residential home into a new reality. It didn't begin
all that new. Somehow, within a few hours of my arrival, I ended up in the
one place I had been told not to go and fell through thin ice into the Seine
River that formed the northeastern boundary of the Hamilton's suburban
farm on the outskirts of Winnipeg.

"Bad, bad," I muttered, after my wet clothes had been removed and
replaced with striped pyjamas, *just like a prisoner's*, I thought at the time.
"I'm still bad. I'm always bad," I yelped at the dinner table.

"No, you are not bad," replied Bill Hamilton, my new father, who had
already astonished everyone at the Children's Aid Society by being the first
man who approached me that I did not hide from or kick. "Karen Fleming
might have been bad. But Karen Fleming is gone. You are no longer Karen

Fleming. From now on you are Sharon. Sharon Hamilton. That is your new name. And Sharon Hamilton is a good girl."

A good girl? Me? All accomplished by simply changing my name? For some reason, I believed the kind words that washed away the dirt of my wrongdoing. It was a start to a new identity, that's for certain!

The next morning, after breakfast, I was told to sit on the chesterfield. Katherine Hamilton picked out a big orange thing from a shelf and swung it in my direction. I ducked and protected my head, accustomed to people swinging objects at me. But this orange thing didn't hit me. With a cosy flourish, my new mother sat down beside me and asked me to open the orange object. I did, and, like Alice falling down the rabbit hole, entered another entirely new dimension of existence, this time the fictive world of nursery rhymes and children's stories.

In this world, children might do bad things but were rarely called bad. Problems could be resolved not by hitting but by talking things through. In this fictive world, the possibilities were endless. Slowly, through stories and poems, I began to learn how to be human, how to talk and smile instead of kicking and hitting and biting.

SECTION 2: PARTICIPANT IN LITERACY

The process of becoming a good girl was neither quick nor easy. Having been abused and neglected by my birth mother and her many male companions, to the point of being taken from her and made a ward of the court at 8 months of age and then moved to 18 different foster homes by the time I was 3, I had no manners, little knowledge, and lots of anger and frustration. I did, however, have a memory, and told my new mother many stories about life at The Greenhouse, my name for the Children's Aid Society residential home. And, whereas the matron was possibly correct in labeling me borderline autistic, since it has taken me decades to learn how to become a compassionate person concerned with the well-being of others, she turned out to be completely wrong about my being uneducable.

When I was 7, my mother had me read every day to my younger cousin, who lived with us while his mother was in the final stages of her fight with cancer. At that time, because most of my classmates read aloud very slowly, I thought reading as quickly as possible was good and skipped along on the surface of the words, not paying any attention to what I was actually reading. "Slow down. Sally is sad and scared because she is lost. Sound sad and scared. Her big sister is trying to help her. Make Jane sound helpful. And Dick thinks it's all a big adventure. Think about what you are reading."

Think about what I was reading? Perhaps other children do that automatically, but the notion was unfamiliar to me. I read the story again, paying attention to the feelings of Dick and Jane and Sally and trying to make those feelings come alive in my voice. What a difference. It was as though the black and white of word on page grew vivid with color and movement. The characters came alive. I began to care what happened to them. If we consider an epiphany to be a moment when a new insight makes us restructure our world view, this moment was an epiphany. I felt in a partnership with the people in the story.

A few months later, my mother introduced me to her Underwood typewriter and suggested I type my memories of life in The Greenhouse. "Who would be interested?" I asked.

"You will be," she replied, "when you are older and have forgotten those years because of all the new memories you will have made and all the ideas you are learning at school. Just type one story or one page a day and we'll keep them all together in a box. Then you can put them together in a book."

A book? My own book! I began immediately with the first memory that came to mind and quickly discovered that each snippet of memory, while not always complete, led to other memories and other stories. I learned, without fully realizing it and completely unaware of the implications, that writing can be a heuristic for more writing and that memories are woven together in such a way that they rarely unravel independently of each other. Every story is threaded into other experiences and events, making an intricate pattern that can become overwhelming. At the same time, I could type only one word at a time and so the act of forming fleeting images and ideas into sentences and those sentences into an ordered narrative automatically forced the ideas to march inexorably to a finite conclusion. I came to know, without understanding, that the surface arc and flow of a narrative, with its beginning, development, and end are by their nature deceptively simplistic, hiding a tangled root system of selected inclusions and omissions, with many possible paths inevitably ignored. Not until the eighth grade, when we learned in school the iconic metaphor of what we know as the tip of the iceberg of what is knowable, did I begin to understand the experiential knowledge I had acquired while typing out simple memories.

It took even longer for me to appreciate that these almost daily episodes of writing were moving me beyond being not only a recipient of literacy, a reader of stories, to becoming a participant in the creation of a literate work. Books and authors were not "out there" in some intellectual remoteness but were rather with me and within me. I would not have identified myself as a writer but rather considered writing to be as ordinary an activity as reading or skipping or watching television.

SECTION 3: YOU ARE WHAT YOU WRITE

Not until the process of earning a PhD in language and literature did I come to understand the extraordinary power of writing, not only through my research of the high stakes exam-oriented focus on writing of sixth form students competing for university places at Oxford and Cambridge but also through my own academic writing. At school I had developed a comfortable approach to writing essays: isolate the key words in the essay question, not just the nouns but also the verbs, in order to determine an organizational direction for the essay. Depending upon the expected length, identify three to five main aspects of that direction and write as though those were the most significant aspects to consider when developing my line of argument. It was a technical process that served me satisfactorily through high school.

My adoptive parents, my father with a grade three education and my mother with Grade 11 plus a year of normal school, agreed I should be self-sufficient and self-supporting by the time I was 18. They gave me the choice of business school or 1 year of teachers college when I graduated from Grade 12. I chose teachers college because I thought it might eventually open doors to a university education. One year later, in the fall of 1963, I began my teaching career in a one-room eight-grade country school on the Canadian prairies.

Narration, particularly autobiographical narration, forces choices. The life portrayed so far in this length-controlled narration suggests that the rotten core of the bad apple known as Karen Fleming has disintegrated into the dust of its origins and that Sharon Hamilton has emerged from the steaming cauldron of early neglect and abuse, teenage hormones and frustrated ambitions with no harm and no foul.

Not quite.

My adoption occurred in an era when most people believed that nature trumps nurture. My adoptive parents earned my lifelong respect and gratitude when I learned how frequently they had been assailed with comments such as, "Born bad, always bad. Blood will out. You watch. She'll murder you all in your sleep." On the other hand, my adoptive parents had their own son, born in their 40th year, who was their pride and joy. "Blood is blood and water is water," is how they explained the significant difference in how each of us was treated. I grew up insufficiently grateful for the security and material support that my parents provided because I became so angry at the absence of emotional connection. I made bad choices. I shoplifted clothing, I lied to avoid punishment, and, predictably, I became pregnant before being properly married. The rotten core had spread like an insidious disease, influencing my attitude and behavior.

In the early 70s, the Manitoba government declared that all teachers had to earn an undergraduate degree in addition to teacher training. With a 2-year-old son and a husband who also had to complete his degree while teaching and coaching basketball, the prospect looked initially bleak. Time and money presented equal challenges. Nonetheless, I was thrilled with the opportunity to go to university. I had to go or I would lose my job and my teaching certification. A passionate but impossible dream of attending university had suddenly become a necessity for earning our living.

We decided that my husband, who already had one undergraduate year of university credit, would continue his full-time teaching and coaching while attending night school and summer school. I would stop teaching full-time, attend university Monday, Wednesday and Friday mornings, substitute teach Tuesdays and Thursdays when possible and take night school and summer school courses. Our goal, which we achieved, was to complete our Bachelor of Arts degrees in 2 years.

Fortunately, my mother-in-law, who worked afternoons, was willing to babysit mornings but I had to scramble for other assistance when I had substitute-teaching assignments. We lived in a small apartment with only one table, so my assignments had to be cleared away for all mealtimes. One of my professors advised me to learn how to divide my assignments into segments of 5 minutes, 10 minutes, and 15 minutes, and to make lists of these segmented tasks. As a result, if I had to wait 5 minutes for something to boil, or if my son had a short afternoon nap or was playing with a toy, I could get something done. It might be making an outline, listing the books for my research, reading a page or two of a textbook, writing a sentence or two, making index cards of information I needed for recall, or entering items in a bibliography. Within a couple of weeks I became adept at segmenting almost every intellectual and household task. It's amazing how focused the mind can become under the pressure of time.

Regrettably, I had no time to play with ideas, to develop alternative lines of discussion, or to explore the implications of discoveries I made while researching essay topics. Building on the technique I had developed in school, my writing was completely mechanical and driven by the ideas of others. I did well primarily because my essays were thoroughly researched, clearly organized, and grammatically conventional.

I was sufficiently self-aware to realize that, even though I was thrilled to be attending university, I would not have identified myself as a scholar, an intellectual, or an academic. When my undergraduate professors critiqued my work, they always acknowledged the clarity and organization and then went on to say that my writing had no heart or passion, no sense of who I was and why my views on this topic were important. I did not understand the point they were making. I had no views on the assigned topic and was merely completing an assignment in as short a time as I possibly could. I had no heart or passion for what I was writing because I was too busy trying to be a wife and mother and not doing very well at either.

Twenty years later, when I completed my first assignment as a doctoral student at the University of London (U.K.), my tutor, Harold Rosen, articulated much the same idea with the words, "You can get by in academe with this third-person objective word-from-God North American dialect if you want to, but why would you want to. Where are you in this? Where is your fire?"

Fire? My marriage had dissolved years earlier, my son was in university in Canada, I was on a 3-year leave of absence from my teaching position at a Winnipeg high school and living in London for the sole purpose of earning a PhD. For the first time in my life, I had sufficient time and energy to light a fire. I just hadn't realized that I had a right to do so. I would go further now and say that I didn't realize I had an obligation to do so. Fire? Finally, I was ready to make sense of that recurring admonition of my writing—of my identity—and follow through with it. It was, as Rosen pointed out, my responsibility as a scholar. And, because he treated me as a scholar, with all the expectations entailed in that identity, I consciously began the process of becoming one.

SECTION 4: AM I WHO I AM BECAUSE I AM WHO I AM OR AM I WHO I AM BECAUSE YOU ARE WHO YOU ARE?

One approach to answering that question emerged from a commemorative lecture at the London University Institute of Education as part of the ceremonies honouring the contributions of Harold Rosen upon his retirement. Wayne Booth, Professor Emeritus of English language and literature at the University of Chicago and author of *The Rhetoric of Fiction* had been invited to pay tribute to Rosen's achievements as a scholar. Booth spoke first of how they had met, not at a professional conference or through professional writing, as is often the case among academic colleagues, but rather as trench-mates during World War II, neither of them thinking beyond surviving the war, much less of becoming globally esteemed intellectuals. Booth went on to discuss his process of becoming a professor, with its tripartite responsibilities for teaching, research, and service, describing it in terms of an imposter syndrome.

He spoke of his first time entering a lecture hall, a freshly minted PhD the only credential entitling him to be the voice of authority in the room. He spoke of feeling inadequate to be dispensing knowledge to those upturned faces anticipating wise stewardship of information, data, statistics, and theory. He felt an imposter, out of place, not deserving his students' respectful expectations. As a teacher, I had felt the same at the beginning of every new class of students. Eagerly I listened, wanting to learn how Wayne Booth had defeated his anxiety. He hadn't. He embraced it. He imagined who, among the best teachers and professors he knew, would be the best person at the front of that lecture hall and he "became" that person. He began by pretending he was that person, with his or her fine teaching attributes and educational brilliance. He analyzed what worked well for himself and for his students and what needed fine-tuning. This dialectic between how he was teaching and how his students were learning became the focal point for ongoing decisions about the effectiveness of his imposter persona. Gradually the pretence of being that other person dropped away as he assimilated the desired teaching and learning values of that professor into his own style. By pretending he was "that person" he became someone different, not quite the other person but a consciously refined version of himself. He *was* what he had become.

The play *Art*, written first as a novel by Y. Reza (1996) and translated for the stage by Christopher Hampton, highlights the significance of others in determining one's identity. Sergei, one of three friends trying to determine essential characteristics of a work of art, is dumbfounded and angry at his friends' rejection of a painting he has purchased and begins to question the integrity of his artistic values, which he considers to be the core of his identity. He asks:

> If I'm who I am because **I'm** who I am, and you're who you are because you're who you are, then I'm who I am and **you're** who you are. If however ... I'm who I am **because** you're who you are, and you're who you are **because** I'm who I am, then I'm not who I am and you're not who you are.

This quandary about identity in the play *Art* led me to ponder more deeply Hannah Arendt's assertion that, for excellence, the presence of others is always required. Are any of our characteristics immutable no matter what happens in whose company? Do we all have a core, an essence that we can rely upon to determine what kind of person we are? When we are bullied or derided, do we believe we are who others say we are? The Myers-Briggs inventory suggests that, when in crisis or danger, people often behave in ways opposite to their normal way of being, a phenomenon I have experienced not only within myself but also have observed in others. In *Mother Night*, Kurt Vonnegut (1962) admonishes his readers that "we are what we pretend to be so be careful what you pretend to be." Considered with Wayne Booth's discussion of the imposter syndrome, the concept that you become what you are is both Platonic and Jungian in its implications. When we choose whom to pretend to be, that choice is already commensurate with our values or we would not have made that particular selection. On the other hand, we all know that, in a group situation that goes beyond the boundaries of our usual behavior, we can choose to pretend to be the kind of person who behaves like the others, often with disastrous consequences.

While I cannot offer a definitive answer to the question in *Art,* I can say that throughout my postadoptive life I have consciously and continually identified people, both in literature and in real life, whose ethical core of compassion and integrity have inspired me to become a better person. I am grateful to teachers who caught me at critical moments and cajoled, coerced, or inspired me to behave more honestly, speak and act more thoughtfully, and think more about others less fortunate. I am grateful to my mother who took me to the ballet, the symphony, and theatre, where I learned the aesthetic consequences of self-discipline. Without the example of others, I undoubtedly would have remained the rotten apple I had been labelled as a little girl.

SECTION 5: HOW YOU RECREATE YOUR PAST DETERMINES YOUR PRESENT AND SHAPES YOUR FUTURE

Having explored my personal history through examining my Children's Aid Society records, recounting memories, publishing a memoir, consulting with psychiatrists, and finding and meeting the 10 siblings my biological mother birthed, only two of whom also have the same biological father, I have spent considerable time and energy dwelling in and recounting my past to others. Over the decades, I have noted a significant change in perspective and its influence on how I characterize the person I have become. In my early years, when my new mother would ask me about The Greenhouse, most of the stories I told her were quite horrific, focusing on the abusive episodes I remember. The only truly positive story was about one kind foster mother who wanted to adopt me but couldn't because she planned to move back to England. I still recall the smell of freshly baked cookies I associate with her and the red, yellow, and green jellybeans she gave me every night so I would dream in color. Later, the stories of my past focused on the inequitable treatment of me and my brother, my adoptive parents' "real" child, primarily his being sent to a prestigious private school and promised university if he completed grade twelve, which he didn't, and my local schooling with the promise of being funded for 1 year past Grade 12 to gain a certificate that would qualify me for a job by the time I was 18.

As I type these words, I feel none of the frustration or resentment I remember dominating my moods as a teenager. Rather I feel respect for my mother's generosity and appreciation for being prepared for a world in which woman work for their financial independence. I could cite other stories that led to severe depression in my youth but that now I can under-stand in a larger context and can see how they have shaped me to become self-sufficient, independent, ethical, and compassionate. The bad little girl with a furious temper, a huge vocabulary of swear words by age 3, and the ethics of a potential criminal must dwell within me somewhere, but she now seems a stranger, both me and not me. My memories of my past are now predominantly pleasant, primarily because most of the events I choose to talk about are the positive ones. I now use the creation of a fictive world to explore the darker regions of my history.

Over the past decade, I have written three novels and a play. Written during my retirement in England, all three novels are situated in a South Devon village. Each novel is set within the context of a significant social issue and explores how circumstances can force normally honest and kind people to commit horrific crimes. I appear in each novel as a Miss Marple sort of person, observing the world around me and attempting to make sense of the criminal acts perpetrated in the most unexpected circumstances, often by kindly-motivated individuals. The connective tissue among the novels is that lawbreakers can be created by social policies and that justice is not always best served behind bars. The trilogy *Fall of a Sparrow* (2013), *Chapel on the Moor* (2014), and *The Doolally Gang* (2016). features Detective Cora Bodkin, recently transferred from the Met at Scotland Yard to the sleepy hills and hollows of South Devon. Her unconventional views of the relationship between justice and the law had limited her promotions in London and ultimately lead to her resignation in the third novel.

Writing is inevitably and inexorably tied up with identity. My professional writing occasionally tilted toward being quirky and creatively idiosyncratic but generally ended up as conventional exposition. Writing fiction has enabled me to discover a core that is not rotten, that values compassion and integrity, and that is optimistic about the world in which we live even as it tells stories of evil within that world.

The play was much more difficult and less satisfying to write. My adoptive parents and their son, my brother, all died within a short time of each other. Their estates went to blood relatives. Having visited and telephoned and cared for my mother following the death of my father and my brother, I was initially more hurt than resentful. I could rationalize that those who inherited were more needful than I was, but money was not the issue. Rejection was the issue and threw me back into the "bad girl" syndrome of my childhood. I had no way to work through the feelings, since everyone directly involved was dead.

I turned to writing to help me sort through my stunned anger at not being considered a "real" member of the family I had called Mom, Dad, and brother for over half a century. I titled the play *My Brother Was My Mother's Only Child* (Hamilton, n.d.) and found it so painful to write that I managed only one speech segment a day. I wrote it as a one-woman show and performed it three times, twice at the Athenaeum in Indianapolis as a fundraiser for educating unwanted female babies in China and once at the College of Education at the University of Texas in Arlington to mark the inauguration of their alumni program. After each performance, people came up to me to say thank you and to tell me that they were going right home to contact their mother or sister or father or brother to try to reconcile differences before it was too late. These responses opened my eyes to a new way to approach the rejection I had been trying to understand.

The storyline takes place in the cemetery where the remains of my adoptive mother, father, and brother rest. In the play, I visit the graves of my parents and brother in an attempt to try to reconcile the war of feelings within me. I acknowledge my understanding of their thoughts and motivations but nonetheless the perspective is predominantly mine. I have decided to give voice and perspective to my parents and brother by creating their ghosts, thereby layering the exploration with more nuanced interpretations. I will not be able to hear their dialogue and opinions, as I never effectively did in life, but they will be able to listen to what I say and respond and interact with each other, while the audience observes and hears it all.

In conclusion, in my mid-seventies, I am still becoming through the process of writing and interacting with others. Literacy in its basic form of being able to read and write is essential. The capacity of literacy to shape who we are and who we become is one of the most powerful forces we can draw upon. With the good fortune to have been adopted by parents who valued reading and writing and with the assistance of wise teachers who helped me at critical points in my life, I have defeated the statistical projections that I would end up either in prison or in an institution for the emotionally challenged. I feel comfortable that I am no longer "a real bad apple."

REFERENCES

Hamilton, S. (1997). *My name's not Susie: A life transformed by literacy*. Heinemann.

Hamilton, S. (2013). *Fall of a sparrow*. Dancing will Dilemmas (DWD) Publications and Amazon via Createspace.

Hamilton, S. (2014). *Chapel on the Moor*. Dancing with Dilemmas (DWD) Publications and Amazon via Createspace.

Hamilton, S. (2016). *The Doolally Gang*. Dancing with Dilemmas (DWD) Publications and Amazon via Createspace.

Hamilton, S. (n.d.). *My Brother Was My Mother's Only Child*. Unpublished.

Phelps, L. W. (2017). Four scholars, four genres. In D. Mueller, A. Williams, L. W. Phelps, & J. Clary-Lemon (Eds.), *Cross border networks in writing studies* (pp. 81–122). Inkshed/Parlor Press.

Reza, Y. (1996). *Art: A Play* (translated by Christopher Hampton). Farrar, Straus & Giroux.

Rosen, H. (1987). *Tutorial*. Institute of Education. London University. Bloomsbury.

Vonnegut, K. (1962). *Mother Night*. Fawcett Publications/Gold Medal Books.

CHAPTER 9

NARRATIVE OF A WHITE MIDDLE-CLASS MALE PRINCIPAL

An Apologia

James F. Lane, Jr
University of Phoenix

INTRODUCTION

Much of current academic literature calls for stories describing success over adversity from members of racially marginalized groups. Those voices have long been suppressed. They must be heard, and I welcome them. I am a white, male, former middle school principal, ensconced in the American middle class. I know that my role group generally has been a privileged class in American culture. I know that my perceptions are filtered through this prism. I believe, however, that as individuals we endure our unique traumas, and that reflection on our resolution of these ordeals may provide insight into challenges faced by others.

Narratives on Becoming: Identity and Lifelong Learning, pp. 121–132
Copyright © 2021 by Information Age Publishing
All rights of reproduction in any form reserved.

In this narrative I trace the process of my perpetual becoming through emotional traumas and ethical dilemmas. I describe how I applied deep reflection to discover and refine my moral purpose as a principal working with students within marginalized groups and with teachers who served them. I bring my personal and professional backgrounds together to understand what I believed and now understand about myself and my work. I present my life after principalship as a novice researcher, academic writer, and teacher of doctoral students. I am constructing a new persona, growing, changing, vulnerable, fearful, expectant, hopeful, resurgent, resourceful, resilient, and productive.

THEORETICAL FRAMEWORK

I've adapted the academic framework of this reflection from the work of Lawrence-Lightfoot (2010), who has done extensive work in studying those in my chronological arc, those from the ages of 50 to 75, a period she described as the "Third Chapter" in one's life. These years, she said, "when we are neither old nor young," can be the most transformative time in our lives, "as long as we have the courage to challenge the ageist stereotypes, the creativity to resist the old cultural norms, the curiosity to be open to new learning, and the adventurousness to pursue new passions and experiences" (p. xii).

This discussion centers around the seminal event of my retirement from a successful career of 37 years in my local school district. During that time, I moved from high school English teacher to district supervisor of language arts to middle school assistant principal to middle school principal. I reflect on life events using what Lawrence-Lightfoot (2010) identified as four dominant themes of adult reinvention:

- Facing new realities: Job loss, decline in earnings, fear, turning crisis into opportunity, risk-taking, and innovation.
- Willing to risk vulnerability and failure, challenging what is *age-appropriate*.
- Needing to "give forward, … to leave a legacy, … to be of service."
- Valuing cross-generational projects … "Young and old learning together." (pp. x–xi)

All of these themes combine to shape my worldview in the past, present, and looking forward. They form what I have been, what I am now, and what I may become.

METHODOLOGY

The methodology for this narrative reflection is autoethnography. Briefly, that is "research, writing, story, and method that connect the autobiographical and personal to the cultural, social, and political" (Ellis, 2004, p. xix). Many qualitative methodologies focus on personal experience. A short list of those that have influenced me includes phenomenology and the work of Van Manen (1990, 2016); narrative analysis and the work of Clandinin and Connelly (2000); portraiture and the work of Lawrence-Lightfoot (1997, 2010, 2012, 2016); personal history and the work of Cole and Knowles (2000, 2001); and the qualitative habits of mind offered by Janesick (2011).

Autoethnography emphasizes the researcher as subject. Often the focus is evocative, revealing epiphanies, powerful experiences that Denzin (2014) described as "moment(s) of revelation in a life" (p. 15). Through these insights, focused on events that are often painful, the researcher comes to understand more about himself or herself, as well as others. While there are many key researchers in this field, those to whom I often turn include Ellis (2004, 2009), Bochner (2014), Denzin (2014), and Poulos (2009). Lawrence-Lightfoot (2010), echoing many life-history researchers, observed, "In the particular lies the general" (p. 16). My hope is that my story of self-discovery and reconstruction can help guide others as I learn more about myself.

My heritage is rooted in the Deep South and predates the Confederacy. A few years ago my wife and I visited a family cemetery hidden in a Georgia wood. Among the graves of my ancestors rested several who had fought for the Confederate States of America, the iron CSA insignia attached to the tombstones. Did they fight for slavery, as many charge? I don't know. I do believe they fought for their homeland and for their honor as they perceived it. After the cemetery, we visited the local archives office, where volunteers had meticulously catalogued documents dating to the early 1800s. I nervously scanned the will of one of my ancestors, looking for the conviction of slavery. Instead, I saw that he left his dresser, his prize cow, and his pigs variously to his wife and children. They were poor farmers. Those are my ancestral beginnings.

My personal history begins in the White middle class. My father was a pharmacist and my mother a teacher. Both were born in South Georgia but emigrated to central Florida during the Depression. His father was shot and killed in a bar fight when my father was an infant. My mother's father was an orange grove worker. He and my grandmother bought some property with insurance money they received when one of their sons was killed in a swimming accident. They cleared the land themselves and planted orange trees, which they maintained until their deaths. They all encountered their own traumas and labored through them.

Like many white middle-class parents of the 1950s, mine settled into a new subdivision and began to raise their family. He worked in a pharmacy while she stopped teaching to raise my younger brother and me. We attended the church in which my mother was raised, went to a newly opened Christian school, and lived in a neighborhood populated with families of similar demographics. When I was 8, however, this seemingly idyllic structure abruptly changed. A victim of asthma and allergies, my mother died of emphysema, an effect, I'm convinced, of my father's smoking. Her death pushed him into an emotional maelstrom from which he never recovered.

After my mother died, my father hired a series of housekeepers to tend to us. He then married a woman with a son from a previous marriage. My new stepmother wanted a more affluent house, and so my father sold our home and moved us to a larger, newer house in a rural setting. That marriage was an unhappy union, and they divorced after 3 years. Within three months he married again, this time to a woman with four children. She quickly became pregnant and, tragically, contracted measles during the first trimester of her pregnancy. As a result, her baby was born legally blind and deaf. Thus, within a year my brother and I had moved from a family of one stepmother and stepbrother, to just ourselves, to another house, location, and family of stepmother, four step siblings, and an infant sister with severe disabilities.

While my father's second marriage was unhappy, this third match was a catastrophe. They fought loudly and often, which was something my brother and I had not previously experienced. All this took a severe toll on my father, who deteriorated both personally and professionally. Perhaps as a result, he committed some actions for which he was legally sanctioned. Although he did not serve any prison time, he carried that stigma for the rest of his life. In addition, he was stripped of his license to practice pharmacy. His life was shattered. He lapsed into acute depression, was suicidal, and did not work for 2 years.

Fortunately, both sets of our grandparents lived nearby, and periodically my brother and I were able to spend time with them. I remember their homes as refuges. I later had this same feeling visiting our Georgia relatives. There we had unconditional acceptance, no judgment, no anger, no jealousy, no malice. We were enveloped by unconditional love, which is a remarkable human phenomenon.

TEACHER AND PRINCIPAL

In college I majored in English education. The reasons were simple. I had always been a reader and writer, and English was easy for me. I also received a full scholarship for becoming and working as a teacher. I had no other resources, so the choice was easy. becoming an English teacher was the right decision for me.

I worked as a teacher in two large, suburban, affluent high schools, both serving overwhelmingly white populations. Although I think I learned to be a reasonably good teacher during that time, the difficulty I faced was that I saw it was going to be challenging to raise a family on a teacher's salary. By then I had married and begun a family that would grow to three children, and I realized that if I was to stay in education, I needed to earn more money. That meant moving into administration. I first served as the district's supervisor of secondary language arts. Following that, I worked as assistant principal of two different middle schools. Both schools served ethnically, culturally, and economically diverse populations, which provided my first experiences in working with marginalized groups.

All these experiences served as precursors to my appointment as principal of high-poverty high-minority Orange Pines Middle School. That event catapulted my journey toward greater self-awareness. The student population was comprised of 70% from low socioeconomic backgrounds, 65% minority, 20% migrant, and 35% with disabilities. The school, which I have identified with a pseudonym, was set in a small town in central Florida and drew students from both the town and rural areas. The buildings, dating from 1948, were in disrepair. Once the flagship of the community, the school carried the reputation of a "ghetto school," avoided by affluent parents who chose private or newer schools for their children. Although not required in Florida, more than 90% of the teachers were union members. Most had worked at the school for many years and were resistant to change.

The 7 years I spent as principal of the school presented many challenges for which I was grossly unprepared. These included deaths of students and staff; teachers involved in personal scandals; substance abuse; claims of racial discrimination; and incompetent teachers and staff protected by a strong union and contract. I remain vague here to protect all participants. I was accused of being ignorant, insensitive, and racially biased. These emotionally traumatic experiences, however, forced me to interrogate my professional and personal values and significantly steered the trajectory of my professional life.

Concomitantly, I learned to negotiate reform within the school structure. I formed study groups of teachers and my assistant principals. We worked to understand our unique student population, to devise strategies to improve the culture of the school, and thus to boost student achievement. We built a learning community that raised student achievement and improved the school's reputation within the community. We established a partnership with a school in China, telecommunicated regularly with Chinese students, and sent 15 teachers and students to Nanjing to teach over two summers. We hosted two Chinese teachers in a Chinese-English summer camp. We hired outstanding teachers. We initiated a complete renovation of the school's physical plant. Students were featured twice on the Nickelodeon television network and several times in local newspapers. Our hard work paid off, and we moved the school from a grade of "C" to "A" in Florida's School Accountability system.

DOCTORAL DERAILMENT

Despite the common life-challenges I have faced, I have met true despair in two distinct phases. The first stemmed from the death of my mother, plunging my brother and I into a miasma of domestic dysfunction that lasted until we both were working, attending college, and had the means to leave home. The second period of despair came decades later when I was trying to complete my dissertation.

In describing personal journeys, Chris Poulos (2009) recalled mythologist Joseph Campbell and his description of the hero archetype and the hero's journey. In what he called a heroic monomyth, Campbell described a structure that can be applied to thousands of stories, from ancient to modern. Briefly, the hero leaves a secure existence on a quest for discovery, spurred by an unsettling discovery or event. The hero encounters a series of adventures and obstacles. The obstacles reach a peak when the hero faces seemingly unassailable dangers. Here the hero encounters despair. Although usually with the help of others, he or she must look within to find the answers, weapons, and strength to vanquish the enemy. Poulos (2009) suggested that the hero archetype can personify one's search for self, and made keen observations about the phenomenon of despair:

> Hope fades, becoming just a trace, a wisp, of a … memory. Gloom settles in. Once Despair takes hold of the human heart … we may slip into that place from which there is no easy release. If we are not careful, Despair can kill us.… There is, in the end, but one way to conquer Despair. We need to breathe again. We need to feel *possibility* (emphasis in the original). (p. 92)

I am not offering my journey as a heroic archetype. I do not, however, find the description by Poulos as hyperbolic. I found myself despondent, frightened, and uncertain of my way forward. After earning two master's degrees, one in English and another in educational leadership, and completing all coursework for a doctoral degree in education. Leadership, my formal education stalled. While attempting to write a case study of a research project at a school where I had been assistant principal, I was unable to complete a satisfactory dissertation proposal. My time in the program expired. If I intended to continue in my university's doctoral program, university officials required me to take a series of refresher courses—in essence, repeating nearly my entire course of doctoral studies. While that is standard procedure in most doctoral programs, it was potentially devastating to me. This was especially frightening because I was entering the final decade of my K–12 career. My plan had always been to earn a doctorate and then, following retirement, teach in a local college. What seemed to be a clear and simple plan lay in shambles.

The reasons for my failure were varied. I had become a principal, a time consuming and stressful job. I wasn't sure about my research project. I had some health challenges. These are common hurdles in many doctoral journeys. While they were daunting, I saw no choice but to persevere if I were to meet my postretirement goals.

The process of reinstatement required me to petition each professor whose course I needed to retake to allow me to complete one or more research papers to demonstrate currency in the topic. I didn't want to spend more time reenrolling in a course, and I certainly didn't want to spend more money. Deep despair raised its head in my emotional reaction to an e-mail from one of the professors I had petitioned. Saying that I would have to completely retake his course, which would not be offered again until the next year, he suggested that I either seek an education specialist degree (EdS) or admission at another university. The EdS is not considered a terminal degree and would have prevented me from teaching doctoral students. Thus, either of those actions would have sabotaged my long-term plans. Reading his comments now, they seem reasonable and direct. Then, however, his words seemed malevolent. I was stunned. Fortunately, another faculty member interceded for me, and the professor allowed me to complete a research project in lieu of retaking his course. I completed eleven course currency demonstrations over a 1-year period to reinstate my candidacy and resurrect my goal of achieving a doctorate. Following that, I changed my dissertation chair and dissertation topic, strategic moves that set me on the path to complete my doctorate.

Reflections on Doctoral Derailment

Those were dark days. A future that I had envisioned was collapsing before me. I had always been a strong student, top of the class, even in graduate classes, but I had lapsed. I had achieved many previous successes: Marrying a supportive and talented partner; raising three terrific kids; climbing the career ladder to a rewarding but challenging job; enduring a bout with cancer and another health crisis from which I nearly died. Although these were experiences that might absolve my failures in the eyes of others, the truth remained that I had not achieved my goal of earning a terminal degree. Without that, I had no sense of what my future after retirement would be. Still young enough to work after my projected retirement, I had always assumed that academia would be my once and future home. That anticipated future was now in serious doubt.

I had no choice. I would complete the projects, complete the course currency demonstrations, find a new chair, a new dissertation topic, and earn the degree. All that did happen, although I completed the dissertation and degree after I retired. Ironically, the professor whom I felt had opposed me has since become a mentor and guide through the academic wilderness and is someone I contact periodically for advice.

That was the wilderness for me. Archetypal or not, my despair was real. By the time I was reestablishing course currency and reshaping my dissertation, I had moved to the principalship of another middle school in the same community. As I struggled to find a topic to research, I realized that my experiences at Orange Pines were the stories I wanted to tell. In those dark moments, I brought my personal and professional backgrounds together to decide what I believed about myself and my work as a principal. The result was a much deeper understanding of educational leadership theory and practical application of qualitative methodology, as well as a more focused life trajectory after retirement.

My dissertation directed me toward a path of self-discovery in which I probed my moral purpose as principal of a challenging school. I used ethical prisms of care, critique, justice, community, and the profession (Furman, 2004; Shapiro & Stefkovich, 2011; Starratt, 2012) to probe my past. I discovered that my values shaped early in my life forged for me an ethic of care for both students and employees that ironically caused me more stress than a different or more balanced focus would have. In my dissertation I described how I applied deep reflection to discover and refine my moral purpose as a principal working with students within marginalized groups and with the teachers who served them. That process of deep reflection prepared me for my current trajectory.

I am a believer in serendipity. Marvelous things have happened to me when I least expected them, sometimes within the wilderness of despair. Had my original proposal been successful, I would not be nearly as reflective and current in educational leadership policy and qualitative methodology as I am today. While I might have secured a college position sooner, I would be less educated, less astute, and less experienced than I am today.

My first position as assistant principal came unexpectedly. I was comfortably ensconced as supervisor of language arts for my district. It was a position that I had aggressively pursued, but I had grown comfortable and sedate. I received a call from a former supervisor. She had been appointed as principal of a nearby middle school and offered me a position as an assistant. That was a large school of nearly 2,000 students with a challenging population. I held that job for 6 years. While there, after applying unsuccessfully for several principal positions, I had given up. After a particularly painful rejection, the principal of a new school called unexpectedly and offered me a job as assistant principal in opening his school. That proved to be a marvelous opportunity. A year later, in another seemingly random event, the assistant superintendent called to suggest that I apply for the principal position at Orange Pines, a job I had not considered.

In addition to the dissertation debacle proving to be the best thing that could have happened to my evolution as an emerging scholar, a dean at a university for which I had been teaching classes as an adjunct offered me a chance to facilitate a research center. The university employs people like me—an earned doctorate, accomplished in their field, often still working, but with limited time to devote to research, publication, and presentation. The job was to encourage faculty to research, present, and publish. Again, I found myself vulnerable, searching, ignorant, and insecure. And yet, I was exhilarated by the opportunity and challenge.

POSTRETIREMENT TRAJECTORY AND REFLECTION: LIFE ROLES AND CHANGE

Van Manen (1990) said we learn only in retrospection and reflection of events, not amid the acts themselves. Qualitative reflective methodologies have given me frameworks to examine, understand, and learn from pivotal professional and personal experiences. Today I remain a novice scholar, although far ahead of what I knew several years ago, and light years ahead of where I would be if that first dissertation proposal had been successful. These are the themes that Lawrence-Lightfoot (2010) drew upon in her study of those of us in the age group 50 to 75, which she identifies as the third chapter of our lives.

Lawrence-Lightfoot (2010) observed that when adults transition from successful careers, they suffer from a lack of identity. I always identified with my job. When my former boss offered me a job as her assistant principal, I first did not accept. I had become identified with the role of language arts supervisor for the entire district. I did not want to become absorbed into the fray of many nameless assistant principals, in my view lost in the anonymity of numbers. However, becoming an assistant principal was the right move and led to a successful tenure as principal of two schools.

Identity and social roles define who we are. These are difficult to relinquish. Separation creates an emotional chasm that must be filled. I live in a small community. It is common for me to encounter familiar faces.

I recently met one of my former assistant principals in Walgreens. She asked, "So what are you doing now?" I replied, "Doing some writing, some research, teaching some classes, staying busy." How do I explain learning, searching, falling, climbing, growing myself, and helping others? I struggle to define my current role, which seems amorphous, even when I write it here.

Psychologist Erik Erickson (1959) believed that for individuals to develop and maintain a healthy personality, they must continue to resolve critical psychological conflicts throughout their lives. Similarly, Lawrence-Lightfoot (2012) observed that to age successfully, people must maintain an active curiosity about a rapidly changing world and adapt to developmental changes in their own abilities. They must be eager to engage new skills and perspectives. They must be willing to take risks, experience vulnerability and uncertainty, learn from experience and failure, seek guidance from others. Like the adults in Lawrence-Lightfoot's *Third Chapter* (2010), I seek new adventures, new goals, and new processes of learning.

Lawrence-Lightfoot (2010) said that those in their third chapter often want to give back to younger generations. My hope is to contribute to the scholarship of my profession. In that vein, another task I have taken on is to work with doctoral students. These are working teachers and administrators completing their doctoral journeys. It is thrilling to see them respond and meet their goals. I see myself as working to develop myself, so that I can in turn provide the same constructive direction to others who follow me.

Poulos (2009) and Lawrence-Lightfoot (2010) argued that we are each shaped by our historical contexts, culture, background, and values. Formative cultural events for me included the Kennedy assassination, Civil Rights upheavals, the assassinations of Martin Luther King and Robert Kennedy, the Vietnam War, the Watergate debacle, and Nixon's resignation. My generation, I was certain, would shape a better world. Several decades later, I'm not sure we succeeded. I can, however, strive to make my own impact.

I have not discussed some prominent life-roles, although they are significant to me. The roles of father and grandfather reign prevalent, as I learn from my children, even as I try to offer them advice. The roles of husband, partner, and lover are important, as my wife and I face our collective third chapter together. My roles as son and grandson carry historical and social context as I view my 21st century world. They have shaped roles seminal to this discussion: seeker, learner, adventurer. All are a part of the tapestry of my journey: past, present, and future.

What am I still blind to? I am a White, middle-aged, middle-class male. I know I have been protected from judgment based on the color of my skin and the country of my birth. Like many others, I have known trauma, fear, and loss. I believe those phenomena are human gestalts that bind us as human beings. I have sought insights into the sufferings of others I worked with, such as English language learners who carried knives used as their tools to eat, work, and survive, who were unaware this tool is considered a weapon and an expellable offense in American schools. I sat on the porch with grieving parents whose child had died. I have worked with children who did not have a bedroom of their own or a safe place to sleep. I also worked with African American families who grew up in the segregated South and believed the system was still rigged, this time against a new generation. As a researcher, writer, and teacher, I believe I can draw on my experiences to help others. I have learned to see others as divine entities evolving through imperfect vessels. I have learned to treat individuals as I would want to be treated. I have come to see that our commonalities greatly overmatch our differences. I have learned that through reflection and perseverance one can succeed.

My professional ride has been frightening and exhilarating, frustrating and rewarding. I have often been forced to admit my ignorance. I have also learned and improved as a scholar and educator, although I am not as polished as I hope to become. I steer through uncharted waters, often turning to those younger than I for mentorship and advice. I am refreshed, renewed, and exhilarated as I strive to make meanings of my experiences and share those insights with others. I seek to experiment, to improvise, to explore, to change, and continue to learn.

Dewey (1933) reminded us, "Education is a social process. Education is growth. Education is not a preparation for life; education is life itself" (p. 17). I look forward to continuing my education and sharing new knowledge with others. My goal is to provide personal reflections and insights that may help improve the work and lives of others. I hope to make a difference.

REFERENCES

Bochner, A. P. (2014). *Coming to narrative: A personal history of paradigm change in the human sciences.* Left Coast Press.

Clandinin, D. J., & Connelly, F. M. (2000). *Narrative inquiry: Experience and story in qualitative research.* Jossey-Bass.

Cole, A. L., & Knowles, J. G. (2000). *Researching teaching: Exploring teacher development through reflexive inquiry.* Allyn & Bacon.

Cole, A. L., & Knowles, J. G. (Eds.). (2001). *Lives in context: The art of life history research.* AltaMira Press.

Denzin, N. (2014). *Interpretive autoethnography* (2nd ed.). SAGE.

Dewey, J. (1933). *How we think. A restatement of the relation of reflective thinking to the educative process* (Revised ed.). D.C. Heath.

Ellis, C. (2004). *The ethnographic I: A methodological novel about autoethnography.* Altamira Press.

Ellis, C. (2009). *Revision: Autoethnographic reflections on life and work.* Left Coast Press.

Erikson, E. H. (1959). *Identity and the life cycle*. W.W. Norton.

Furman, G.C. (2004). The ethic of community. *Journal of Educational Administration, 42*(2), 215–235. https://doi.org/10.1108/09578230410525612

Janesick, V. (2011). *Stretching exercises for qualitative researchers* (3rd ed.). SAGE.

Lawrence-Lightfoot, S. (1997). *The art and science of portraiture*. Jossey-Bass.

Lawrence-Lightfoot, S. (2010). *The third chapter: Passion, risk, and adventure in the 25 years after 50*. Sarah Crichton Books.

Lawrence-Lightfoot, S. (2012). *Exit: The endings that set us free*. Sarah Crichton Books.

Lawrence-Lightfoot, S. (2016). *Growing each other up: When our children become our teachers*. University of Chicago Press.

Poulos, C. (2009). *Accidental ethnography: An inquiry into family secrecy*. Left Coast Press.

Shapiro, J. P., & Stefkovich, J. A. (2011). *Ethical leadership and decision making in education: Applying theoretical perspectives to complex dilemmas* (3rd ed.). Routledge.

Starratt, R. J. (2012). *Cultivating an ethical school*. Routledge.

Van Manen, M. (1990). *Researching lived experience: Human science for an action sensitive pedagogy*. SUNY Press.

Van Manen, M. (2016). *Phenomenology of practice: Meaning-giving methods in phenomenological research and writing*. Routledge.

CHAPTER 10

WALKING (BACKWARD)

Giving Identity a Moving Place

Kate McCabe
Simon Fraser University

Walking calms turmoil. Prisoners circumambulate the yard, animals exercise back and forth in their cages, and the anxious pace the floor—waiting for the baby to be born or to hear news from the board-room. Heidegger recommended the path through the woods for philosophizing. Aristotle's school was called "Peripatetic"—thinking and discoursing while walking up and down; monks walk around their closed gardens. Nietzsche said that only thoughts while walking, *laufenden* thoughts, were of value—thoughts that ran, not sitting thoughts.

—James Hillman, "Pleasure of Walking"

We begin on a beach in Tofino, Canada. I recuperate there following surgery for breast cancer. I am acutely aware of the uncertainty of my future even though I am identified as "survivor." My bones creak with the rhythms of

Narratives on Becoming: Identity and Lifelong Learning, pp. 133–138
Copyright © 2021 by Information Age Publishing
All rights of reproduction in any form reserved.

this tide. The weightiness, pressures and pains of heteronormativity, childhood trauma and cancer rush at me, through me. I have been "surviving" for so long that I doubt my own feelings, my own experiences. My thinking seems muddled and I lean into the little spirit that is left to get me through these next few months. Exhaustion penetrates the rhythms of my breathing; I am close to losing my capacity for resistance. I am vapor where past, present, and future are bound to my cells. I whisper: "I want a big love."

> This is not an instance of begging.
> This is not even a request.
> I am ready.
> It is already here. It arrives in hesitations.

I started a journal the day of the diagnosis. Since then, writing has become one way that I am coming to know myself. My academic circles have encouraged me. Through life writing (Hasebe-Ludt et al., 2009) I am learning that cancer, as an emotional and physical wound, can create its own wound, its own opening for life events to spill out and onto the page. Writing helps that which was roiling to work its way out. My identity is allowed to "waver and tremble" (Caputo, 1987, p. 7) like those cardboard paper dolls with clothes that clip and unclip.

****

The Myth of Sisyphus (Camus, 1983) session of the philosophy conference draws my attention. I have carried the myth with me since I was young. It is as though the grey coolness of the stone presses itself against my hands as I enter the conference room aware of the smell of the grass and dirt upon the land. I see Sisyphus, moody, as he rolls the stone back up the hill. My thinking wanders as I listen to the speaker. Memories flutter in and out of view while snippets of the presentation land on my notepad. At the end of the presentation, as the clapping of appreciation brings me back into the room, I turn on my phone to check for messages. I have been waiting on a call from the doctor about the outcome of my biopsy. I see she has left me a message. I leave the room and find a small outer sitting area to make the call. "I don't like to give information like this on the phone," the doctor says, "but it's your information and you deserve to have it as soon as possible. You have cancer." She pauses. I hold my breath. "Come into the office as soon as possible so we can plan." In that instant I let go of the boulder. It rolls by me. I don't turn.

In that short telephone conversation, unlike Sisyphus, endlessly toiling, I am relieved of the burden of pushing the boulder up the hill. I don't look as it rolls away. In that diagnosis, "you have cancer," I am released of the burden of identifying myself with the repeated, futile struggle of pushing, again and again. Resistance. Compliance. Instead, I unclip. Instead, I breathe.

> Seeing the frailty of your life through seeing the breath is the meditation on the recollection of death. Just realizing this fact—that if the breath goes in but does not go out again, or goes out but does not come in again, your life is over—is enough to change the mind. It will startle you into being aware. (Chah, 2001, p. 44)

Images collide: Mountains. Pacific silver fir. Water. Sand. Body. Wound. Clip-unclip. Sisyphus. Opening. Silence.

> What do they want of me?
> I don't turn.
> The Weight. The Light. The Breath.
> All here. All along.

****

It is time to walk. I wonder if I am ready. "Once I can get some distance from the doorstep of my own exhaustion, a glimpse is possible" (Jardine, 2019, p. 17). Do I have the courage to walk into what is emerging about identity, illness, myself? The walking is necessary. One foot in front of the other, in order to go on. Going on isn't about moving forward and forcing change. It is more about the growing awareness of the *possibility* to change and of the directions some of those changes might take.

> Opportunities are not plain, clean gifts; they trail dark and chaotic attachments to their unknown backgrounds, luring us further. One insight leads to another; one invention suggests another variation; more and more seems to press through the hole, and more and more we find ourselves drawn out into a chaos of possibilities. (Hillman, 2013, p. 94)

Unlike the predictable pushing of the boulder, this kind of walking is filled with risk. The unpredictable circumstances that show themselves are part of the call to know the *other* in me. The force of the boulder against my hands is the force of customs, requirements, and expectations handed down through laws and traditions. The boulder is also my apathy. The release, stepping aside, stepping back, gives me a chance to see if and how the laws might make it back up the hill, without me falling in line. They are being held accountable, as am I.

Deciding not to fall in line is one step toward a more compassionate way within this messy, risky life. My life cannot wait. The commitment is made the moment stepping away happens. "There are times when we have all the information we need and we just have to decide" (Caputo, 2018, p. 211). So, I walk, acknowledging past experiences, joys, successes, abuses, and oppressions. The ties loosen, giving a wide range of experiences and identity a place to move. Attempting to dismiss the ropes that bound me and that I used to bind myself has not resulted in their elimination. What was imposed had become belief, and the release of these beliefs about who I am has been both painful and humbling. As the cool sand gives way under my bare feet, muscles support and give strength to my movements as I work out the stiffness, the outcome of ceaseless toiling and nightmares that cramp not only my legs but the self I am opening to.

There is as much cure for cancer in walking as in the time spent on the radiation table. "Walking can be meditative therapy—not an idyllic hike by the ocean (Hillman, 2006, pp. 252–253). Walking back and forth along the edge of the sea can be as tumultuous as the water itself. I squirm under the memories that make their way to the surface like toxic flotsam. But there is also calm. Walking backward isn't about walking back into memories, attached to places, people, and ideas of the past. It is not sinking into the depths of that muck. In this act, the memories and their weightiness are slackened. Walking backward has more to do with slowly navigating the place I find myself in, attending to it by lending it space. In releasing myself to this physical act, I find that I am given room to show up, to find myself. I breathe: in and out.

There are no guarantees as I respond to the voices of the other-in-me.

****

Sitting a little behind me, on the beach, is my white plaster bust. I created it the night before the surgery as a marker of the changes that were about to happen. Seeing it there against the logs, I feel the strips of wet, plaster-infused cotton that I layered on my skin and that heated and hardened. I feel the panic that came over me as I pulled the white impression away at midnight and later tossed it in a corner of my bedroom. Now, I *find* myself with it on this beach.

Finding myself involves locating my body here, on the sand, with the rush of ocean, its waves assaulting my ears. As I look out onto the horizon, the dense coastal forest soars behind me. The reclining bust is there too, supported by a log-strewn beach. Even now, some of my skin cells, dotting its cavity, are taken up by the wind. Where will they land? Where will I? The sharp, sweet scent of fir, cedar, and hemlock and the rush of waves hold my attention and hold me as I wobble back and forth at the edge of the foaming sea. Suddenly, "I belong here. I live here. The Earth is my home.

I can finally experience my being as resonant, indebted, and interwoven with these things" (Jardine, 1998, p. 99).

I see myself in the whipped and aerated waves. I realize that my call for a big love was here all along. Earth. Sky. Wind. Tidal rhythms. Silver fir and the single, soft, high-pitched note of the eagle as she glides above the sea are with me, part of me. My sea-soaked bust, still reclining, still waiting, reminds me of a *me* that has been here all along and that I can now turn toward with compassion. Now, awakened to love, I walk toward myself, recognizing the entwined net of relations all around me. This is the attachment I welcome. This is a landscape so large that even Sisyphus, with his endless toiling, has room to breathe.

With compassion, I have space to walk and to be with the changes all around me. With this view of myself and of my relation to the land, I see the gaps, the places where I too am opened by these earthly rhythms rather than being wrung out or tossed aside by them. These gaps, these spaces, give me the strength to see myself anew. They give me strength to bear witness to the white-hot flashes of childhood trauma. They give me strength to rise up and out against oppressive traditions and beliefs. They give me strength to see my stillness on the radiation table, not as weakness or powerlessness, but as a will to live, to love, to thrive, and to remember. Forgetting and forgetfulness have kept weighty, welded structures in place. Unforgetting, and reclaiming my life beside the vibrant rhythms of the earth, draws attention to the fullness of me, where the old is made anew.

Months later, images push themselves with more persistence into this intimate, raw opening. Frightful flashes of corridors, car washes, black polyester, canoes, and dusty bookshelves push up from their burial. Now that I have ceased pushing the rock, there is nothing to keep them down. The acts of looking and listening remind me that they were never truly gone, never truly forgotten. Heart and breath quicken when I dare to look, to listen. But as I unforget these alarming, difficult moments, as I let them pass through me, the Earth asserts itself and sustains me.

The stored images seem to be working their way out while I practice working my way back in—into life and my body.

I've found that walking gives wildness and sorrow and pain and suffering their due. Walking gives thoughts of identity a moving place, a territory where it can "take steps." Life, like love, "doesn't just sit there, like a stone, it has to be made, like bread; remade all the time, made new" (Le Guin, 1971, n.p.). Listening to the beings around me—the wind, the trees, the ocean, the machines, the friends—makes identities in this life possible but not necessary. In this way of walking, life—identity—is not fixed but rather livable.

I have lived my experiences. I have lived the identities imposed on me. I have lived the often overwhelming feeling of being little more than a paper doll. Now I begin to chart the way out by walking. I follow paths I had not noticed before. I shape some of my own. Wildness is a place of decay and creation. In that walking, backward and forward, especially into the wild, I find that *livable* identities are beautiful and generative. They don't limit the possibility of change when something comes along to shake up what's becoming fixed. Some things *stand* for us and call us to them, and as a result, our bodies open to include them. We become expansive. No longer am I limited by the identity of "survivor." I am love, filling and releasing.

REFERENCES

Camus, A. (1983). *The myth of Sisyphus and other essays*. Random House.

Caputo, J. D. (1987). *Radical hermeneutics. Repetition, deconstruction, and the hermeneutic project*. Indiana University Press.

Caputo, J. D. (2018). *Hermeneutics. Fact and interpretation in the age of information*. Random House.

Chah, A. (2005). *Everything arises, everything falls away*. Shambhala.

Hasebe-Ludt, E., Chambers, C. M., & Leggo, C. (2009). *Life writing and literary métissage as an ethos for our times*. Peter Lang.

Hillman, J. (2006). *City and soul*. Spring.

Hillman, J. (2013). *Senex and puer*. Spring.

Jardine, D. W. (1998). *To dwell with a boundless heart. Essays in curriculum theory, hermeneutics, and the ecological imagination*. Peter Lang.

Jardine, D. W. (2019). *Asleep in my sunshine chair*. Dio Press.

Le Guin, U. K. (1971). *The lathe of heaven*. Scribner.

CHAPTER 11

OUR BRIEF
SHARED NARRATIVE

Identity Development in the Context of our Shared Environment and Individual Generational Experiences

Kathryn Medill
Arizona State University Museum

Anne Medill
Northern Arizona University

THE BEGINNING

This narrative essay examines two generations of women from the same family whose identity development has been shaped through the intertwining of shared space, personal beliefs, and social history. Our voices provide selected glimpses of developmental milestones and shared or individual

Narratives on Becoming: Identity and Lifelong Learning, pp. 139–151
Copyright © 2021 by Information Age Publishing
All rights of reproduction in any form reserved.

experiences that have shaped our professional and personal identities. The older woman (Anne) has been a lifelong learner who returned to higher education to complete her doctorate in her late 30s. The younger woman (Kathryn), her daughter, is currently in her mid-20s and has recently completed her doctorate. One foundational influence for both women is their mother or grandmother. Her name is Barbara or Mom or Nana.

Barbara Also Known as Mom or Nana

Barbara viewed the role of higher education as twofold: first, it offered a way to cultivate one's intellectual capacity and second it created avenues to achieve financial stability. For these reasons she saw it as a necessary experience for her children and grandchildren. Barbara also believed in supporting her community—both her immediate and extended families as well as, the larger community. Barbara lost her mother at a young age and was raised by her father. However, when sharing her own life narrative, Barbara emphasized that her extended family had taken care of her from a very early age and influenced who she was, or her identity. Barbara was raised in a time when male roles were strongly tied to the identity of the breadwinner, and female roles were tied to the identity of the caretaker of the home. While Barbara chose to give up a career as a nurse to fulfill the caretaker role but instilled a desire in both her female and male children to pursue higher education. As both a mother and grandmother, Barbara exposed her family members to multiple cultural, social, educational, and arts sectors like museums, galleries, the ballet, theatre, the symphony, and social work agencies. Barbara's focus on education as a means to support oneself, her commitment to the arts sector as a means for self-enrichment, and her ability to think openly and critically about the world and the reciprocal nature of being a member of the world, are values that both authors cite as being important grounding points for our own lifelong identities. Our current identities reflect the shifting trends in family size, economic mobility, and the real impact an individual's lived environment has on identity development.

THE MILLENIAL: KATHRYN (KAT)

This narrative grants me the opportunity to unpack two aspects of my "self" identity: (1) the influences my Nana and mother have on my cultivated sense of self identity and career interests, as well as, (2) the label I have been given, "millennial," as a result of my year of birth. These relationships and the millennial label both inform and are informed by each other and contribute to my personal identity in a nonlinear fashion. For the purpose of clarity in this narrative I will do three things: (1) discuss each influential woman discretely, (2) unpack the label millennial and how it impacts my identity, and (3) reflect on how points one and two have impacted my educational identity and career endeavors.

The Women and the Environment: Nana and My Mother Anne

My grandmother, Nana, gave me many things: my middle name, Nellis, my love of the ocean, and my wry sense of humor. But a passion for the arts sector and my desire to propagate an "educated and well rounded" identity are the two most cherished attributes I received from Nana. They are the traits that have influenced my identity and career interests the most. My summers were spent in Upstate New York, where my grandparents would take the grandchildren to symphony performances, theatre, and local art galleries—a privilege my grandparents were proud to offer us. A common game during our summertime breakfasts was to name the play or opera a song was from before it finished playing on the kitchen stereo. Nana was also very proud of the fact that her aunt Geraldine was an accomplished self-taught artist and often pointed out her artwork that was in the home. Once I expressed interest in art Nana set up a drawing station for me at her kitchen table so I could look out onto her back garden and sketch. She always supported my creative interests.

Our identity formation is influenced by the messages we receive from significant others in our environments throughout our lifespan, and my experiences have reinforced this fact. I remember clearly when I was a young child and my Nana introduced me to her friends, they would often politely comment on some aspect of my aesthetic qualities, for example, "She is pretty/cute/beautiful." While these were meant to be compliments, my Nana would always retort, "And she is smart too." This message of being proud of my curious nature, especially as a female, has been embedded in the way I identify myself when I am in a professional role or social gathering.

Later, when I developed an interest in pursuing a career in the arts sector, Nana bought me a book on influential female artists and wrote on the front cover, "Dear Kat, I thought you'd like this book. It is good for one female talented artist to have a book about another. Love you, Nana" (B. Nellis, personal communication 2005).

One critical memory from my 20s was when I visited her in the Alzheimer care facility she lives in and shared that I had been accepted into a master's program in the United Kingdom. Despite her inconsistent connection to the present, she discussed the program requirements and shared her excitement about my continued intellectual development. This was 45 minutes of lucidity I will never forget. While Nana is no longer cognitively present enough to understand that I have just completed my PhD, I will still respond to any compliment based off my aesthetic qualities with, "Yeah, and I'm smart too."

My mother, Anne, also champions the idea of being educated as an integrated part of her self-identity, a narrative I imagine she acquired from her mother. In addition to a focus on education, my mother instilled in me a sense of civic responsibility, an understanding of systemic inequity and a desire to interact with individuals or groups from diverse social and economic demographics. I spent my youth observing her practice as a social worker and a professor. When she would do workshops with the local domestic violence shelter, I would be in a separate room with the children of the families attending the sessions. First, I saw myself as a peer to the children; as I grew older, I became the one who facilitated the children's art-making activities.

This experience demonstrated to me the privilege that came with being a part of a family that had the interest, money, and time to help me to create a self-identity that maximized my intellectual capacities and personal interests. While I saw my contribution to the domestic violence shelter as a civically minded gesture, my mother helped me to realize that my positionality in the community made my experience in the shelter very different from the experiences of the other children. I was able to leave the shelter after the hour of art making and return to what I knew as my "normal." But, for the other children, the shelter was their "normal," complete with its own set of implicit and explicit identity expectations and implications.

I also observed my mother as a professor. She is someone who can discuss difficult topics like domestic violence and suicide with potential social workers in an empathetic and informed manner. She made it clear to me through her lived example and verbal messages that earning her doctorate afforded her many opportunities: (1) the chance to teach direct practice-based topics to potential future practitioners, (2) personal financial independence and security, and (3) access to resources and institutions that are not given to many individuals in the general community. My mother has cultivated a career that is symbiotically community-minded, civically focused, and intellectually fulfilling to her—a path I am working on emulating in my present environment.

The Label: Millennial

Millennial is a label that others apply to me. According to market research (Adkins & Rigoni, 2016; Bump, 2014; Gallup, Inc. 2016; De la

Cruz, 2012; Howe & Strauss, 2006; Stein, 2013; "Who Are Millennials," n.d.), the term millennial indicates several things: (1) I was born between 1977 to 2004, (2) I am civic-minded, (3) I am tech-savvy, (4) I am interested in community building, (5) I crave close contact and immediate feedback with my work supervisors, (6) I have accumulated a substantial amount of personal debt ($45,000 on average), and (7) I am part of a demographic that makes up 25% of the U.S. population.

While these traits are only a few of those attached to millennials, they have created stereotypes about my generation. Nevertheless, these seven traits do resonate with my self-identity. I was born in 1990; I am interested in the concept of community on a personal, social, and academic level; I feel fulfilled in my workplace when my ideas are heard, and I am able to have a meaningful conversation with my supervisors and I rely on my technology to keep my schedule organized.

Yes, my life lens is grounded in the idea of "me," but not in the sense of what I get from others and the environments that will benefit me; instead, I wonder: what can I do benefit my community and the environment? I am a pragmatic idealist; that is, I recognize the existence of systemic modes of oppression. I also believe that these systems can be deconstructed internally and externally, and my hope is to contribute to this deconstruction with the work I do as a part of my career. With the help of technology, I see community as both a local and global concept. With the influence of the important women in my life, I see education as a tool to create the life and career I envision; an instrument that is attached to my sense of identity.

The Professional Path: Furthering Identity

Given my social history, my decision to pursue a career in art education and museums seems fitting. Since the 1960s the museum sector has experienced a shift in ideology. Museums are no longer univocal cabinets of curiosity; rather, they are striving to become multivocal laboratories that reflect community interests and needs (Ambrose & Paine, 1993; Falk et al., 2007; Silverman, 2010). The rise in socially engaged practice in the arts sector and constructivist learning trends in education since the 1980s makes a museum the ideal space to question, reconsider, and deconstruct art and visual culture as well as the role of museums as institutions that shape identity (Falk & Dierking, 2013; Simon, 2010).

My experiences with Nana and my mother inspired me to question the role of the museum by pursuing a degree and developing an empathetic lens. The current ideological shift in museum theory is multifaceted and will take years to activate on a large-scale level. My role as Audience Experience Coordinator at a university museum is the ideal entry-level position for me in both a pragmatic and academic sense. I can see where the gaps between theory and practice emerge and have learned that textbook concepts exist differently in a practical setting. Additionally, in my role I manage and mentor student workers who act as our front of house staff, providing tours and work events. During my three years in this position, I have expanded the student worker role from a work-study position to a program in which students help us create our content for the public, receive on-the-job insight into the different roles of internal museum positions and continue to shape their own professional identities.

A strong sense of self is a trait I have acquired from my Nana and my mother. It, along with financial privilege, has given me the courage and passion to pursue higher education in both the United States and the United Kingdom. My confidence in learning, operating, and contributing to new systems is a direct reflection of my strong sense of self and my support system. I see my Nana and mother as progressive women for their respective eras, and I feel an obligation to continue this tradition in my own personal and professional practice.

THE BABY BOOMER: ANNE

When my daughter and I first discussed writing about our identity narratives, I took time to reflect on how I got to this point in my professional and personal self-identity. I am a 62-year-old professor with a doctorate, who additionally possesses the following abilities that my mother trained me in: (1) I know how to clean house with a vengeance, (2) make meals for my husband, and (3) take care of others' needs continually without hesitation. Yes, I am also a baby boomer. We baby boomers are often labeled the sandwich generation. A generation that identifies with caring for our elderly parents, launching our children, and having to work longer to ensure some quality in our living standards and health care in our "golden years."

The Professional Path: My Mother's Lived Example

My mother Barbara (or Nana) instilled in me the social responsibility of taking care of family members, providing service in the community, and engaging in opportunities to learn about diversity. When I was a child, my family hosted children from the inner city as summer visitors as part of the Fresh Air program. These children were economically disadvantaged African Americans who arrived on a bus in our community. Fitting an eighth child into our already crowded home was a challenge, but it worked;

we all learned from our guests as much as they did from us. I learned about the concepts of social privilege and having unmet needs.

I continued to learn about helping others, advocacy, and social justice in my adulthood through watching my mother's civic engagement and engaging in my own social work practice. In the early 1990s, my mother worked as a volunteer nurse at one of the city's first hospice centers for individuals who were dying from AIDS. She worked tirelessly and with an ability to accept the individual who was dying as a fellow human in need, rather than seeing them as a member of socially stigmatized population in her community. As a young adult, I worked the annual ice cream social to raise funds for this program, and I engaged with those change agents who were creating constructive solutions to gaps in the social welfare system.

My mother Barbara also volunteered to work with children in the inner city to assist them with their reading skills. She was in her early 70s when she was doing this work and had developed mild Parkinson's. One day she asked me if her head shaking was that noticeable because one of the boys she was reading with said, "Hey lady, why does your head shake?" This was one of the only times my mother referred to her mild Parkinson's. Generally, she was not aware of her Parkinson's because her needs were not her primary focus in any situation either in our home or when she was in the community.

Furthering Professional Identity: Social Work

I believe it is no accident I am a social worker because of my lifelong exposure and education in civic engagement in diverse settings with culturally different populations. As a member of the baby boomer generation, I have a developed sense of collaboration, a strong work ethic and a strong sense of self-assurance. My mother Barbara nurtured these ideals through her own consistent community action.

Much like my mother's messages to my daughter, my mother consistently told me I was intelligent and that I should never rely on a man to make my way in the world. I grew up watching her care for and manage seven children and a husband who was engaged in the family in what I consider the typical hands-off style of the 1960s and 70s. My mother knew about the "women's liberation movement," but she was too wrapped up in the daily demands of keeping eight other people moving in the right direction to formally educate herself on the ideals attached to the movement. However, I suspect she would have loved to enroll in a women's studies class. In a memory book she completed for Kat she wrote, "Women today work hard at home and in their professions but still have not received equal recognition with male professionals" (B. Nellis, personal communication, 1990).

Higher Education

My mother instilled in me the belief that I was as physically capable and as intellectually able as a man. I was repeatedly given the message to do my best work, and I find that mantra has been carried into my present teaching approach with undergraduate and master's level students. I have always done my best academic work, and this enabled me to attend a PhD program on full grants and work study. Today I encourage the next generation of millennials to differentiate themselves by doing their best work in the classroom and their field placements. I ask them how they want to be identified.

I went back for my PhD after over a decade of direct social work practice, but it was not a planned journey. Instead, it was more of a "I will try to get admitted to a program approach" since we were moving back to the East Coast. I also had always been comfortable in the classroom and loved the engagement created through discussion. In my liberation as a woman of the mid-90s, I fooled myself into thinking that liberation meant working in a university teaching discipline that had been predominantly male and maintaining the traditional roles ascribed to my gender as a woman. I had married a man who maintained a hands-off engagement style in the family that I was familiar with from my childhood, and I found myself part of the glorious second shift generation (Hochschild & Machung, 2003). Taking classes during the day, working as an instructor, and teaching assistant and then going home to my 2-year-old, making dinner, giving her a bath, reading her books, and then beginning what I saw as the third shift. I am still perplexed by those who have asked me: "You only have one child?" Internally there must have been a part of my identity that saw this fact as a symbol of my failure to do it all as a woman because my consistent response became: "My PhD program is/was my second child." I now accept that it was my decision to have one child and that I did not need to make excuses for my own identity. In my 50s my identity was liberated when I accepted that not having any children was acceptable for both genders. This shift was caused in part from by my many discussions with my daughter's female millennial friends, who recognized children were not a requirement to live a fulfilled life or to complete their individual identity.

Lifelong Learner

My educational identity as a lifelong learner was shaped early in observable ways. In my childhood home, homework was a priority and television was limited to 30 minutes each day. We generally watched TV as a family and shows that my mother thought presented women as objects, such as

Laugh-In, were prohibited in the house. She would talk to each of her daughters about weighing the decision to have children and the number we might have. She stated in her memory book for Kat, "I do want you as you grow older to think of your grandmother as a woman who thought for herself. I am a woman from my time with a mind of my own. A bit of me is in your mom." She was frustrated that she had to minimize her career as a nurse to take care of the home, but she did her best work as a homemaker. She taught me to have pride in whatever it was I did for work and in my role as a family member. This belief translated into my being able to understand that each woman in the community is doing her best in the role she selected or was assigned. I also understood I was privileged to have choice and other women were not.

On more than several occasions when I was a young adult, I encouraged my mother to return to school to complete her BSN or to take classes. She expressed her sense of insecurity and concern about being too old to return to the classroom. In my own educational process, I learned that you are never too old. I see this as a shift in my sense of self-empowerment that is different from that of my mother, who is from another generation. Reflecting on my mom I realize that, without having read the books, she lived the tenets of women's liberation within the cultural constraints of her generation.

My family's economic situation while I was growing up was quite different from what my daughter has experienced. My father was a social worker and my mother worked part-time as a nurse, which created limited finances. The arts, theatre, and symphony were all important activities that my mother wanted to expose us to. Instead of the paid venues Kat and the other grandchildren have been afforded, our exposure was limited to free concerts in the park, free theatre through our own public education, the library, and art activities at home. I remember our parents taking us downtown to see the architecture of the beautiful mansions in the city. My mother always pointed out their doors and gardens. My daughter Kat knows when we travel that there will be a garden tour or two because of my identity with nature-cultivated through my mother and her desire for us to be exposed to the natural environment. When I was a child or young adult, my mother and I would identify the names of the flowers. I laugh today when I find myself asking my husband and daughter which flowers, they can name in a garden because I can hear my mother's voice asking me the same question.

I have continued to be an engaged learner and have expanded the tools I use to learn by developing a global learning focus. My parents always encouraged us to travel, but it was not until I was living independently that I first was able to afford travel to Europe, Africa, and Central America. I remember sitting in the theater in London for a production of the *Lion*

King and being overwhelmed emotionally because I realized I had achieved what my mother wanted for me. I was experiencing an art form in a new country in a venue that I had never experienced. I felt lucky, fortunate, and privileged. My travels have continued for the last 10 years, with Kat joining me on international educational programs. I have created a study abroad program for undergraduate students because I believe knowing about the world has gotten easier as technology advances and international travel becomes more available. The millennial generation has instant access to international events, social and political changes, and news that was not previously possible.

The summer of 2017 in Madrid I was able to participate in the World Gay Pride gathering on the streets and in the Plazas. I witnessed several million people from around the globe being accepted by businesses while displaying the Gay Pride flag and other symbols. Churches and diverse families also opened their doors to travelers in need during this parade and true celebration of diversity. Throughout the weekend I found myself energized, excited, and humbled by what I was witnessing in terms of the increased level of acceptance around diverse ways of self-identifying. I was standing in the Madrid, Chamartin train station watching this steady flow of people arriving to participate in the parade. I thought about my parents and our long-ago trips to Provincetown, Massachusetts, which was one of the first East Coast communities in the United States to welcome gay individuals openly. I had to acknowledge that the global social environment is not the same as it was in my 20s and that my life experiences continue to shape my self-identity. But I also know because of my interest in global politics that many members of the LBGTQ community are still labeled as outcasts in their home spaces, and that we as educators and citizens have the civic responsibility to work on global acceptance of difference.

My mother wrote in her memory book to my daughter that what she remembered most about my teenage years is "Knowing deep in my heart that your mom would leave home and go far away. I knew it from the time she was very young." I continually reflect on her insight and know that I have only been able to go far away and continue to cultivate my self-identity because of the strong belief in self and education that was shaped in my childhood by my mother and that has grown in my adulthood and been passed on to Kat.

BARBARA NOW

Kat and I continue to be shaped by my mother or her Nana. My mother's nursing background helped her care for my father or Kat's Papa until his early death from cancer. She continued to do her best work as a wife and caretaker, making sure all his needs were met until he died. Today, she has Alzheimer's and lives happily in a full-time care facility. Her memory is intermittent, and her family members have become the staff of the facility in many ways. She is demonstrating now through her actions and not so much in her words, how to be dignified in engaging and making connections with others. She continues to give of herself and ask for nothing. She will always reach for a hand to hold and offer a smile. She has influenced who both Kat and I are as women today and her other daughters and their children.

LESSONS LEARNED

In closing this narrative reflection Kat and I both found it interesting that we wanted this section to be titled: Lessons Learned. Of course, we thought this makes perfect sense when looking at the influence learning has had on both of us. Our shared use of language reflects how we both identify "self" through learning as a continual process.

Kathryn (Kat)

On a micro level, for me (Kat), writing this article highlighted the fact the while market research can synthesize aspects of generations and create nicely packaged labels, they do not address a critical element of my self-identity-my family. I define my success and motivation as a direct result of not just my lived experiences but the experiences of my Nana and mother. On a macro level, I recognize that this rhizomatic family dynamic has been a positive influence in my life but that feeling, or experience is not true for everyone.

Anne

As Kat's mother I learned that she does embody the best aspects of being a millennial, and the two generations of women before her. She knows that she is smart, shaped by her environment, and believes in the importance of reciprocal sharing in the lifelong learning process. I see her sense of civic responsibility in the professional work she does, and this motivates me to do more community work and to continue teaching about our shared responsibility to others in the undergraduate and graduate social work programs. We agree that we are fortunate to be related to one another and privileged to have been influenced by Nana or mom or Barbara. We will continue to act on our collective commitment to teach ourselves and others about the life lessons learned by women before us and to reflect upon our own identity based on our lived experiences.

We encourage the readers of this article to either: (1) have a conversation with someone who they feel safe with who has impacted their identity formation and ask them how they crafted their own identity and/or, (2) reflect on their identity formation process and visually represent it using whatever artistic process they enjoy.

FINAL THOUGHT

As we edit this chapter for the final time my mother and Kat's grandmother Nana is one of the thousands of individuals who finds herself in quarantine because of the COVID-19 pandemic in a nursing facility without the comfort of her family members. We miss her and know that thousands of other family members miss their family members who represent their history and the foundation of their identities. We are grateful to be lifelong learners.

REFERENCES

Adkins, A., & Rigoni, B. (2016). *Managers: Millennials want feedback but won't ask for it.* Retrieved March 23, 2018, from https://www.gallup.com/workplace/236450/managers-millennials-feedback-won-ask.aspx

Ambrose, T., & Paine, C. (1993). *Museum basics.* ICOM in conjunction with Routledge.

Bump, P. (2014, March 25). Here is when each generation begins and ends, according to facts. *The Atlantic.* https://www.theatlantic.com/national/archive/2014/03/here-is-when-each-generation-begins-and-ends-according-to-facts/359589/

De la Cruz, N. (2012, March 22). *Today's 20-something is carrying an Average $45,000 in debt.* Retrieved March 23, 2018, from https://www.businessinsider.com/millennials-are-carrying-an-average-of-45000-in-debt-2012-3

Falk, J. H., & Dierking, L. D. (2013). *The museum experience revisited.* Left Coast Press.

Falk, J. H., Dierking, L. D., & Foutz, S. (2007). *In principle, in practice: Museums as learning institutions.* Alta Mira Press.

Gallup, Inc. (2016). *How millennials want to work and live* (Rep.). Retrieved March 23, 2018, from Gallup, Inc. https://www.gallup.com/workplace/238073/millennials-work-live.aspx

Hochschild, A., & Machung, A. (2003). *The second shift: Working families and the revolution at home.* Penguin Books.

Howe, N., & Strauss, W. (2006). *Millennials rising: The next great Generation /by Neil Howe and bill Strauss; cartoons By R. J. Matson.* Vintage Books.

Silverman, L. H. (2010). *The social work of museums.* Routledge.

Simon, N. (2010). *The participatory museum*. Museum 2.0.

Stein, J. (2013, May 20). Millennials: The Me Me Me Generation. *Time*. http://time.com/247/millennials-the-me-me-me-generation/

Who are millennials. (n.d.). *Millennial Marketing*. http://www.millennialmarketing.com/who-are-millennials/

CHAPTER 12

DEVELOPING A PROFESSIONAL IDENTITY AMONG YOUR PERCEIVED OWN

An African American Woman's Journey From Public School Educator to HBCU Professor

Denelle L. Wallace
Norfolk State University

INTRODUCTION

As a new faculty member transitioning from the public school environment to the university setting, it was extremely important for me to maintain a close connection with practitioners in the classrooms of urban school districts, while establishing a research agenda as required for a tenure-track professor. The need to maintain this close connection stemmed from a desire to avoid an ivory tower mindset and provide solutions that merged research, theoretical frameworks, and real-world experiences. From my

Narratives on Becoming: Identity and Lifelong Learning, pp. 153–163
Copyright © 2021 by Information Age Publishing

viewpoint, this was the missing connection needed to ensure authenticity in research-based solutions to public school system issues reflected in the classroom. This close connection served as the driving force behind my transition from public school educator to historically Black college/ university (HBCU) professor.

IVORY TOWER MINDSET:
FROM CLASSROOM TEACHER TO UNIVERSITY PROFESSOR

As a former public school classroom educator, the transition from a public school environment to a university setting was an extraordinary opportunity for marrying research-based knowledge and real world professional experience, but a shift in mindset was essential and required a structured plan for success (McLeod, 2008). Both the public school classroom educator and the university professor serve the same purpose, which is to impart knowledge to students. Based upon Erikson's social identity theoretical framework, our professional identity is constructed by our societal affiliations. Group membership, whether voluntary or involuntary, profoundly impacts the development of our professional identity as cues from the groups to which an individual belongs provide the basis for defining appropriate professional roles and responsibilities (Byrd-Poller, 2013). Hogg et al. [New rule] (1995) defined role identity as "distinct and diverse parts of self that are reflected in roles individuals perform in society and that provide meaning for self" (p. 257). However, society views the expertise of the public school classroom educator much differently from that of the university professor. The university professor is elevated to a higher position within the hierarchy of professional expertise. When problems related to maintaining accreditation in a school district arise, the public school classroom educator directly dealing with the daily needs of a diverse student population is called to the decision-making table with far less frequency than university researchers with a grant. As a former classroom educator in an urban public school district, I find that the list of grant-funded initiatives, research projects, and experts utilized to "fix" a problem is far too long to recall in detail. To this day, the magic one-size fits all cure for what ails a school division has yet to be discovered. However, for me, gaining the credentials to be an expert in the field was a way to amplify the voices of public school classroom educators everywhere—or so it seemed.

The concept of guiding youth to become productive citizens serves as a key motivating factor in an individual's desire to enter a teacher preparation program and gain the state licensure to become a classroom educator. Until recently, teaching has been considered a noble profession garnering community respect. The primary role of a public school educator is the effective delivery of the content using school district approved textbooks and materials selected by a body of experts, which may or may not have included a current classroom educator. The experts housed in state and school district central offices also prudently lay out the pace of the delivered content, and they provide a scope and sequence for the educator to follow. While professional learning communities are often a part of the public school environment, there is little to no pressure on the public school classroom educator to conduct research that adds to the body of knowledge. In fact, the classroom educator's action research determines the best approach for maximizing student understanding and progress, but it rarely goes beyond ensuring positive academic achievement for every student crossing that classroom's threshold. In other words, the classroom educator in a public school has little control over the curriculum, the textbooks, the sequence for delivering course objectives, or the selection of formal assessment tools.

What the classroom educator in a public school does have complete control over is the creation of a positive classroom environment conducive to learning, which is essential for academic success (Jackson, 2011). Administrators conducting observations to evaluate teacher effectiveness simultaneously note the classroom educator's ability to deliver the course content while managing the environment. An educator must not only demonstrate content knowledge, but also the disposition necessary to inspire students to excel academically. The most interesting aspect of being a classroom educator is the ability to positively impact students without having complete autonomy over curriculum, instruction, or assessment (Milner & Laughter, 2015). While society in many ways respects a great classroom educator, there is a hierarchy that says the expertise of the classroom educator pales in comparison to other experts. Within the school division, the hierarchy begins with the district central office and flows down to the individual schools. The hierarchy begins with the division superintendent, followed by the assistant superintendents and curriculum specialists, followed by the school principal and assistant principals and finally the classroom educator. The existence of this hierarchy leads to the ivory tower mindset. *Merriam-Webster* defines "ivory tower" as "a secluded place that affords the means of treating practical issues with an impractical often escapist attitude; *especially*: a place of learning" ("Ivory Tower," n.d.). In the ivory tower known as academia, university professors often remain secluded and research the public school environment from afar. This distance allows the ivory tower mindset to exist. For me, ivory tower mindset refers to university professors who rarely, if ever, step foot inside an actual classroom in a public school to provide the research-based instructional delivery or classroom management techniques being prescribed, but who accept the title of expert regarding matters associated with the public school environment.

Saud McLeod (2008) explained that categorization is a natural cognitive function that allows humans to make sense of the world. While categorization can be beneficial and is often benign, the human need for a sense of purpose and meaning leads to exaggerated and skewed notions about group differences. Social identity theorist Henri Tajfel explained that to increase our own self-image, the status of the groups to which we belong must be elevated (Hall & LaFrance, 2012). The approach to establish this elevated status is the catalyst for discrimination, prejudice, and stereotypes. This theory relates to the elevated status of the university professor in relation to the classroom educator. The university professor is an expert in his or her field based upon contributions made through research and writing peer-reviewed articles and books to be used by practitioners. Therefore, the university professor in the field of education can be elevated to a higher status of expertise than that of a practicing classroom educator without the benefit of any public school classroom experience simply because society perpetuates this notion. A doctorate, particularly from a respected institution of higher learning, provides the credibility needed to be labeled an expert.

My effort to maintain connection with the real world of the public school while attempting to settle into the ivory tower proved far more difficult than I anticipated. The support needed to maintain a strong connection and opportunities for collaboration between the public school and the university would not present itself for quite some time. I needed to overcome obstacles through extensive involvement with professional organizations and community service projects as well as through soliciting support from within and outside of my university department. This approach included finding interested parties to work with outside of my discipline, which could only be accomplished through learning the new rules for professional socialization. Strategic planning in this area included attending activities sponsored by other campus departments and volunteering for university-sponsored initiatives that were seemingly outside the focus of my department but were closely aligned with my research. The road to learning the rules of engagement for my university setting was filled with moments of ambiguity and rejection. However, perseverance and having clear professional goals grounded in my values and beliefs led me to overcome most obstacles.

New Playground Rules: Socialization and Finding a Safe Haven

Transitioning from one teaching environment to another should be simple. After 17 years in urban and suburban schools at both the elementary and secondary levels, I was ready for a change. I had obtained my doctorate

4 years prior to the transition from public school to the university. A challenging year as an assistant principal in a middle school changed my desire to remain in the public school environment. While the student population of the school was diverse, the implicit and explicit biases related to race and gender from a core group of central office administration personnel, school board members, and parents added to the stress of being in the position of a school building level administrator. I wanted a new adventure and decided to move from a racially, ethnically, and socioeconomically diverse suburban public school in the southeastern United States to an ethnically diverse historically Black university (HBCU) in the same geographic region. In my mind, the experience would be akin to episodes of the classic show, *A Different World*. As Williams (2017) highlighted, this show featured the fictional HBCU known as Hillman College, where professors worked together to connect with the students and better the community in a close-knit environment of camaraderie and mutual respect. Unfortunately, as an African American woman lacking a frame of reference for the norms and values of a historically Black college or university campus, I found the phenomenon of cognitive dissonance experienced upon entry into the university setting to be stifling. Cognitive dissonance is "the feeling of uncomfortable tension that comes from holding two conflicting thoughts in mind at the same time" (Gladding, 2013, p. 387). There was no sage professor to greet me and provide words of wisdom about the inner workings of the university. My expectation of meeting over a hot meal to discuss research to benefit the students and community was not fulfilled. The mutual desire to band together to benefit our community and in turn honor the traditions of our ancestors was not enthusiastically displayed either.

After months of observation, the greatest obstacle seemed to be the preponderance of faculty members working in silos. Working in silos is not unique to the university setting, but according to Gleeson and Rozo (2013), silos negatively impact morale and reduce productivity. The administration must cultivate and support a culture of collaboration, which at the most basic level requires the support of the dean and the department chairs. Unfortunately, my quest for tenure and promotion while juggling a full teaching load left little time for collaboration and relationship building. It was not so much that my fellow department colleagues did not want to work with me, but the emphasis on teaching and university service overshadowed the development of my research agenda. With faculty members working in silos, there was little information available about the research interests and active projects of tenured faculty who may be open to working with me. The silos limited the open communication of ideas and areas of interest. Furthermore, the sharing of completed publications and successful grant programs only occurred during a couple of meetings at the midpoint and end of the academic year. This approach provided no opportunity for me to be made aware of and gain access to opportunities for collaboration. A removal of the silos is what I needed to thrive.

Silos cannot be eradicated without personal effort. The benefit of cognitive dissonance as Gladding (2013) so eloquently explained is that experiencing this kind of stress can serve as the catalyst for change and thus present an excellent opportunity to learn. As a member of an organization, gaining valuable insight about its culture, norms and values is best done through socialization (Smith & Hatmaker, 2014). The approach I took as an African American woman scholar was to seek opportunities to socialize with professors within and outside of the field of education who had a profound interest in building relationships with classroom educators, specific schools in need, and urban school districts. It seemed that this approach would provide the bridge needed to maintain a clear understanding of the challenges in real-world classrooms and the research that professors needed to appropriately assist classroom educators. My initial thought was that surely, this approach would neither be that complicated nor meet with any opposition, but I was about to experience a rude awakening.

In public school environments, novice educators learn to avoid the teachers' lounge at all costs before completing a teacher preparation program. The teachers' lounge is mainly for listening to gossip and negativity regarding everything from state mandates, to unpleasant administrators, to disgruntled parents/guardians, and more (Powell, 2016). Socialization at the university level is quite different, and the rules of engagement change as you move across the campus from one department to another. Though there are university-wide assemblies and committee meetings, the structure of the university setting regarding tenure and promotion creates a vibe that is unfamiliar to a newcomer, but must be understood to avoid working in isolation with limited emotional and professional support. University-wide assemblies often morph into griping and negativity, just as an educator may experience in the teachers' lounge of a public school. In my experience, these meetings are not opportunities to build relationships and seek support. One of the five basic needs identified in Maslow's Hierarchy of Needs is to be appreciated and accepted as a member of the group (as cited in Berger, 2014). Thus, suggestions for finding and creating a social network that provides a haven for creativity and exploration are valuable.

Two approaches proved beneficial in developing my professional identity as a university professor. Through considerable trial and error, the first approach was to seek and cultivate relationships with professors who shared my worldview. The most difficult aspect of this search was gaining access to these professors. The silos created limited opportunities for discussions concerning shared interests. In other words, faculty engaged in their office hours, taught their classes, and advanced their research agendas in solitude. Taking a cue from the public school environment, I put my concerns in writing and presented them to the department chair prior to department meetings, which was the first step in limiting the silos' effects. Gradually, the chair incorporated time into each department meeting to recognize scholarly endeavors and encourage discussion concerning research interests. While the chair did not go so far as to assign junior faculty to senior faculty with similar interests, the chair was open to allotting time for discussion and provided suggestions along with the rationale for collaboration.

The second approach involved identifying professors within and outside of the university that demonstrated my definition of an outstanding university professor. Again, this approach required borrowing from my previous public school experience. As a novice university educator building my professional identity, I modeled my teaching style after the educators of the past and present whom I admired. I studied their dispositions, instructional delivery styles, classroom management approaches, and community service. The list of professionals included educators throughout my K–12 experience, mentors provided to me through the school division, and famous educators such as Marva Collins (1992) whose work I studied. I also took cues from classroom educators who were not the type of professionals I aspired to be. The latter individuals provided examples of dispositions and practices to avoid. These guides provided the scaffolding needed to develop a professional identity uniquely aligned with my own personality, interests, values, and beliefs. This approach had worked well in the public school environment and proved to be an excellent approach in a university setting—with one exception. The silos made it fairly difficult to identify the dispositions, instructional delivery styles, and scholarly endeavors of professors within my own discipline as well as across the campus. So, my initial approach involved maintaining relationships with doctoral program professors who continued to serve as mentors well after I attained my doctoral degree. This meant restructuring my professional identity began outside of my university. However, the approach proved beneficial in maintaining my values and beliefs. This approach also helped me to avoid an ivory tower mindset and to amplify the voices of public school educators.

Flourishing Versus Surviving: The Value of a Mentor

Reflecting upon the road leading to tenure and promotion, it is evident that the selection of mentors played a vital role in my success. I was striving for tenure and promotion, which is contingent upon effective teaching, frequency of publications, attainment of grant funds, and university service in the form of committee participation. As an African American woman scholar at a state-supported public HBCU, for me the research support afforded to colleagues at other research-focused, private and public, non-HBCU institutions was nonexistent. This lack of support created a conundrum regarding an understanding of the protocol associated with conducting research, gaining access to resources to strengthen writing for publication, and, most importantly, identifying a mentor to serve not only as a guide, but also as a motivator. The networks of a tenure-track professor serve as a dominant influential factor in productivity, job satisfaction, and ultimately professional identity development (Clarke et al., 2013).

The selection of a mentor cannot be done haphazardly. An arbitrary assignment of a mentor by a department chair or other supervisor may not yield the results anticipated, if there is not a clear understanding of research interests, academic strengths, and professional goals. The importance of careful selection was made clear to me through participation in a grant writing endeavor that yielded funding for a 5-year project. The participants for the grant writing and subsequently the research project were selected without input from the members. Thus, the grant writing approach was disjointed, confusing, and frustrating due to a lack of understanding among the members concerning research interests, writing styles, academic strengths, work ethic, and personal preferences for completing tasks in a timely manner. Once the grant was awarded, more chaos ensued that could have been avoided if each member had been vetted to determine professional fit. Out of this experience, my resolve to identify mentors who were a good fit intensified, and my search continued with laser focus.

In some cases, balance can only be obtained through the selection of two mentors. The first mentor could be a member of another organization, but shares similar research interests, has a demonstrated record of scholarly activity, and provides the motivation necessary to accomplish professional goals (Clarke et al., 2013). The second mentor is a member of the current organization with similar interests and a keen understanding of the culture, norms, and values of the organization. My first mentor was a member of another university who shared my research interests, values, and beliefs as well as had an extensive record of scholarly activity and effective teaching practices. Additionally, we shared an interest in research activities that would be mutually beneficial to the classroom educator and the university researcher. This mentor and I shared the concept of working alongside classroom educators and respecting their expertise as comparable with our own. While this mentor could not help me with understanding my organization's culture, the nurturing relationship provided the motivation and guidance needed to create a sound research agenda, clarify professional goals, and strengthen instructional delivery at the university level. The outside of the organization mentor also served as an excellent sounding board and guide for remaining focused even amid opposition or chaos.

Aside from professional guidance, the emotional support was priceless. For a junior faculty member, there needs to be a safe place to vent frustrations, acknowledge fears, discuss concerns, and celebrate triumphs without worry of retaliation, judgment, jealousy, or pity.

The selection of a mentor within my organization began with an invitation to lunch offered by a department colleague after a meeting. This lunch included the colleague that extended the invitation to me as well as another colleague within my department. This meeting of the minds over a meal served as the first blow to existing silos. These two colleagues shared similar beliefs, values, and professional goals while also expressing an interest in working directly with classroom educators in school districts close to the university. Both colleagues had several years with the university and could therefore provide guidance in understanding the organizational culture. Additionally, they served as the liaison with members of other departments and provided insight regarding professional organizations to join and university services in which I should increase my involvement. One colleague graciously agreed to serve as the mentor I was seeking. My professional identity began to take shape, strengthen and blossom, which was the impetus for conducting the scholarly activity needed for tenure and promotion. John C. Maxwell said, "One of the greatest values of mentors is the ability to see ahead of what others cannot see and to help navigate a course to their destination" (Maxwell, 2015, p. 212). The continued evolution of my professional identity enabled me to withstand conflicting administrative policy changes, resist attacks against my professional character, and advocate for self when necessary.

Maintaining Nirvana: Steps to Weather Change

Beijaard et al. (2004) describes professional identity development as an ever-evolving process that encompasses the interpretation of multiple experiences over time that serve as a guide for who we wish to become. As an African American woman who has experienced all formal education, from kindergarten through a doctoral program, through the lens of a member of an underrepresented population, becoming a part of the faculty at a HBCU ushered in the hope of being guided and nurtured by individuals with similar experiences. I hoped that these individuals would embrace my desire to grow as a scholar and assist me in navigating the waters of research and publication that lead to tenure and promotion. While I began this journey with this rose-colored glasses notion, a few harsh realities, which created a sense of isolation, confusion, and frustration proved to be quite beneficial overall.

I now use these experiences to assist incoming junior faculty in an effort to lessen for them the stressors I encountered, as my mentors did for me. As a lifelong learner, my mentors have played a key role in enabling me to open myself up to professional development experiences focused on being an effective mentor. I feel more comfortable serving as a mentor to junior faculty and enthusiastically embrace the role because of my own mentors. As a result, the department and the college in which this department is housed now have a stronger support system. While silos have not been totally eliminated, there is a better understanding of collaboration and support. We are moving in the right direction.

REFERENCES

Beijaard, D., Meijer, P., & Verloop, N. (2004). Reconsidering research on teachers' professional identity. *Teaching and Teacher Education, 20*, 107–128. https://doi.org/10.1016/j.tate.2003.07.001

Berger, K. S. (2014). *The developing person through the life span* (9th ed.). Worth.

Byrd-Poller, L. D. (2013). *Exploring the relationship between role conflict, role ambiguity and general perceived self-efficacy: A quantitative study of secondary assistant principals* (Doctoral dissertation). The George Washington University.

Clarke, M., Hyde, A., & Drennan, J. (2013). Professional identity in higher education. In B. M. Hehm & U. Teichler (Eds.), *The academic profession in Europe: New tasks and new challenges* (Vol. 5, pp. 7–21). Springer.

Collins, M. (1992). *Ordinary children, extraordinary teachers*. Hampton Roads.

Gladding, S. T. (2013). *Counseling: A comprehensive profession* (7th ed.). Pearson.

Gleeson, B., & Rozo, M. (2013, October 2). *The silo mentality: How to break down the barriers*. Forbes. https://www.forbes.com/sites/brentgleeson/2013/10/02/the-silo-mentality-how-to-break-down-the-barriers

Hall, J., & LeFrance, B. (2012). "That's gay:" Sexual prejudice, gender identity, norms, and homophobic communication. *Communication Quarterly, 60*(1). https://doi.org/10.1080/01463373.2012.641833

Hogg, M. A., Terry, D. J., & White, K. M. (1995). A tale of two theories: A critical comparison of identity theory with social identity theory. *Social Psychology Quarterly, 58*(4), 255–269. https://www.jstor.org/stable/2787127

Ivory tower [Def. 2]. (n.d.). In *Merriam-webster*. https://www.merriam-webster.com/dictionary/ivory tower

Jackson, Y. (2011). *The pedagogy of confidence: Inspiring high intellectual performance in urban schools*. Teachers College Press.

Maxwell, J. (2015). *The leadership handbook: 26 critical lessons every leader needs*. Thomas Nelson.

McLeod, S. (2008, September 17). Erik Erikson. *Simply Psychology*. https://www.simplypsychology.org/Erik-Erikson.html

Milner, H. R., & Laughter, J. C. (2015). But good intentions are not enough: Preparing teachers to center race and poverty. *Urban Review, 47*, 341–363. http://dx.doi.org/10.1007/s11256-014-0295-4

Powell, L. (2016, August 09). Why I avoid the 'teachers' lounge' and you should, too. *Ed Week*. www.edweek.org

Smith, A. E., & Hatmaker, D. M. (2014). Knowing, doing, and becoming: Professional identity construction among public affairs doctoral students. *Journal of Public Affairs Education, 20*(4), 545–564. https://doi.org/10.1080/15236803.2014.12001807

Williams, S. (2017, September 24). 'A *Different World*' still a key cultural force 30 years later. NBC. https://www.nbcnews.com/news/nbcblk/different-world-still-key-cultural-force-30-years-later-n804336

CHAPTER 13

TEACHING AS BECOMING

A Relational Way of Working With Undergraduate Students

Zitong Wei
China Women's University

INTRODUCTION

For 6 years, from the beginning of my graduate education to my PhD commencement, I primarily played the role of a student in education. Having learned pedagogical content knowledge as fluid praxis, I reflected on my new teaching and mentoring role as a full-time teacher in a women's college in Beijing. As a woman who graduated from the same college but just returned from the United States after 6 years of graduate study, I share similarities with the first-year students and have different experiences. Like most of them, I am a woman from a working-class family. I also studied on the same campus. However, as a new teacher and a person who spent 6 years in a different culture, I encounter role differences as well as a reverse

Narratives on Becoming: Identity and Lifelong Learning, pp. 165–176
Copyright © 2021 by Information Age Publishing
All rights of reproduction in any form reserved.

cultural shock. From a holistic perspective (Bieler, 2013), I regard teaching and learning as bidirectional coconstructions of knowledge. I argue that mentoring relationships not only involve intersubjective cultural relationships in teaching and learning (Mullen, 2009) but also include reciprocal growth and identity transformation (Healy & Welchert, 1990). Based on the similarities and differences, I have explored the relationship between my freshmen and me. I was curious about what my students and I learned, in addition to answers on exam papers and evaluation feedback. What differences could my students and I make that are meaningful to our lives? This is the question that drives me to rethink learning as transformative.

MENTORING RELATIONSHIPS

Before attending the women's college, these freshmen had to pass the College Entrance Exam (Gaokao), a nationwide standardized test. Because personal achievement is prioritized, they were used to learning by completing practice tests and asking for correct answers from their high school teachers as experienced authorities. The systematic skill-based learning and power relationships the freshmen experienced previously reflect core ideas of traditional mentoring.

Traditional mentoring is identified by goal-directed learning and hierarchical relationships. The mentoring relationship involves a reinforcement of systematic rules and instrumental values (Mullen, 2009). In professions that are traditionally male dominated, standards prioritize personal achievement (Chandler, 1996). The emphasis on standardization and achievement in high schools indicates that masculine culture is valued. In addition, mentors and mentees are regarded as two parties. Whereas mentors act as experienced seniors who offer guidance, mentees are seen as inexperienced help recipients (Bona et al., 1995).

In contrast to standardized tests in high schools, college evaluations allow more flexibility and enable a relational way of mentoring that is holistic and transformative. I incorporated formative assessment into my course policy, talked frequently with my freshmen about their feelings and expectations, and asked for timely feedback. During their learning over the first semester, these young women also made efforts to establish a new order. My way of teaching and their process of learning reflect ideas in feminist relational mentoring. According to relational cultural theory (RCT), individuals as members in relation coconstruct social identities in contexts. Mentors and mentees share their roles based on their different expertise and cocreate authentic and meaningful experience (Beyene et al., 2002). Building on equality and mutual respect, power is bidirectional from within through dialogical communications. The reciprocal relationship fosters mutual growth and leads to five outcomes: "zest, empowered action, increased sense of worth, new knowledge and desire for more connection" (Fletcher & Ragins, 2007, p. 386). While I facilitated discussions and reflections, I was also reminded of culturally meaningful signs in the right process.

IDENTITY DEVELOPMENT IN A CHINESE CONTEXT FROM A FEMINIST PERSPECTIVE

Whereas RCT is developed as a Western theory, its emphasis on feminist relationships, cultural contexts, and situatedness makes it an appropriate analytical framework in the context of my teaching and mentoring in China. The women's college I work for is located in a Confucian cultural context, and Confucian culture shares similarities with feminist relational mutuality. Whereas Confucianism emphasizes interdependence and connections, the Confucian cultural way of teaching and learning also values heuristic dialogue (Kim & Kim, 2013). Instead of delivering standardized answers, teachers are expected to engage students and elicit thinking. It is natural for members in the community to take responsibility for each other and think in a relational way. In addition, the mission of the women's college shares similarities with feminism. The women's college highlights gender equality and encourages women's social participation. In the past, only males were allowed to receive formal education in China. Even in recent decades, the field of higher education has long been male dominated. Mentoring and women's experience in higher educational institutions in China is under-researched, especially from a qualitative perspective. It is therefore not only appropriate but also pivotal to understand socially coconstructed mentoring experiences and identity transformation in the Chinese context from a feminist perspective.

TRANSFORMATIVE LEARNING

The narratives that follow are based on the reflective journal I kept during my first semester of teaching. My first pedagogy class, an introductory course on educational foundations, curriculum and teaching in fall 2016 was for students in applied psychology. Most of the students came from working class families in different provinces in China. Within the Confucian cultural context in Beijing, I look at the mentoring relationships using RCT. Because RCT attaches great importance to holistic experience, I use narratives to show the process of growth and present a vivid description for situatedness. Based on transformations in identities and changes in power relationships, the narratives are organized in three sections below: "A relational way of thinking"; "Good girls—changes in motivation"; and "Being adults while still having dreams—identity reconstruction." These mentoring episodes provide contextual descriptions of the changing process during the semester.

EPISODE 1: A RELATIONAL WAY OF THINKING

Oct. 14, 2016: Grouping as a Start for Increased Cultural Understandings

Having spent 6 years in a coeducational research university in a Midwest state in the United States, I had not taken grouping as a serious task. While it was typical to group students based on their preferences, it is not the case in the women's university in Beijing. At the end of my class, I provided my students with six topics. Instead of writing down their preferences, most of them said they preferred to present with members in their dorms. After a while, some students showed signs of understanding, because they found there were five dorms but six topics. Others still hesitated to write their preferences down. Considering the cultural and relational way of thinking, I adjusted my plan and suggested they choose five topics to group by dorms. Everybody was released. Each dorm parent sent me a note with names of their dorm members and the chosen topic.

Nov. 4, 2016: PowerPoint Presentations and Reflections

The PowerPoint presentations and student reflections showed that the students view individual identity as relational. The presentation prepared by each dorm had a different style and expressed a different but harmonious and artistic feeling. Also, described in their self-evaluation notes were their collaborative efforts. They frequently used "we" and focused on their relationships when describing both successful and challenging situations. For example, one student used "we" to show her feeling of competence: "We did a good job working together. We shared our views, and everybody contributed in searching for resources and making the PowerPoint. I felt great that we were all engaged, working towards a same goal" (translation). Another student also used "we" to express her feeling of guilt as a dorm parent: "We did not do a good job preparing for the presentation.... As the dorm parent [group leader], I felt guilty about not engaging everybody in the process" (translation). These reflections indicate that the students first identified themselves as a member in the dorm, and they valued relation-ships and responsibilities.

DISCUSSION

Engagement in pedagogical relationships is an important characteristic of feminist praxis (Hammond et al., 2015). When I first divided groups by dorms, my first year students and I had not established a shared under-standing. Although we showed the desire to engage each other, we were only able to make assumptions based on our unique cultural experiences. Whereas I thought of them as individual choice makers responsible for their own learning, they assumed that I took dorm as a unit following their relational way of thinking. Their efforts to understand me based on their cultural perspectives were shown in some students' interpretations of the difficulty in dividing six topics by five dorms. Our initial communication suggested a disconnection based on different understandings.

However, my students and I made adjustments and experienced an increased sense of competence during the process of forming groups. Forming groups became a starting point for making connections. On the one hand, I learned both their different dorm styles and their views of responsibilities, especially from the feedback from dorm parents. I felt accepted and empowered when they opened themselves up to me with their reflections on achievements as well as challenges. As the first-year students conceptualized "we" instead of "I" as a basic unit based on their experience, their responses to the initial grouping and reflections after presentations showed that they took responsibility for their own learning. Based on my relationships with them, I not only achieved my teaching goal but also increased my sense of competence as a new teacher. On the other hand, the group development process enabled the freshmen to work and share with people they felt comfortable relating. They affirmed their assumption that I respect their ways of thinking. The students' frank reflections on their sense of competence and guilt indicated that they unin-tentionally saw me as a part of them.

During the course, we supported each other to learn and grow by co-cre-ating a community of learning. Our adaptations took place simultaneously and naturally. The changes we made embodied our mutual willingness to trust each other. Seeing their motivation to engage in learning from their request of grouping by dorms, I assumed that the changes I made to groups would encourage collaboration. Similarly, receiving the sign that I intended to help them become better learners, they were willing to share their thinking and expose their relational identities to me. Although we manifested the relationship differently, we made efforts to arrive at a shared understanding. Based on bidirectional acceptance and collaboration, the grouping and presentations went beyond the realm of teaching and learning to be meaningful activities.

EPISODE 2: GOOD GIRLS—CHANGES IN MOTIVATION

Oct. 21, 2016: Good Girls

I gave my students Dewey's *My Pedagogical Creed* (2013) to read the week before and asked them to submit a short reflection based on their schooling experience. To understand their motivation, I made it an optional assignment. I did not expect a high response rate, but I was still disappointed by the fact that only one woman who seldom expressed herself submitted her work. I remembered that all of a sudden, the class quieted down. Also, I noticed that one of the hardworking students who usually sat in the front row was embarrassed, worrying that she may no longer look good. As a "good girl," this student sent me an e-mail the week after with a summary of the reading and a WeChat note, explaining her shortcomings in writing a reflection this time. Even though the assignment did not count toward the final grade, in the following weeks several students explained to me their different reasons for not completing the assignment.

Dec. 2, 2016: Changes in Motivation

I went over the content and facilitated discussions as usual. At the end of the class, I planned a quick clean-up after their departure. When I said "class is over," however, I heard all students saying goodbye to me together, a response by the whole class in most high schools as a way of showing respect to teachers. Before I cleaned the blackboard, one of the students rushed to the front to help me. Also, I found it unusual for a Friday afternoon class that all other students remained in their seats. I walked around, hearing them discussing the questions and examples shared in class. I was impressed by their changes from passive learners as "good girls" to active meaning cocreators. Later, a student told me that although only a few of her classmates sent their reflections to me, many were reading and discussing Dewey's (2013) *My Pedagogical Creed* together with other optional readings in their dorms. I did not know how well they understood the content based on the few responses I received. However, I was sure that they started to reflect on their experiences and establish connections, which according to Dewey are critical for building a sense of real community.

DISCUSSION

At the time I assigned the reading reflections, I had not established relationships with the first-year students. Several students' explanations of different reasons for not completing the assignment showed their hidden "good girls" identities of obedience. Also, although the students did not make it apparent, their instrumental value was displayed through their choice of not completing the optional reading reflection and their responses after seeing their peer who submitted her reflection. It was apparent that they were extrinsically motivated by outcomes rather than by processes of learning. At that time, I was disappointed that the freshmen did not have the willingness to take responsibility for their own learning and make connections. While they were skilled at fulfilling official course requirements, they did not share with me an internal motivation for learning.

During the process of teaching and learning, we made efforts to understand each other. Especially after the freshmen's presentations and reflections, I gradually discovered their hidden identities as active learners in relationship to others. I encouraged them to reflect throughout the course, and their practices became more self-motivated. When the students asked questions based on their experience and shared with me their career plans, I felt most of them started to treat the class as more than a means for them to get a good grade. In contrast with their initial responses, their reactions at the end the semester showed some changes in their motivation. Their discussions after the class on December 2 suggested that they implicitly accepted my way of teaching and were motivated to reflect on their own learning. They were also willing to exchange ideas with classmates outside of their dorms. The student who rushed to help me clean the blackboard showed her respect and acceptance of me as a teacher. At the end of the semester, no one was playing the role of a "good girl." Instead, they started to read optional assignments and share during their leisure time. The students' different reactions during the semester suggested changes in their identities from passive learners to active meaning cocreators. Their new responses also suggested changes in their understandings of power relationships. While they enjoyed the atmosphere, they no longer needed me as an authority. I felt competent that the students and I gradually established a learning community within which knowledge was valued for its own sake.

Before entering college, the students spent 3 years in high school. Learning standards and college entrance exams reinforced instrumental value and top-down relationships. Whereas high school teachers were regarded as powerful authorities who delivered knowledge and prepared students for tests, students were expected to obey as listeners. Since those who spent more time on what counts for tests would win in the competition and get access to better universities, it was not difficult to understand why the students hesitated to complete optional reflection tasks at the beginning of the semester. However, during the semester the freshmen and I coconstructed a different teaching and learning relationship. They showed identities of intrinsic learners, and I encouraged their active learning. Supported by an environment that welcomes active learning and questions, the first-year students started to learn for themselves and contribute to their own learning. Power was no longer a directing force but rather emerged as a bidirectional property. What counted the most for them went beyond tests to their growth in the learning community and relationships with each other. The relational way of thinking made their learning relevant to their lived experience a holistic integrity.

EPISODE 3: BEING ADULTS WHILE STILL HAVING DREAMS—IDENTITY RECONSTRUCTION

Dec. 9, 2016: Identity Reconstruction

After class, I met two students on a transit bus, the new and the only one that connects the suburban campus with the subway. Ten years ago, when I was a student on the suburban campus, I had to walk for 20 minutes to catch a bus into town. We started to share our experience. After a while, I asked them to comment on my teaching, expecting feedback. However, our conversation changed when the students talked about two other female teachers and their ways of teaching. According to them, Ms. Gao (a pseudonym), the first teacher, never engaged students. She usually asked a question, stopped for a second, and then gave a correct answer. Although Ms. Gao only delivered the content, she was very generous in grading. In contrast, Ms. Li (a pseudonym) taught quite differently. She gave vivid examples and encouraged students to participate in group activities. The only problem with her was that what she taught had nothing to do with the syllabus and the tests. As a result, many students failed her class each year. To my surprise, what the students expressed was that every teacher has her drawbacks. Since in their minds female teachers are supposed to either find someone to marry or take care of their family after getting married, they thought I do not have to be perfect. While they valued relationships and responsibilities, they persuaded me not to spend extra time on preparing to teach more innovatively. It was clear that they were aware of what it means to be an adult and a woman.

As our conversation went on, however, they started to share their desires for making a difference in everyday life. Their hidden identities of equality seekers started to unfold. One student said that each week she felt exhausted spending 4 hours on a single trip home. Because her parents were not well educated, she also had to help her younger sister with her homework. It was difficult for her to imagine that a woman like her would make a difference. By working with me, a woman from a similar socioeconomic background and an alumna, she started to imagine herself becoming a college teacher in the future. She said, "you brought us hope." Although higher education has long been a male-dominated profession, the student expressed her desire to break the boundary. We waved goodbye at a subway station, but I noted to myself how meanings are continuously coconstructed at bus stops, on subways, and right in moments of daily life.

DISCUSSION

Regardless of feminists' efforts for equality, differences in social expectations and gender stereotypes shape women's roles in society. With low self-efficacy and self-worth, women silently take their assigned social roles and passively reify them in practice. During my teaching, I have been told different stories about the difficulties of receiving higher education by the students who came from the working class and economically challenged families. For some parents in remote areas in China, sending their daughter to college is still an optional and risky investment. Female students from these families usually work part-time or apply for loans to pay their tuition, because all their parents' money goes to their brothers. Although the students in the above case were lucky enough to attend college, their social background made them hesitant to make changes. In most of the classes that are disconnected with their experience of doing housework and taking care of family members, their goal was to pass based on the standards. Given their previous socialization experience and a relational way of thinking, it is not difficult to understand why they persuaded me, a new member in their community, to fit into the social role of a woman to balance my life rather than spending too much time on innovative teaching.

However, mentors have an influence on students' academic success as well as their long-term development (Maryann, 1991). Through dialogue we broke silence. Although we only met once a week for a semester, our relational way of thinking and shared commitment increased the intimacy in our relationship. Our conversation also constituted discourse for equality. I read from their sparkling eyes the desire for a better life. Teachers play roles of both mentors and friends (Semeniuk & Worrall, 2000). As a woman and a friend like them, my role as a college instructor and my way of teaching showed them possibilities for change. They started to challenge dominant discourses and socially constructed gender expectations. Their actions to learn for themselves about their dreams contributed to the formation of equal communities. Through conversations with my students, I felt the time I spent on teaching preparation rewarding. I not only helped them to learn knowledge and pedagogical skills required for preservice school counselors, but I also supported them to think independently, challenge the assumptions and standards behind the required content in textbooks. I became confident that I can make teaching and learning meaningful for them. Our coconstructed discourse showed our increased self-worth as women and members in society. Going beyond teaching and learning in classrooms, the relationship provided us emotional support for mutual growth.

THE EPISODES

The three sets of episodes above represent three mentoring relationships and involve different degrees of transformation in power relationships and identities. In the first set, "A relational way of thinking," the freshmen and I made interpretations from our own cultural perspectives. Although we made efforts to establish a relationship, none of us showed a dramatic change of identity. While the freshmen regarded each dorm as a unit and made efforts to maintain relationships by questioning the way of grouping, they did not keep challenging when they found there were six topics for five dorms. Their responses imply that they still took the topics as a "given" for them even at the expense of their relationships. Based on their responses, I knew more about them and slightly shifted myself from a novice outsider to a teacher within. The second sets of episodes, "Good girls—Changes in motivation" show an explicit change in social identity. Based on our understandings, we formed a mentoring relationship for both parties to grow. The students moved from passive knowledge receivers to active learners. I also played a more authentic role as a teacher and mentor in facilitating their learning. Because both parties were willing to share, the power relationship changed from an external formal connection to a cocreated relationship that became mutually empowering. Instead of fitting into the "good girl" stereotype, the students attached more importance to what they learned from their dorm discussions. The third episode, "Being adults while still having dreams—Identity reconstruction" represents a moment of our identity transformation through conversations. No longer were the students silenced according to their belief of what it meant to be women in the local context. They changed from passively fitting into the roles of socially expected working class women to innovators with better self-worth. I also felt competent by not only fulfilling the teaching requirement but also engaging in a relationship that empowers. Maybe this is what it meant to be women and teachers who influence and inspire.

In all three sets of episodes, my students and I transformed simultaneously. The pedagogy class went beyond knowledge and skills in classrooms to become a part of the identity formation process. While our ways of understanding were disconnected at first, we established connections by transforming our learning. The freshmen changed from passive learners for making a living to active learners for a better life. I also changed from a novice teacher who had limited understanding of the context to a community member. This transformation was based on mutual understanding and trust, coconstructed through a bidirectional mentoring relationship within a relational learning community.

CONCLUSION

Analyses of the episodes suggest that within the Confucian context wherein students learn from life experience and reflections, relational mentoring is both culturally appropriate and innovative. Compared with unidirectional teaching and learning and standardized testing, bidirectional communications and relational mentoring contributes to transformative learning. In a standardized and globalized time, it is important that we engage women in traditionally male-dominated professions. It is not only knowledge and skills but also relationships and mutual support that enable women to grow and to make contributions as equal members in a larger community. My experience suggests the possibility and necessity of international collaboration in reframing mentoring relationships in higher education. Given differences in cultural understandings, it is expected that we enrich the dialogues on transformative learning with diverse models of mentoring.

REFERENCES

Beyene, T., Anglin, M., Sanchez, W., & Ballou, M. (2002). Mentoring and relational mutuality: Proteges' p erspectives. *Journal of Humanistic Counseling, Education and Development. 41*, 87–102. https://doi.org/10.1002/j.2164-490X.2002.tb00132.x

Bieler, D. (2013). Strengthening new teacher agency through holistic mentoring. *The English Journal. 102*(3), 23–32. http://www.jstor.org/stable/23365369

Bona, M. J., Rinehart, J., & Volbrecht, R. M. (1995). Show me how to do like you: Co-mentoring as feminist pedagogy. *Feminist Teacher, 9*(3), 116–124.

Chandler, C. (1996). Mentoring and women in academia: Reevaluating the traditional model. *NWSA Journal, 8*(3), 79–100.

Dewey, J. (2013). *My pedagogic creed* (P. Zhengmei, Trans.). Shanghai Renmin Chubanshe.

Fletcher, J. K., & Ragins, B. R. (2007). Stone center relational cultural theory: A window on relational mentoring. In B. R. Ragins & K. E. Kram (Eds.). *The handbook of mentoring at work: Theory, research, and practice* (pp. 373–399), SAGE.

Hammond, S., Powell, S., & Smith, K. (2015). Towards mentoring as feminist praxis in early childhood education and care in England. *Early Years, 35*(2), 139–153. https://doi.org/10.1080/09575146.2015.1025370

Healy, C. C., & Welchert, A. J. (1990). Mentoring relations: A definition to advance research and practice. *Educational Researcher, 19*(9), 17–21.

Kim, Y., & Kim, J. (2013). *The great equal society: Confucianism, China and the 21st century*. World Scientific.

Maryann, J. (1991). Mentoring and undergraduate academic success: A literature review. *Review of Educational Research, 61*(4), 505–532.

Mullen, C. A. (2009). Re-imaging the human dimension of mentoring: A framework for research administration and the academy. *The Journal of Research Administration, 15*(1), 10–31.

Semeniuk, A., & Worrall, A. M. (2000). Rereading the dominant narrative of mentoring. *Curriculum Inquiry, 30*(4), 405–428.

CHAPTER 14

TRANSFORMATIVE LEARNING AS TEACHERS

The Narratives of Two Teachers Becoming Critical Pedagogues

Injeong Yoon
University of Arkansas

Benjamin Ramirez
University of Arizona

INTRODUCTION

Our stories of becoming teachers are not in the least similar. On the surface, one of us grew up in a big city in South Korea, and the other grew up in a small Midwestern city in the United States. Our educational experiences in two different countries were also not alike, aside from the amount of time we spent in school. Our family backgrounds as well as the level of support that we received from our teachers differed significantly as well.

Narratives on Becoming: Identity and Lifelong Learning, pp. 177–192
Copyright © 2021 by Information Age Publishing
All rights of reproduction in any form reserved.

One of us started their first teaching job as a multiple subject teacher for sixth graders in a public school, and the other started as an English teacher in a private institution that served K–12 students. The South Korean city where we first began our teaching careers was the only commonality in our trajectories as teachers.

Although we had extremely different schooling and teaching experiences in addition to our social identities, we have both been questioning what it means to be a critical pedagogue. Each of us has 6 years of teaching experience in different education settings, and these experiences led us to deeply reflect throughout our graduate school educations on social issues entangled with schools and students' lives. When we were introduced to critical pedagogy in a graduate course on social justice education which we both took, we immediately found that it resonated with our own questions and reflections on our teaching experiences. Even though our areas of study are not completely similar, we shared many readings and thoughts on implementing theories of critical pedagogy, social justice, and feminism throughout our journey in the same school. As educators who share teaching experiences in both South Korea and the United States, it was important for us to collaboratively reflect on our positionalities and teaching experiences. Additionally, our common interest in our roles as educators to promote social justice and challenge the status quo specifically brought our works in different fields together.

We are currently working with preservice teachers separately in teacher education programs in two public universities. These new roles add another layer of our identities as educators. As we share our own teaching experiences with our students, we constantly ask ourselves in what ways our teaching is in line with critical pedagogy, how we envision our pre-service teachers' futures as critical pedagogues, and what we can do to support their growth. It is undeniable that all professions entail multidimensional roles and meanings. Nonetheless, our experiences with and in schools as students, teachers, mentor teachers, and teacher educators, allow us to reconsider our teacher identities in particularly complicated and ever-changing manners. In this sense, our journeys to becoming educators consist of intermingled stories of our respective experiences and how we make sense of those stories or experiences. As He (1995) described, our teacher and teacher educator identities are not a collection of static attributes. Rather, they are a process of continuous emerging and becoming.

From this perspective, this chapter shares these stories of becoming educators who constantly ponder what it means being critical pedagogues and feminist teachers. Our teacher-selves are sites of conflict and negotiation, which are continuously constructed vis-à-vis sociocultural contexts and power relations. As Zembylas (2005) argued, our experiences of becoming teachers are infused with negotiating our subjectivities in relation to normalizing power. Thus, this chapter highlights how our teacher identities are necessarily intertwined with our sociocultural identities as well as ongoing social interactions and daily experiences. Ultimately, we argue for the significance of narratives addressing the intersection of teacher identity construction and sociocultural identities.

Our narratives were collaboratively written and are meant to be read together. In the beginning of our collaboration, we decided to write each of our schooling and teaching experiences separately. When we completed our first draft and put them together, we found that our stories were interconnected through similar topics and thoughts. After having several conversations about our narratives, we rewrote our stories in a way to respond to the common threads we found. This process was dialogic in the sense that we cocreated meanings by reading each other's narratives and discussing what we found (Ngunjiri et al., 2010). By writing our stories and perspectives together, we attempt to demonstrate how the process of making sense of our educator identities is necessarily social and interconnected. This collaborative process of writing and reflecting can possibly serve as a vehicle to reimagine our identities in connection with others and society beyond the omnipresent individualist perspective.

This chapter is organized based on the common threads we found through our collaborative meaning-making process. They include (1) the background of how we became teachers, (2) the process of reflecting on our teaching practices, (3) awareness of our social positionalities that influenced our teacher identities, and (4) intellectual works and ideas that shaped and are still shaping our practices as critical pedagogues. Each section includes a few snippets of our experiences to provide the context of our teacher selves. The intention of sharing these stories is to describe how we came to understand our sociocultural differences in relation to our teaching experiences. We conclude the narratives by illuminating how collaborative reflectivity continuously prompts us to reorient the process of becoming and growing as critical teachers.

BECOMING A TEACHER

"Teaching is Perfect for a Smart Working-class Girl Like Me." (Yoon)

I decided to go to a college of education to become an elementary teacher when I was 18 years old. Due to the admission process in South Korea, I had to decide in my senior year of high school regarding which college and teacher education program I would attend. I was not completely sure whether I truly wanted to become a teacher, especially a multiple subject teacher for first through sixth graders. Some of my high school teachers were apprehensive about my decision and believed that I would better thrive in other areas of study. However, my parents tenaciously persuaded me to choose elementary education since they believed a public-school teaching job promised an overall stable life for women, myself included.[1] The tuition was extremely low for the national university of education where I was admitted, and the job situation after graduation appeared optimistic. Despite my initial apprehension, I thought that becoming a public-school teacher might be the best option for a young woman like me, who was from a working-class background.

As soon as I graduated from the college, I started working full time in an elementary school without fully realizing what it meant being a teacher. It took me a while to gain a sense of my teacher identity, despite having completed 4 years of a teacher education program that prepared me well regarding curriculum design and instructional strategies. The everyday routine of my teaching job, including teaching classes, organizing school events, and running after-school programs, equipped me with the skills and knowledge to be an effective teacher. And yet I was still wrestling with my own teacher identity: I constantly asked myself what kind of teacher am I becoming and want kind of teacher I want to be.

Although I started my teaching career without a lucid understanding of what it means to be a teacher, I spent a lot of time with my students, which allowed me to think about the meaning of teaching. As a classroom teacher, I would spend an entire year with the same group of students. Throughout these years, I was able to intimately connect with the students by having conversations with them about their lives. I learned more about their families and the numerous factors affecting their school experience. I realized that teaching is more than what I teach in the classroom; teaching is about building authentic relationships with the students (Harrell, 2009). Working in three socioeconomically different schools also showed me that educational opportunities are not necessarily offered to everyone on the same level. In the low socioeconomic schools, my teaching job became more complicated and challenging with multiple roles of counselor, therapist, social worker, and sometimes legal guardian in addition to teaching. I spent my evenings every so often talking to my students' parents and helping the students resolve their personal issues. The compound social factors shaping the students' opportunities and academic success made it hard to believe in the simplistic notion of the meritocracy.

In retrospect, I developed the central part of my teacher identity around this array of experiences. I learned that students were more engaged when the content of my teaching was relevant to their lives. This is the reason why getting to know students and their communities became a key part of my teaching. When I was introduced to multicultural educators' work, such as that of Banks and Banks (2010) and Grant and Sleeter (2009) in my Master of Arts program, I found that their theories concretely explained my teaching experience and what some of my students went through. Moreover, the educational theories about equity and justice led me to be more conscious about my role as a teacher and everyday practice. I started considering my role as not simply as a knowledge transmitter; the agency of teaching which can make an impact through raising consciousness also became clear to me (Freire, 2003). I became enthusiastic about possible changes I could bring beyond the classroom. I started focusing on developing students' consciousness about their relationship to others and the world through my teaching.

"You Need to Speak Only English to Your Students." (Ramirez)

In June of 2007, I moved from the United States to Daejeon, South Korea to begin what would be a 6-year teaching journey. This unexpected opportunity came through a close friend who was already working at the private institution I was to begin working at. As a young college graduate, I dove into this opportunity without knowing the expectations of the position. When living in South Korea, I taught English as a Second Language in different topic areas which included reading, writing, speaking, Business English, social studies, and basic biology to K–12 students and adults. The classes at the private academies I worked at typically started in the early afternoon and would finish in the evening. I worked in two affluent areas and one lower socioeconomic area. The first 3 years, I worked as a teacher, but for the last 3 years, I earned the title of head foreign teacher. Although I did not intend to stay for 6 years, I am glad that I did as it provided a foundation for my understanding of education and offered a career path for my future. Additionally, it provided the preliminary groundwork for my teacher identity.

When reflecting on my first year of teaching experience in South Korea, I realize that the private academy that I worked for presented a teacher-centered approach, which I naively accepted as ideal since its philosophical positioning understood all students as being the same and that the students' success was contingent on the lessons I provided. For the remainder of that first year and for the following 2 years—I was convinced that this was a legitimate approach that my surface-level understanding of educational success in South Korea supported. One of the main expectations of the directors, teachers, and parents focused on the practice of English-only classrooms as this was understood to generate the most success for the students. This was a perspective that I too accepted without any form of critical engagement and that was exacerbated by the invisibility of English language ideology.

Despite student success being part of my responsibility as a teacher, the danger of this particular teaching approach was that it allowed me to blame the students for their lack of understanding rather than consider how my acceptance of the teacher-centered approach was problematic for the students. The combination of the English-only policy and a teacher-centered approach, coupled with unfamiliar content for students, created problems. I found the problems primarily surrounded communication and the suppression of the Korean language in the classroom. For example, the grammatical explanations I provided the students in English caused confusion. When the students asked for an explanation in Korean, as the teacher under strict English-only rule, I had to refuse their request. I remember the disappointment and frustration the students expressed and began to think carefully about these issues along with beginning to question why these practices were not producing the promised results.

Moreover, these problems were exacerbated by the idea that the students were all expected to succeed in these conditions that did not favor language learning. When a lesson failed, I could blame it on students' lack of concentration or any other excuse that focused on the students' performance. This blame created a negative learning environment and therefore most of the students were disengaged.

For the first 2 years, my naivete consumed my sense of what it meant to be a teacher. My preconceived notions of what it meant to be a teacher and my early experiences at the private English academy informed my teacher identity. I was convinced that teaching can, and should be, reduced to a series of actions by the teacher in relation to the content. I understood teachers, myself included, as automatons who worked diligently to get through the material in a timely manner. I accepted this conception of teachers and was initially happy to be a cog in the machine. The regimented teacher-centered approach filled me with a sense of accomplishment as I completed my tasks day by day. Becoming familiar with the everyday routine also solidified this sense of accomplishment, which further fed into my teacher identity.

When I compared my experience learning Korean to my students learning English, I began to empathize with my students. As a beginning Korean language learner, I needed a mix of English and Korean explanations to move forward, so surely my beginning students needed this too. This experience contradicted the English-only environment I was immersed in and subsequently advocated for. The lack of critical engagement played a significant part in the early formation of my teacher identity. However, as I continued to teach, I slowly began looking into second language acquisition to find strategies that would both help my students learn English and assist me with learning Korean. It was at this point that I began to reexamine the teacher-centered approach I had been deeply invested in. A new foundation was beginning to form, and my identity as a teacher was in the process of changing.

BECOMING A "DIFFERENT" TEACHER

"What if I Looked Like My Students and Spoke Like Them?" (Yoon)

When I moved to the United States as a graduate student, my teacher identity dramatically shifted. In the first semester of my doctoral program in a public university located in the Southwest, I had an opportunity to teach a general education course. I had to jump into my new role as a graduate teaching assistant (GTA) without any proper preparation. The role of a GTA was vague and unfamiliar for me; as Muzaka (2009) described, it occupies an ambiguous niche. There were ongoing tensions between my roles and responsibilities as a student and a teacher within the hierarchical structure of the university. In addition, my racial, gender, and linguistic identities added complicated layers to my teaching. I was frequently asked where I was from, and people tried to decipher my accent. I thought my differences would alienate me from the students. I felt pressured to fit into the persona of a stereotypical academic authority figure. My inner struggles as well as occasional hostility from the students turned my teaching into an everyday battle. It was a battle with my own internalized oppression as well as a battle with racist, sexist, and nativist narratives surrounding female teachers of color in the U.S. academy. I was caught up with the concerns about how my students would perceive my differences. I was also afraid that differences would be perceived as incompetence (Baker & Copp, 1997).

The effect of internalized oppression often reinforces self-fulfilling negative stereotypes (Padilla, 2001). Self-doubt is one of the consequences of internalized oppression, in company with helplessness, frustration, mistrust, and so on (Harro, 2010). I perceived my linguistic and cultural identity as a deficit in my teaching practice, rather than an asset. As a doctoral student studying social justice education, I was introduced to many different critical theories, such as critical pedagogy, critical race theories, and feminist theories, to challenge the oppressive thoughts and systems. However, reading these theories did not automatically dissolve my self-doubt and self-loathing. On the one hand, I felt my experiences and struggles were validated by critical scholars' voices. Nonetheless, I was still trying to reduce my "differences" so I could be assimilated. I was constantly judging myself and how I would be perceived by my students, who were at that time dominantly White (Lee, 2006; Rodriguez, 2009). Instead of considering my presence as an agent of change that could challenge prejudices about teachers of color (Vargas, 1999), I considered my difference as my weakness to overcome. This dissonance between what I was understanding intellectually and what I was feeling caused pain, anger, and frustration. As I gained critical languages and tools to tap into my own colonial ways of thinking and internalized oppression, the feelings of guilt, shame, and anger engulfed me. I sometimes had to step away from critical thinking to take a break from my emotional turmoil.

As much as the reflective process was painful, this process rearranged my thinking on my positionality as an Asian cisgender woman in the academy in connection with the racial and gender power relations in U.S. society. By deconstructing my own colonized ways of thinking and performing my Asianness, femininity, otherness, and difference, I started considering the new layers of my identity as a source of liberation and transformation of myself as well as my relationships with others. The rigorous self-reflection became a critical part of my teaching practice. When I came back home from teaching, I tried to spend time either reading the writings of the other female teachers of color or writing a short reflection in my journal. The active reflexivity shifted my thoughts on how I viewed myself in U.S. academia and what I could contribute towards the efforts for social transformation.

When Sites of Contention Collide: Constant Identity Negotiation (Ramirez)

Like many other urban and ethnically mixed Native people (Amerman, 2010; Dunbar-Ortiz & Gilio-Whitaker, 2016), I did not have many opportunities while growing up to acknowledge and appreciate my native side of racial and cultural identities. However, some of my earliest memories with my father included Ojibwe language lessons and introductions into Ojibwe culture through pow-wows and other cultural events. As a young boy, I began to learn how to dance and make prayer ties and these, of course, are fond memories. I became disconnected from my indigenous heritage after my parents' divorce and was further disconnected as I was indoctrinated into Christianity from another family member.

As a young child, I welcomed and embraced my indigenous heritage. I remember my fellow students having a genuine curiosity as to who I was. During these early times, the historical content of American Indians focused primarily on how people lived in different regions of the United States, the incredibly generalized material items that indigenous groups created, and the use of American Indian "hieroglyphics," that when spoken, represented a stereotypical form of speaking in which articles and other parts of speech were removed. Not knowing any better, I remember being so enthralled with lessons like that because I was convinced that this was an "authentic" form of writing and speaking for Native Americans. My other memories include learning about first contact with the western world, romanticized stories of westward expansion that included popular lore around Sacajawea, and conflicts with indigenous peoples. These events assisted in the construction of settler colonial narratives that serve to maintain settler society through the (in)visibility of American Indians. The same dehumanized stories were retold in a slightly modified manner. The (in)visibility refers to what is said when American Indians are absent/present in a settler colonial curriculum (Calderon, 2014). The (in)visibility of American Indians in curricular contexts allows access to several common American Indian stereotypes. It was/is through those stereotypes where people would frame their questions or comments.

All of these early memories and experiences have made an impact on my choice of not only becoming a teacher but also becoming a teacher educator. As my identity was, and to a point still is challenged, I carefully considered in what ways I might have a more positive, humanizing impact on educators and curricular materials. The major transition of my teacher identity took place when I started learning more about critical theory, indigenous philosophies, critical indigenous pedagogy (Garcia & Shirley, 2013; Lee, 2006), and the process of cultivating a different way of being. Although this list is not complete, it provides a stronger foundation for my thoughts on what it means to be a teacher. Despite my previous years teaching in private English academies, it was not until I attended graduate school that I reexamined this question with a profoundly different perspective than when I originally started my teaching career. The intellectual and emotional turbulence of understanding, and coming to terms with my experiences, proved to be a powerful incentive for pursuing a career in education. It also provided a powerful, yet philosophically different, teacher identity.

It is important that I discuss part of my past influences in order to explain the current iteration of my teacher identity. My indigeneity is a continued site of contention. I have to contend with not only mainstream understandings of who Indigenous peoples are but also academic, religious, and legal definitions. The problem with these conceptualizations is that Indigenous voices are usually ignored or relegated to nonacademic or "illegitimate" ways of knowing. For me, these specious definitions came primarily through education. I was plagued by the ebb and flow of different conceptualizations of who I am, which came from an amalgamation of various academic sources in history, sociology, and anthropology; from curricular materials including textbooks and educational documentaries;

and from personal opinions of the general public, family, and friends. When engaging with these perspectives and the people who were presenting them, rarely were my thoughts or explanations accepted as legitimate. Instead, I was presented with reductive counterpoints, pseudo-intellectual explanations, and other information that caused a conflicting understanding of who I am as a person from people on all sides of the political spectrum. These conversations would typically end with people expecting me to conform to their conceptualizations of who or what an Indigenous person *should* be. Being overwhelmed by these pseudo interpretations, and not having the critical knowledge or the language to combat these explanations, many times I either conceded or conformed to what they expressed.

BECOMING A CRITICAL PEDAGOGUE

The Intersection Between Critical Pedagogy and Critical Race Feminism (Yoon)

"Diversity Issues in Art and Visual Culture Education." This course, which I taught in my 4th year of my doctoral program, became the turning point in my teaching. The course was designed to engage students in various topics of diversity and social justice through art-based projects. I was competent in the content as well as theories of multicultural and social justice education, as they were my main research interests. My major concern was student engagement: What are the ways to engage the students in meaningful conversations about social justice across their and our differences? How can I help the students critically reflect on their positionalities? In what ways can I encourage them to move out of their comfort zones and empathize with other people who have different social experiences? When I walked into my classroom the first day, I was a bit surprised by my students' enthusiasm about the topic of social justice. One third of the group was students of color, and there were several nontraditional students. When I collected their precourse survey answers on their interests and backgrounds, I saw their hope that we could have interesting and provocative conversations in class.

However, it was not easy to encourage the students to participate in the conversations in the first couple of weeks. When it comes to the topics of racism and heteronormativity, I found that many students choose to remain silent rather than voice their thoughts. To help them feel less intimidated about talking in class, I started sharing my personal stories about the topics. I sometimes talked about my own guilt, embarrassment, and shame about my own internalized oppressive thoughts. I tried to keep these stories short and honest. My goal was not to make the students understand my vantage point, but to contextualize and model the reflective process. I often included humorous moments in my stories to make the students laugh and approach difficult topics in a less intimidating way. I noticed that the students started sharing their experiences more openly in the middle of the semester. Some students thanked me particularly for my vulnerability and courage to tear down my academic façade.

I later found this practice of sharing my own stories was in line with what bell hooks (1994) described as mutual vulnerability. Many other female teachers/scholars of color have explained how feminist ways of teaching are more about creating a learning community even when conflicts exist in the classroom (Berry, 2006; hooks, 1994, 2010; Ng, 1993; Vargas, 1999; Wing & Willis, 1999). In my earlier graduate program, I was determined to be equipped with theories of critical pedagogy and social justice curriculum to voice my critique of the current inequitable educational system. Through critical pedagogy, I learned in what ways my pedagogical practices could raise critical awareness and ultimately lead to actions for social transformation. Along the same line, what critical race feminist (CRF) educators/scholars demonstrated was how I, as a female teacher of color, can unapologetically practice critical pedagogy, sustain my energy, and work as a critical feminist teacher, and engage students in deeper conversations.[2] More importantly, their works explained how teachers can connect to their students across and beyond conflicts and difficulties. Critical pedagogy and CRF together opened a new pedagogical possibility for me to raise critical consciousness by finding and building interconnectedness between stories of myself and the students.

Considering the influences of critical pedagogy and CRF, my teaching goal was not to make the students believe what I believed, but to encourage them to see other sides of their perspectives and to make sense of the linkage between their everyday lives and the system of (in)justice. To do so, I first opened up myself and revealed my vulnerability in the classroom. As bell hooks (1994, 2010) reminded us, I constantly told the students that every single one of them was a member of the learning community and was encouraged to contribute to our collaborative knowledge production. I also explicitly acknowledged emotional responses to what we learned in class and encouraged my students to embrace their emotions as a part of learning (Ahmed, 2015; Zembylas, 2005). After years of feelings of disconnection and alienation in U.S. higher education, I felt strongly connected to my students for the first time. Although teaching this way was challenging and sometimes instilled fear as an already vulnerable GTA, I felt rewarded through reconceptualizing my role as a female teacher of color working for liberation.

The Intersection Between Critical Pedagogy and Indigenous Philosophy (Ramirez)

"we need to tend to the embers ..."

Graduate school has made a positive impact on my identity both personally and professionally. The theoretical and conceptual frameworks I learned have reshaped my perceptions of education and students. Moreover, the critical indigenous frames allow for survivance and resilience in education. The survivance and resilience responds to settler colonial curricular materials and deficit perspectives that some teachers hold and continue to profess. It was in graduate school where I witnessed examples of how Indigenous epistemologies and ontologies played an important role in influencing my teacher identity. The discussions I have shared with numerous mentors, both in class and in private, prompted my own investigation into Ojibwe philosophy, which includes its own unique and powerful epistemological and ontological perspectives. These examples were inspiring, and they opened new paths of exploration, particularly into my own Ojibwe heritage.

As I learned and continue to learn more about critical theory and how it complements Indigenous philosophical traditions, the more I can critically reflect on who I am as a teacher. The language and ways of thinking provided a new understanding of my experiences. My frustration and anger at times would convince me that I needed to not only continue working with critical indigenous perspectives but would also inspire me to help preservice teachers work through their understandings about Indigenous peoples. This includes how their perspectives can potentially impact their students' respective identities and requires both a personal and curricular analysis and reflection. This learning happens not through traditional lecturing or inundating students with fact after fact but through sharing different perspectives from various sources where empathy is brought to the forefront. Empathy, from an Ojibwe perspective, is part of love and compassion and has powerfully impacted my identity as a teacher.

Being mired in Western thinking, I needed time during graduate school to reflect on my own understandings of students. There was a point where I would become frustrated with my students if they did not understand a concept or pushed back on specific topics. I remember my frustration with students who would say problematic things in class and would make other students upset as well. Since critical self-reflection and engagement are naturally part of Ojibwe philosophy, I needed to take the time to remember that I, too, was not born a critical thinker and that this process of grappling with ideas that challenge our positions takes time. Thus, the recoupling of myself to my Ojibwe heritage and philosophy have positively influenced how I perceive students and how I understand my job as a teacher. In short, my Ojibwe heritage has strengthened my identity as a teacher and has ushered in different teaching practices that highlight this strength.

Mino-Bimaadiziwin is an Ojibwe philosophical tradition that informs how Ojibwe people should interact with the surrounding world. Mino-Bimaadiziwin is usually translated to "the good life," but it has some different connotations in English that seem to focus on material goods and notions of luxury. A better translation would be "many ways of living a good life." Every Ojibwe person will have a different perspective on Mino-Bimaadiziwin, and due to this, different themes emerge for different people (Gross, 2014; McCoy, 2007). Mino-Bimaadiziwin also stretches into every aspect of one's life (Gross, 2014; McCoy, 2007). Gross (2014) stated that Mino-Bimaadizi win is a life-long learning process and is rooted in storytelling or the sharing of parables, which offers an explanation as to why there is tremendous diversity of thought about and in Mino-Bimaadiziwin (p. 208). This philosophical tradition is also intimately connected to the Ojibwe language, epistemology, and ontology. Thus, it is crucial that this philosophical tradition and the cultural context are not reduced to a series of actions, values, or practices nor ascribed stereotypical, romanticized attributes.

Furthermore, the seven grandfather teachings influence the notion that education is a life-long process where lessons can come from experiences, observations, events, various peoples with different perspectives, etc. The seven grandfather teachings are values that are interconnected, and the movement among them is nonlinear (Benton-Benai, 1988, p. 64). Mino-Bimaadiziwin and the seven grandfather teachings have played an important role in reframing my teacher identity. These concepts accentuate a humanist perspective on life in general and inform how a humanist approach is also brought to educational settings. Humanism in Mino-Bimaadiziwin is one of the key elements that has altered my understanding of what it means to be a teacher, which has assisted in reframing how I engage with students.

These philosophical approaches encourage different ways of being that are necessary in the modern era. To me, these philosophical inclinations allow for a reconceptualization of what it means to be a critical pedagogue from an Ojibwe perspective. They provide a different set of critical questions that take Indigenous peoples and perspectives that are in relation to settler colonial states into consideration. Numerous questions stem from an engagement with Ojibwe philosophy such as, what does compassion look like in the classroom? What does it mean to be a compassionate educator? What does it mean for a teacher to have humility? These questions and my (re)engagement with the Ojibwe perspective allowed for a new conceptualization of who I am as a teacher. They also point to the idea of becoming as a continual process of change.

My graduate school education provided difficult, yet honest, conversations about race. My mentors who are Indigenous scholars interweave their indigeneity into their personal and professional lives, my other mentors who are nonindigenous and have worked with different peoples have also inspired change through their compassion and knowledge, and my own reacquaintance with my indigenous heritage are just a few areas that have impacted what it means to be a critical pedagogue and a person. The characteristics that create my teacher identity will undoubtedly change as I continue to interact with people, books, and different ideas. What exactly the future holds for me as a teacher and how it will impact my teacher identity, I do not know, but I look forward to learning, engaging, and changing.

CONCLUDING THOUGHTS

Through our collaborative writing process, we found that reflexivity has played a significant role in making sense of our respective teacher identities. Critical reflexivity prompted us to investigate the ways power relations, oppression, and privilege shaped our teacher identities and how our practices have evolved through continuous reflections (Harrell, 2009; Warren, 2011). Furthermore, the collaborative meaning-making process allowed us to recognize and ponder our experiences from different angles that we were not able to see otherwise. Our identities as teachers clearly incorporate numerous intersectional aspects that include gender, class, race, and ethnicity and the various philosophical engagements that have assisted with our continuing transformation as teachers. Our collaborative reflective works bring us to another level of criticality by creating and sharing new meanings we found from each other's narratives. hooks (1994) reminded us that teachers who want to grow as critical thinkers should talk to each other and collaborate in discussions which cross borders. Likewise, we hope that our narratives, which were written out of our transformative conversations, can invite educators to continue their reflective works collectively in and out of their communities. In so doing, we can envision collective reflexivity in education that weaves our different experiences and various ways of knowing together to cross borders.

REFERENCES

Ahmed, S. (2015). *The cultural politics of emotion* (2nd ed.). Routledge.
Allard, A., Bransgrove, E., Cooper, M., Duncan, J., & Macmillan, M. (1995). 'Teaching Is Still a Good Job for a Woman': The influence of gender on career and

life choices. *South Pacific Journal of Teacher Education, 23*(2), 185–194. https:// doi.org/ 10.1080/0311213950230205

Amerman, S. K. (2010). *Urban Indians in Phoenix schools, 1940–2000*. The University of Nebraska.

Baker, P., & Copp, M. (1997). Gender matters most: The interaction of gendered expectations, feminist course content, and pregnancy in student course eval-uations. *Teaching Sociology, 25*(1), 29–43. https://doi.org/ 10.2307/1319109

Banks, J., & Banks, C. A. M. (2010). *Multicultural education: Issues and perspectives* (7th ed.). Wiley.

Benton-Banai, E. (1988). *The Mishomis book: The voice of the Ojibwe*. Indian Country Communications.

Berry, T. R. (2006). What the fuck, now what? The social and psychological dilem-mas of multidimensional being as a woman of color in the academy. In T. R. Berry & N. D. Mizelle (Eds.), *From oppression to grace: Women of color and their dilemmas in the academy* (pp. xi–xix). Stylus.

Calderon, D. (2014). Uncovering settler grammars in curriculum. *Educational Studies, 50*(4), 313–338. https://doi.org/ 10.1080/00131946.2014.926904

Dunbar-Oritz, R., & Gilio-Whitaker, D. (2016). *"All of the real Indians died off" And 20 other myths about Native Americans*. Beacon Press.

He, A. W. (1995). Co-constructing institutional identities: The case of student counselees. *Research on Language and Social Interaction, 28*(3), 213–231. https://doi.org/10.1207/s15327973rlsi2803

Freire, P. (2003). *Pedagogy of the oppressed* (30th anniversary ed.). The Continuum.

Garcia, J., & Shirley, V. (2013). Performing decolonization: Lessons learned from Indigenous youth, teachers and leaders' engagement with critical Indigenous pedagogy. *Journal of Curriculum Theorizing, 28*(2), 76–81.

Grant, C. A., & Sleeter, C. E. (2009). *Turning on learning: Five approaches for multicul-tural teaching plans for race, class, gender, and disability* (5th ed.). Wiley.

Gross, L. (2014). *Anishinaabe ways of knowing and being*. Ashgate.

Harrell, M. (2009). Social justice teaching: Being fully present in relationship. In R. D. Davis, A. London, & B. Beyerbach (Eds.), *"How do we know what they know?" A conversation about pre-service teachers learning about culture and social justice* (pp. 187–197). Peter Lang.

Harro, B. (2010). The cycle of socialization. In M. Adams, W. Blumenfeld, C. R. Castaneda, H. W. Hackman, M. L. Peters, & X. Zuniga (Eds.), *Readings for diversity and social justice* (2nd ed., pp. 45–51). Routledge.

hooks, b. (1994). *Teaching to transgress: Education as the practice of freedom*. Routledge.

hooks, b. (2010). *Teaching critical thinking: Practical wisdom*. Routledge.

Lee, T. S. (2006). Balancing the margin is my center: A Navajo woman's navigations through the academy and her community. In T. R. Berry & N. D. Mizelle (Eds.), *From oppression to grace: Women of color and their dilemmas in the academy* (pp. 44–58). Stylus.

McCoy, A. C. (2007). *Minobimaadiziwin: Perceiving the good life through Anishinaabe language* (Doctoral dissertation). Retrieved from ProQuest Dissertations & Theses Global. (UMI Number: 1451580).

Muzaka, V. (2009). The niche of graduate teaching assistants (GTAs): Perceptions and reflections. *Teaching in Higher Education, 14*(1), 1–12. https://doi.org/10.1080/13562510802602400

Ng, R. (1993). "A woman out of control": Deconstructing sexism and racism in the university. *Canadian Journal of Education/ Revue Canadienne de l'éducation, 18*(3), 189–205. https://doi.org/10.2307/1495382

Ngunjiri, F. W., Hernandez, K.-A. C., & Chang, H. (2010). Living autoethnography: Connecting life and research. *Journal of Research Practice, 6*(1), 1–17. http://jrp.icaap.org/index.php/jrp

Padilla, L. M. (2001). "But you're not a dirty Mexican": Internalized oppression, Latinos & law. *Texas Hispanic Journal of Law & Policy, 7*, 59–113. https://doi.org/10.1525/sp.2007.54.1.23

Rodriguez, D. (2009). The usual suspect: Negotiating white student resistance and teacher authority in a predominantly white classroom. *Cultural Studies ↔ Critical Methodologies, 9*(4), 483–508. https://doi.org/10.1177/1532708608321504

Vargas, L. (1999). When the "Other" is the teacher: Implications of teacher diversity in higher education. *The Urban Review, 31*(4), 359–383. https://link.springer.com/journal/11256

Warren, J. T. (2011). Reflexive teaching: Toward critical autoethnographic practices of/in/on pedagogy. *Cultural Studies ↔ Critical Methodologies, 11*(2), 139–144. https://doi.org/10.1177/1532708611401332

Wing, A. K. (2003). Introduction. In A. K. Wing (Ed.), *Critical race feminism: A reader* (2nd ed., pp. 1–19). New York University Press.

Wing, A. K., & Willis, C. A. (1999). From theory to praxis: Black women, gangs, and critical race feminism. *La Raza Law Journal, 11*(1), 1–15. https://doi.org/10.15779/Z38DQ04

Zembylas, M. (2005). *Teaching with emotions: A postmodern enactment.* Information Age Publishing.

NOTES

1. The rhetoric about teaching as an ideal job for women is not uncommon in both Korean and U.S. societies. The idea reflects the intricate relationship between gender expectations, class issues, and career choices (Allard et al., 1995).

2. Richard Delgado, who is the leading scholar in critical race theory (CRT), consciously coined the term "Critical Race Feminism" to emphasize its significant focus on women of color and the strong connection to critical legal studies (Wing & Willis, 1999). The CRF scholarship particularly pays attention to certain groups of people who are women, disproportionately poor, and racial minorities. Thus, its racial intervention is rooted in feminism. Many CRF scholars employ storytelling as their analytic methodology in order to bring the voices of women of color (Wing, 2003).

ABOUT THE EDITORS AND CONTRIBUTORS

EDITORS

Emilie Clucas Leaderman is a higher education scholar-practitioner specializing in assessment leadership, centering student voices in institutional data, faculty development, and strategic planning. She recently transitioned from California to her home state of Massachusetts and currently teaches for Woods College of Advancing Studies at Boston College. Emilie has over 13 years of higher education experience leading institutional assessment, teaching education and psychology courses, providing leadership in student affairs, and promoting equitable and inclusive learning environments through consulting for colleges and universities. She presents nationally on a collaborative and relationship-based model of assessment practice. Her published writing and current scholarship also include learner-centered teaching, mentoring, adult learning, professional identity in assessment, and assessment leadership in higher education. Dr. Clucas Leaderman earned her EdD in Educational Leadership in Higher Education from Endicott College, and both her Master of Arts in Rehabilitation Counseling and Bachelor of Arts in Social and Rehabilitation Services from Assumption University.

Jennifer S. Jefferson, EdD, currently teaches graduate and undergraduate courses for Endicott College. During 2020 she served as the Interim Vice President of Academic Affairs at Manchester Community College in

New Hampshire. A longtime instructor of undergraduate writing, for 11 years Jennifer directed writing and learning centers at Endicott College, the University of New Hampshire at Manchester, and MassBay Community College. Dr. Jefferson has also taught graduate courses in educational leadership at Endicott College. Her publications have focused on women in academic leadership, writing center theory and pedagogy, and collaborations between academic libraries and writing centers. Jennifer earned her EdD in Educational Leadership in Higher Education from Endicott College, her Master of Arts in English (Composition and Rhetoric) from Northeastern University, and her Bachelor of Arts in English Literature from Hamilton College.

Jo Ann Gammel, EdD, is an Adjunct Faculty member in the PhD program in Educational Studies at Lesley University in Cambridge, MA. She earned her doctoral degree in Adult Learning and Leadership through the AEGIS program at Columbia University Teachers College. She has a master's in International Administration from the School for International Training in Brattleboro, VT. She teaches courses in adult learning, leadership, and qualitative research methods. Jo Ann was founding director for Endicott College's first doctoral program in Educational Leadership and collaborator on three subsequent doctoral degree programs. She was an early collaborator designing a hybrid online and residency doctoral degree option in Adult Learning at Lesley University. She recently transitioned from Massachusetts to Florida where she continues to teach online and sponsor dissertation writers. Her research and teaching interests include doctoral education and relational mentoring, coaching, advising and mentorship, program design and evaluation, and adult learning and leadership theory and research. Jo Ann has mentored doctoral students across a variety of educational and adult development topics, coached writers in various stages of development, and is committed to supporting adult learners in their quest to doctoral study.

Sue L. Motulsky, EdD, is an Associate Professor in the Division of Counseling and Psychology at Lesley University in Cambridge, MA. She teaches graduate courses in vocational development and career counseling, developmental psychology, and research methods, including doctoral courses in qualitative research as well as advising doctoral students. Her teaching, research, and writing interests include feminist, relational psychology, gender, multicultural and LGBTQ identity development, career development and transitions, and qualitative, constructivist, and narrative research as well as social justice issues in counselor education. Sue publishes and presents on relational career counseling and career transition, transgender career issues, qualitative methods in psychology, and social justice in counseling psychology. Sue earned her doctorate in Human Development and Psychology from Harvard University, where her studies focused on adult development and transition, feminist and cultural perspectives on identity and development, and relational psychology. She also has master's degrees in Culture, Gender and Relational Development and in English Literature. She maintains a private practice in career counseling and has an extensive background in career development and transition in university, community, and human services settings. Sue's approach to teaching and counseling is based on a relational definition of a healthy psychological self as being in connection with the self, with others, and with the world.

Amy Rutstein-Riley, PhD, MPH, is the Interim Dean of the Graduate School of Education at Lesley University in Cambridge, MA. She is an Associate Professor of Sociology, and Principal Investigator of *The Girlhood Project* (TGP). Amy teaches courses in girls' and women's studies, sociology, qualitative research methods, and adult learning and development. She is the Co-chair of the Women's Studies Steering Committee and Women's Center where she has initiated programming focused on women's health, sexual assault prevention, and most recently, a leadership enrichment and development study group for core women faculty. Amy is the Vice Chair of the American Council on Education National Network of Women Leaders in Higher Education of Massachusetts. The work closest to Amy's heart is *The Girlhood Project*, a multilayered community-based service learning and research program focused on the exploration of intersectional girlhoods in the context of intergenerational feminist girls' groups. As TGP enters its 12th year, Amy has mentored over 200 undergraduate and graduate students and is currently writing about the emerging girlhood scholar model, a central component of TGP. Amy can be found presenting locally, nationally, and internationally about this unique program. Amy's current research areas include girls' and emerging adult women's health and identity development, relationship-centered teaching and mentoring, feminist pedagogy, and leadership development of women faculty. It is the relationship between feminist theory, pedagogy, and praxis that is the essence of Amy's work with her students and faculty peers. Amy holds a PhD in Educational Studies with a focus on Sociology and Women's Health from Lesley University, a Master of Public Health Degree in Epidemiology and Sociobehavioral Sciences from Boston University School of Public Health, School of Medicine, and a Bachelor of Arts in Psychology from Simmons University.

CONTRIBUTORS

Susan R. Adams is Associate Professor of Middle/Secondary Education in the College of Education at Butler University. A former secondary ESL teacher and instructional coach, Susan's research interests include race, critical pedagogies, and transformational adult learning. Her publications are included in *Theory into Practice, Critical Literacy, English Journal, Writing and Pedagogy, The Brock Education Journal, SAGE Sociology of Education,* and *The New Educator.* Her 2016 book, *Race and Pedagogy: Creating Collaborative Spaces for Teacher Transformations,* coauthored with Jamie Buffington-Adams, is part of the Lexington Books series, *Race and Education in the Twenty-First Century,* editors Kenneth Fasching-Varner, Lori Latrice Martin, and Roland Mitchell.

Diana-Lea Baranovich is a United States certified teacher, supervisor, curriculum specialist, school psychologist, and diagnostician. She also holds additional qualifications in Jungian-based expressive arts therapies, archetypal play therapy, dance/movement therapy, and sand tray therapy. Diana runs a private psychotherapy practice and specializes in helping traumatized children, at-risk youth, families in transition, and family reunification. She has been based in Kuala Lumpur, Malaysia for the past 12 years and teaches full-time at the University Malaya in the Department of Educational Psychology and Counselling. She has published articles, presented papers, and delivered experiential workshops in international conventions throughout Asia and the Middle East. She authored the following books: *Understanding and Caring for the Hurt Child* (2013); *Understanding and Mentoring the Hurt Teenager* (2017); and *Bonding through Play* (2019). Her research areas are education, counselling, and psychology.

Maria Aurora (Maya) C. Bernardo has worked in higher education for over 26 years, as lecturer, researcher, and higher education manager in the Philippines, Malaysia, Australia, and New Zealand. She has a PhD in education, with a concentration in leadership and management, a Master's in Business Administration, and a Bachelor's degree in Business Management. She is a qualified adult religious educator and an online learning facilitator and designer. She has devoted most of her career to the study of leadership and developing leaders for schools and not-for-profit organizations. Maya is a recipient of the Australian Leadership Award Fellowship in 2008 and was conferred Honorary Fellow for the Australian Catholic University from 2010–2018. Her areas of research are in education, leadership, and community engagement. Maya is based in New Zealand. She has currently shifted careers from academia to work in adult religious formation with the Archdiocese of Wellington.

Gail Simpson Cahill, EdD, joined Lesley University in 2010 after working many years in the public education sector in suburban and urban school systems. She currently holds a faculty appointment in the Graduate School of Education, Special Education Department. Dr. Cahill teaches and mentors courses in assessment, curriculum, seminar, school practicums, and individual education programs (IEPs). Throughout her career, Dr. Cahill has taught at various grade levels in K–12 schools as well as held several administrative positions, including in special education administration and school-based administration. She also has worked at private facilities, including McLean Hospital and the Guild for the Blind, and she holds numerous educational certifications in Massachusetts in areas that include special education, reading, school psychology, and administration. Dr. Cahill holds a doctorate in Educational Leadership, Master's degrees in School Psychology as well as Reading and Language, and an undergraduate dual degree in Special Education and Elementary Education.

Gabrielle Comeau is a junior at Old Dominion University in Norfolk, Virginia where she is studying Biology. She graduated from Poland Regional High School in Poland, Maine in 2015 and started college at Central Maine Community College the following semester. There she finished two associate degrees, in Life Science and General Studies. She currently works as a nationally certified pharmacy technician and lives just outside of Norfolk.

Allyson Eamer is a sociolinguist who researches primarily in immigrant and Indigenous communities in the area of language and identity construction. Additionally, she is interested in the use of mobile technologies in language instruction, and in supporting students from disadvantaged backgrounds in higher education. Recently she has researched, written, and presented on the impact of trauma and mental illness on language learning for refugees and people with psychiatric disabilities. She has served as Graduate Program Director, TESL Program Director, and Assistant Dean at Ontario Tech University where she has been a Faculty Member since 2008.

Yesenia Fernandez, PhD, Assistant Professor of School Leadership, Cal State Dominguez Hills, is a first-generation college student and faculty who earned her PhD in Education at Claremont Graduate University. She studies how systemic racism in the K–16 school system perpetuates segregation and precludes minoritized students from higher education as well as the experiences of first-generation college students. She has been an educator/student advocate for over twenty years. She recently served as an urban school district leader and led initiatives to develop systems which improved equity and access to higher education. She is dedicated to working with school leaders, policymakers, and community members to ensure equity and justice in our urban schools. She is also a member and board president of the East Yard Community for Environmental Justice (EYCEJ) Board of Directors and is involved with other grassroots organizations focused on protecting and healing our communities.

Patrick Flynn, PhD, is the Assistant Principal at Poland Regional High School in Poland, Maine. He started working in public secondary education in 1998, serving as a teacher, a mentor, a department chair, and an administrator. He teaches at University of Maine at Farmington in the Educational Leadership department with a focus on ethical leadership. His research interests include the postsecondary First-Year Experience, restorative practices in education, ethical leadership, and college student development. He lives outside of Portland, Maine, with his family and a pair of Labradoodles.

Kitty M. Fortner, EdD, is an Assistant Professor at California State University Dominguez Hills, College of Education School Leadership Program. For over 20 years, she has been involved in K–12 education in public and charter schools. She received her Doctorate in Educational Leadership for Social Justice from the University of Redlands researching social class and student engagement. Before her work in higher education, she founded two successful charter schools in Southern California. Her passion is providing students with effective personalized learning experiences. She believes that leadership plays an imperative role in fostering academic success for all learners. Her research focuses on identity and its role in effective school leadership. In addition to her current research on urban school leaders' skills, knowledge, behaviors, and dispositions needed for student success, she draws on research looking at the intersection of identity and leadership for liberation and justice education.

Lorena Germán is a Dominican American educator working with middle and high school students in Austin, Texas. Her master's degree is from Middlebury College's Bread Loaf School of English. Lorena has been published by NCTE, ASCD, Heinemann, National Writing Project, *EdWeek*, and featured in *The New York Times, Embracing Equity,* and others. Most recently, she coedited the anthology *Speaking for Ourselves* and self-published *The Anti-Racist Teacher: Reading Instruction Workbook.* She is proudly a two-time nationally awarded teacher. Lorena is Co-Founder of the Multicultural Classroom, as well as Co-Founder of #DisruptTexts, and Chair of NCTE's Committee Against Racism and Bias in the Teaching of English.

Sharon Hamilton, Chancellor's Professor Emerita, taught composition at Indiana University–Indianapolis for 21 years. Born and educated in Canada with a PhD in Language and Literacy from London University (U.K.), she has published four novels, a literacy memoir, and over a hundred academic articles, chapters, and edited volumes. Throughout these diverse genres for equally diverse audiences, one theme asserts itself continuously: the relationship between writing and social issues. Her chapter on the evolution of her academic identity illustrates how her life experience has provided the fodder for her theories on language and literacy. She began teaching in a one-room eight-grade schoolhouse on the Canadian Prairies and ended her academic career as Associate Executive Vice Chancellor (Academic Affairs) at a major American university. She began writing her four novels at age 70. How she began this path to literacy defies expectations.

Antonia Issa Lahera, EdD, found HeartSpace and now it is her home. She strives to live in a just and equitable world where communities create the space and place for all. As an educator and leader with more than 40 years of experience she continues to try to get it right and hopes she is contributing, building, inspiring the next generation. As an educator, author, and presenter she hopes to save the world, or at least impact those she encounters. She has worked all over the nation with the Literacy Leadership Collaborative, the National Urban Alliance, and as a professor and K–12 school administrator. With over 50 publications she is a voice of advocacy for leadership, education, equity, and truth. Toni can be reached at aissalahera@gmail.com

Maria Khristina (Tina) Manueli taught Linguistics, Filipino, and English in the Philippines and Malaysia. She has a PhD in Linguistics, Master's degrees in linguistics and theology, and a Bachelor's degree in linguistics. She was the former head of the Linguistics department at the University of the Philippines, where she served for 10 years before migrating to Germany. During her academic stint in Malaysia and the Philippines, she has published articles and presented papers in international conferences, as well as organized international meetings and conferences. She was a recipient of the Luisa Mallari Fellowship for PhD Research in Southeast Asian Studies (2005–2008) and the Luisa Mallari Language Training Grant (2001) of the SEASREP Foundation, as well as a recipient of the 2009 ASEAN Research Scholars Fellowship (National University of Singapore). She is currently working as administrative coordinator of the Methodist e-Academy and a freelance linguist.

James F. Lane, Jr., EdD, served 38 years as a public-school educator. His roles included high school English teacher, language arts supervisor, assistant principal, and principal. He now teaches beginning doctoral students in the Center for Doctoral Studies, University of Phoenix. He also conducts educational research projects within the university's Center for Educational and Instructional Technology Research. His interests include ethical frameworks, school leadership, school organization, K–12 curriculum, autoethnography, and narrative inquiry.

Kate McCabe is a doctoral candidate at Simon Fraser University in British Columbia, Canada. The working title of her dissertation is *Walking Backward, Out into the Wild*. She teaches preschoolers, school age children, and Early Childhood Education candidates. When not teaching, she walks along the Sumallo River, in the Cascade Mountains east of Hope, B.C., stepping over long, dark green slugs stretched across the path while listening for the breath of bears that are out and about these early mornings. She and her partner live in what is now called Vancouver.

Anne Medill has been a social work professional for 40 years. Her work has included direct practice experiences with adolescents, families, and several Native American communities in the Southwest. She was able to transition from providing direct practice services in these communities to teaching at the university level. Anne finds being able to translate social work knowledge, values, and skills into classroom content and back into the community is the essence of preparing students to work with people on the micro, mezzo, and macro levels. She continues to engage in learning new strategies for working with people to share with her students. Having both Kathryn her daughter and her mother in her life has shaped her identity as a woman and as a member of the communities she engages with.

Kathryn Medill is an art and visual culture educator with an emphasis in museum education. Her practice is grounded in cultivating an open dialogue and utilizing constructivist learning models. Whether it is touring a group of kindergarteners through a museum or discussing a reading with undergraduate and graduate students, she firmly believes that conversation is the key to creating a productive space for both the facilitator and the students. For her, art and visual culture are the ideal channels through which we can both discuss contemporary cultures and reflect on past iterations of culture from micro, mezzo, and macro levels. In the past, Kathryn has worked for art gallery and museum education departments in Spain, England, and the United States. She is familiar with creating curricula that connect to museum content for K–12 students as well as undergraduate and graduate students.

Anthony H. Normore, PhD, is professor of educational leadership in Graduate Education at California State University Dominguez Hills. Dr. Normore obtained his PhD from the Ontario Institute for the Studies in Education (OISE) at the University of Toronto. His multi-pronged research focusses on (a) the *(mis)*-interpretation and *(mis)*-use of leadership and management in higher education, and (b) leadership development of urban school leaders in the context of ethics and social justice. He is the author of more than 25 books including the most recent—*Your Moral Compass: A Practical Guide for New Wave Leaders* (2020, New Wave Publishers); *The Handbook of Research on Strategic Communication, Leadership, and Conflict Management in Modern Organizations* (2019, IGI-Global*), Voices Leading from the Ecotone* (2019, Word & Deed Publishing). He spent 40 years as an educator, published numerous professional articles, and presented many conference presentations. Tony is the 2019 recipient of *International Award for Authentic Leadership,* 2015 recipient of *Willower Award of Excellence in Research* awarded by UCEA Consortium for the Study of Leadership and Ethics in Education, and the recipient of the AERA 2013 *Bridge People Award* for Leadership for Social Justice SIG.

Benjamin Ramirez is a doctoral candidate in the College of Education at the University of Arizona, where he is studying the prominence of settler colonialism in education. He received a Master of Arts degree in Anthropology & Education from the University of Arizona and a Bachelor of Science degree in Anthropology from Central Michigan University. He is interested in settler colonialism, indigenous studies, language, and literacy.

R. Joseph Rodríguez is a literacy educator and researcher in the Texas Hill Country. He is the author of academic research articles, books, and chapters. Joseph has taught English and Spanish language arts in public schools, community colleges, and universities. His areas of research include children's and young adult literatures, language acquisition, and socially responsible biliteracies. Currently, Joseph is coeditor of *English Journal.* Catch him via Twitter at @escribescribe.

Denelle Wallace received a PhD in Urban Services with a concentration in Academic Leadership from Old Dominion University. Her current research focus involves diversifying public-school educator populations, creating culturally proficient school environments, ensuring academic equity and access for diverse student populations, and promoting effective leadership in public school reform. Since 2008, Dr. Wallace has been a full-time faculty member in the Secondary Education and School Leadership Department of the School of Education at Norfolk State University, where she enjoys providing instruction to graduate students interested in becoming exemplary school counselors and exceptional school administrators. During her time away from campus, she enjoys traveling and spending time with her husband, family, and friends.

Zitong Wei received her PhD from Indiana University Bloomington. She has been teaching as an instructor in China Women's University for over three years. Her research interests include early childhood education, qualitative methodology, teacher education, and curriculum studies. She has several independent presentations for AERA and publications with SAGE and IGI Global. She recently published the book *Constructivism and Teachers in Chinese Culture: Enriching Confucianism with Constructivism*.

Injeong Yoon is an artist, teacher, organizer, and writer. She is currently an Assistant Professor of Art Education and Affiliate Faculty in Gender Studies at the University of Arkansas. Before she started teaching at the university level, she worked in public schools as a teacher of multiple subjects for five and a half years. Her doctoral degree in Art History and Education from the University of Arizona shaped her identity as a female teacher-scholar of color working toward social justice. Her recent scholarly works center on decolonial pedagogy, decolonial aesthetics, transnational feminisms, critical race feminism, and social justice art education. In addition to her academic work, she founded a translingual community program, "InterWeave," in Springdale, Arkansas in collaboration with a local nonprofit organization. As an organizer and teacher of the program, she works with adult immigrants to create a translanguaging space and build a bilingual community through art.

CPSIA information can be obtained
at www.ICGtesting.com
Printed in the USA
LVHW061533190122
708626LV00002B/9